RETIRING
Retirement

RETIRING
Retirement

RODNEY MACREADY

HENDRICKSON PUBLISHERS

THEOLOGY OF WORK PROJECT

Retiring Retirement

© 2016 Hendrickson Publishers Marketing, LLC
P. O. Box 3473
Peabody, Massachusetts 01961-3473
www.hendrickson.com

ISBN 978-1-61970-808-2

Printed in the United States of America

First Printing—August 2016

Library of Congress Cataloging-in-Publication Data

Names: Macready, Rodney, author.
Title: Retiring retirement / Rodney Macready.
Description: Peabody, MA : Hendrickson Publishers, 2016.
Identifiers: LCCN 2016022421 | ISBN 9781619708082 (alk. paper)
Subjects: LCSH: Work--Religious aspects--Christianity. |
    Retirement--Religious aspects--Christianity.
Classification: LCC BT738.5 .M33 2016 | DDC 248.8/5--dc23 LC record available at https://lccn.loc.gov/2016022421

CONTENTS

Foreword

A good book provides a conversation partner. A good conversation partner provides a dialogue. A good dialogue provides the opportunity to learn, think, grow, change, and develop.

There is little point in reading a book to confirm your opinions. Often it is best to listen to a conversation partner with whom you disagree. Yet it is most valuable to dialogue with somebody who shares the same fundamental assumptions, who speaks the same language and inhabits the same thought world but disagrees on a particular point.

Such a conversation partner is like a teacher—opening up new worlds of thought. This is the case with Rodney Macready's book *Retiring Retirement*.

A few years ago, an American friend of mine, Dr. Phil Burgess, told me he was writing a book against the common culture of retirement. I thought it sounded interesting and strange. It had never occurred to me that there was any alternative to retiring. I put it down to Phil's zest for life and his American work ethic. But Phil insisted it was a matter of Christian commitment. When Phil returned to America, I lost my only goad to think afresh on this topic, though his challenge continued to spur me to think about the whole Christian philosophy of work and especially retirement. I suspected Phil was right, but my life was too busy for me to thoroughly investigate the Bible's teaching on retirement.

I saw a number of Christian friends "retire," but continue in active service of others. Their financial arrangements changed, their workplaces changed, but their productive service of the community did not diminish; in some cases it increased. I came to the conclusion that we "resign" rather than "retire." We resign from one employment in order to work differently for the good of the community.

Then Rod's manuscript arrived at my desk.

Here is the conversation partner I've been looking for. This book goes back to basic principles, assuming only the general theological position of the average evangelical believer regarding biblical authority and method.

There are no holds barred as Rodney wrestles with the question of retirement. The very topic forces him back into the Bible's view of work and rest and so back to creation, the eschaton, and all stops between. It's exactly the right way to tackle a question such as this, for so many of our ideas and values about retirement are derived unconsciously from our culture.

As an Australian, it is so easy to take our affluent Western way of life for granted, and worse, to generalize it to all people; worse still, to find it in the Bible! There is always this danger in exegesis: that we read the Bible from our life instead of reading our life from the Bible. Those reading this book from outside the Australian context will be particularly helped by its different perspective as well as its biblical awareness of universal principles. Again, that is the advantage of a good conversation partner, who can point out our unwitting biases and help us look at ourselves from the viewpoint of the Scriptures.

Rod helpfully takes time to tell us about himself, so that his readers can join him in evaluating how his cultural and personal biases may be clouding his judgment. Apart from being personally interesting, this is of great benefit, because it confronts the reader with his or her own particular assumptions about work and retirement.

This is not the book for those who want "ten essential tips for a happy Christian retirement," nor "the best way to a fulfilling retirement." It's a book that raises serious questions about our ready acceptance of the world's values about retirement. And whether you agree or disagree with the argument, it is a discussion that is long overdue. Rod Macready is to be thanked not only for raising the topic but for doing it in such a thoughtful and biblical way.

Phillip D. Jensen, Bible Teacher and Evangelist
Two Ways Ministries, Newtown, Australia

INTRODUCTION

Let me be clear from the outset. I don't think retirement is a biblical concept—especially the way it's practiced in my Australian culture. And since my Australian culture is part of a larger animal known as Western culture, I suspect it's the same for that broader context. Since I don't have personal experience of those other cultures, I can't say for sure, but a few others who do live within those cultures have assured me this is the case.

THE PURPOSE OF THIS BOOK

My aim is to challenge you to think about retirement and what the Bible has to say in relation to it. You don't have to end up agreeing with me—although, of course, I think it'd be nice if you did. My big concern is that we Christians have simply adopted our culture's thinking about retirement without examining it to determine whether it fits with our profession to acknowledge Jesus as our king. And that, it seems to me, is dangerous. We've allowed the world to squeeze us into its shape and dictate to us all our dreams, goals, and aspirations about this increasingly lengthy period of our lives.

Occasionally you hear about some areas of the retired lifestyle that are "baptized" with an element of Christian religion—like Christian seniors' golf days or Christian seniors' tour groups. I can sympathize with the sentiment behind such activities and appreciate the evangelistic thrust of many of them, but I think they fail to deal with the underlying beast. Such activities simply accept retirement and its accompanying cultural values as a given and seek to somehow Christianize them. I think that's a bit like trying to Christianize greed. We need first to get to the root of the issue. That involves investigating what God-honoring values imply about retirement itself.

I know the Australian image of enjoyable, leisured retirement resonates with something in the very depths of my being. It doesn't take much for me to picture (and anticipate with great desire!) a lifestyle of overseas holidays, playing golf, reading novels, and enjoying fine cuisine. You can substitute your own pet pleasures if those particular things don't take your fancy. Does the Bible promote that sort of lifestyle for Christians? I think not. It's not that those things are sinful in themselves. Indeed, they may each have a place in the Christian life. They could be considered examples of enjoying God's good creation with thanksgiving. But, as a lifestyle in this current age, there's something there that clashes sharply with Christian values.

In effect, my aim in this book is to achieve a paradigm shift—to get you thinking that retirement (at least as we normally think of it) is not God's best for your life. And so I challenge you to think seriously about this great Australian (or Western) dream. Is it a dream you should desire? Should you put your time, money, and effort into pursuing it?

If you're under fifty, I wish to challenge you to take the opportunity to develop godly goals that will continue into your senior years. Rather than accepting a vision of your life that divides it into working and nonworking years, I hope you will develop a vision of serving others no matter your age. You may reach an age where the nature of that service transitions. That may happen at several ages during your life. But the underlying, driving vision should always seek ways to serve others rather than ways to indulge yourself.

If you're over fifty, still in the workforce, and anticipating the approach of your retirement, I want you to think carefully about your choices at this point. That same vision of serving others is just as relevant for you—but it's far more likely you already have a significant stake in this great retirement dream. It'll be tough for you to shift your thinking. Indeed, without God's help, you won't be able to do it. I want you to actively consider how you can best continue to serve others beyond your official retiring age. For some, that will mean not retiring. For some, it may mean a change of paid employment. For some, it will mean voluntary work in the community or overseas. The options are wide-ranging. But I don't think full-time leisured self-indulgence is among the options available to Christians.

If you're already retired and in the middle of a self-indulgent binge, I want you to repent. You may think you're entitled to this—that it's your God-given right after years of hard work. I don't think you'll find that in the Bible.

Now, I know that's simplistic and doesn't cover all the issues. That's why there's a book and not just an introduction (though I'm sure the book also won't cover all the issues). Our bodies do change as we age. Some of the options previously open to us for serving others disappear as our wrinkles increase and our bodies deteriorate. But the definition of our Christian values doesn't change with age. The depth of our understanding of them and how we express them practically may grow and change, but the underlying values remain constant.

I do need to stress one important qualification to my purpose and acknowledge that some people either can't work or can only work with very limited capacity. This is part of living in a world that's impacted by human sin. The reasons some people can't work are many and varied. Some people are born with physical conditions that either prevent them from working or allow them to work only in a very limited capacity. Some may be involved in accidents or become the victims of violence, and the results are the same: their injuries either prevent or significantly reduce their capacity to work. Still others develop mental conditions that bring about the same results. Those sorts of situations are a separate issue, often accompanied by significant pain. I certainly don't intend to add to that pain and sincerely hope my writing does not inadvertently do so.

For some, their very work situations bring about a similar result. They discover that the physical or mental effort they've put into their work over a period of forty or fifty years takes a toll on their bodies or their minds such that they're no longer able to continue. They find that the spirit is willing, but the body is weak—or sometimes they feel that even the spirit is no longer willing. I don't wish to cause you undue stress if you're in this category. At the same time, I hope you won't avoid the challenge of thinking through this topic. The fact that you can't continue in your previous work (or can work only with reduced capacity) doesn't mean you can do no work—you can still continue to find ways to serve others.

All of us develop reduced capacity to work as part of the aging process. Our bodies slow down and wear out. Our minds aren't as sharp as they used to be. This is the reality we all face. And so, yes, I do wish to change how you think about the subject of retirement, but I don't wish to do so in a way that denies that reality. How does that work in practice?

On the one hand, it means developing a changed mind-set—one that devotes the whole of one's life to serving others and doesn't expect to cease doing that upon reaching "retirement age." On the other hand, it means recognizing our human limitations, especially in light of the aging process. Our ability to serve and the way in which we serve will need to adjust to our changing abilities. Like all our abilities, these vary from person to person. And so, it's up to each individual to assess their own abilities and how these can best be used to serve others at each stage of life. For each of us, there may indeed come a time in our lives where our human limitations are so great that we can no longer serve others—or only do so in a very limited way.

Likewise, some people experience difficulties obtaining paid employment[1]—a highly significant aspect of work within Western cultures. This results in significant problems for such people, including emotional pain, anxiety, and stress. That too is a separate issue from what I address in this book. Again, I don't intend to add to that pain and sincerely hope my writing does not inadvertently do so.

THE PLAN OF ATTACK

So, how do I plan to achieve this aim? First, I want to set the scene by briefly describing what I think are three key elements for understanding our current cultural situation.

1. How did we get here? That is, where did the concept of retirement originate and how has it developed?

2. What is retirement?

3. What are our current expectations about retirement?

Given the cultural reality of retirement, it seems natural to then ask: How should Christians evaluate this concept? That question could be answered from several angles. In this book, I limit myself to exploring the Biblical material that could be used to argue for or against the concept of retirement.

Although I don't particularly like doing so, chapter 2 talks about me: my background and my presuppositions—at least, as far as I am aware of both. I think the former is important so you can weigh any vested interests I may have in this subject and their likely impact on my analysis. I think the latter is important so you recognize the theological tradition in which I place myself and can make any relevant adjustments where it differs from your own.

Chapter 3 explores some major cultural issues. Our world is very different from that in which the Bible was written. There are vast gaps of time, language, geography, culture, and so on. Sometimes we forget those differences when we read the Bible, and automatically read our culture into the text. There are two major areas where I think it's important to be aware of those differences in relation to our current subject: family and work. These were arguably one and the same in the cultures of Bible times.

I believe chapters 4 to 7 form the heart of my argument. Chapter 4 presents the case for a presumption in favor of *work*. Work was part of life in the Garden of Eden. It continues to be part of life after humanity's fall—though there are some significant changes. It's part of life after Jesus' resurrection. I believe it remains part of life in the new creation. Thus it seems to me that if we stop work for an extended period of time, we need to be able to give a reason for our inaction.

Some argue that the Bible's teaching on *rest* provides one such reason. This is understandable, since rest appears to be an important part both of God's original design for creation and of his renewed promises to believers. Those who take this view argue that since God's rest is the climax of the creation narrative in Genesis 1:1–2:3, humans should follow the Creator's example by "resting" from work at the end of their lives. While I agree that entering into God's rest is our ultimate goal, I disagree that the achievement of this goal excludes human work. Instead, the fully biblical view of human "rest" can include work and enjoyment of God's creation. The development of this argument forms the content of chapters 5 to 7.

Chapters 8 to 14 then deal with various other scriptural passages that address aging and work, exploring whether they validate the concept of retirement. The danger here is that I've omitted relevant passages. I've thought through the issue over several years. I've also raised the matter with others. As far as I'm aware, my coverage is comprehensive. Yet, it's still likely I've omitted some relevant passages. I think I've covered all the relevant passages—but I realize that not everyone sees things the same way I do and so it's likely there will be other people who come up with passages they consider relevant. For that, I can only apologize in advance. Like you, I'm not infallible. Hopefully, there is sufficient material in the discussion of the passages that are included for you to evaluate whether adding others would alter my overall conclusion.

I should warn you that these may seem to be the least exciting chapters. The people who kindly read the draft of this book used words like "academic," "thorough," and "weighty"—you get the general drift. Yet, they saw no way of avoiding the problem. These Scripture passages (some of which are rather obscure and not well-known) require exploring, and a superficial treatment would create its own problems. And so, although I'm conscious that many these days want instant information in snack-size servings, I believe it's important to aim for completeness in my presentation of this topic. It's my hope that each of these chapters will help to develop further the overall biblical understanding of work, and address many of the possible pitfalls of interpreting what the Bible has to say on this topic.

The penultimate chapter deals briefly with some passages that appear to favor non-retirement. Because I believe the Bible presumes that work is the norm for human beings, I have not dealt with these passages in as much detail. However, I think it is worthwhile to draw attention to these other passages that lend support to that presumption.

The final chapter starts to deal with the question: So what? While this book is just the first step in considering this issue and thus only comes to an initial conclusion, I think it's worthwhile to begin the process of thinking through the possible implications of that conclusion for our own lives. I don't want this to be simply an academic exercise. Personally, I think the very nature of the topic prevents that, since it impacts how we in the Western world map out our lives in terms of our time, our money, and our dreams. It touches our attitudes toward work and leisure. So, on the one hand, it's hard to imagine this being a purely academic book.

On the other hand, I do find that I have a tendency to love generalities. I'm good at reading general conclusions, agreeing with them, filing them away in my head (or, more likely, on my computer's hard drive), and then doing nothing about them. I find it helpful when an author or speaker fleshes out his or her conclusion with some concrete proposals. Those particular proposals may not work for me in my individual circumstances—that's the danger with specific applications. But I still find those proposals are often more effective in stimulating me to action than the generalities on their own. I hope this final chapter will do the same for you—that it will help you think through the practical implications of what it would mean for us to reject this particular cultural value.

THE JOURNEY

So, I invite you to come on a journey with me as we explore several Bible passages. From my perspective, in looking back over the journey I've undertaken, I have noticed two things. First, I discovered most of the texts I looked at were more difficult than I anticipated. Second, the journey was at least as much about how to interpret the Bible as it was about retirement.

I certainly struggled at times. At times, it wasn't obvious where I could find answers to the questions I had. Much of the reason for that is that I'm asking questions these texts weren't designed to answer—modern retirement didn't exist when the Bible was written. That's probably also why the various commentators often don't answer my questions.

I've tried to leave something of my journey in how I've written. I know that makes for a longer book. I hope the payoff will be that you grow in your ability to interpret the Bible—as well as thinking through the concept of retirement.

1

HAVE YOU THOUGHT ABOUT RETIREMENT?

Retirement is big business in most (if not all) Western economies. It's likely to get even bigger and better. Life expectancies continue to increase. Modern health-care services produce expectations of relatively active lifestyles in retirement years. Today's seniors realistically anticipate twenty years of post-work leisure. They're cashed-up with excess time on their hands. What entrepreneur wouldn't salivate at the prospect? It's a market ripe for the picking.

But they aren't the only ones salivating. Someone trained the rest of us to long for these golden years—and most of us will get there. This is life's goal—the carrot we eagerly crave. It's the new Garden of Eden—leisured, desirable, idyllic. What could be better? No stigma attached to not working. No pressure to meet deadlines. No one telling you what to do. Free to follow your fancy. It's so attractive that many scheme to get there as early as possible. Where's the catch?

For me, the catch is that this seems to be an unexplored segment of Western thinking, especially from a Christian perspective. Now, at first glance, it doesn't look that way. All sorts of magazines, journals, and books deal with issues surrounding retirement and gerontology (a fancy word that disguises the fact it's about old people). You can readily find material that explores:

- How to finance your retirement
- How to cease employment well
- How to cope with a leisured lifestyle
- How to prepare for the life changes involved
- How to handle the aging process
- How to deal with the issues of ageism
- How to develop new hobbies

- How to run a retirement village

- How to treat the elderly with dignity

- How to survive the death of a spouse

- How to deal with a whole host of things that wouldn't otherwise enter my head

Scholars have developed theologies of aging and theologies of ministering to the aged.

But, as far as I can tell, the theology of retirement itself is a neglected field. In particular, it seems that few have stopped to ask the question: Should we retire? Is retirement consistent with the values of our Christian faith? Does God endorse the concept of retirement?

Because that's such a rarely asked question, I don't want to leave it too quickly. Retirement is a subject very dear to most of our hearts. I think it's important to consider why this is so. How is it we've come to this point? Why does this concept attract us? What's our vested interest in longing for retirement—and does that influence what we think the Bible says about it? And so I want to tease this out a bit further—to explore why we seem to have this cultural blind spot. I want to do this by looking briefly at three areas.

1. The history of retirement (for those who abhor the "h" word, I promise to keep it brief)

2. The definition of retirement

3. The expectations surrounding retirement

Having said something about those three areas, I'll then briefly outline the issues involved in understanding what the Bible may contribute to our evaluation of the concept of retirement.

THE HISTORY OF RETIREMENT

So, when did retirement originate? American Express began the first private pension plan in 1875. German Chancellor Otto von

Bismarck began the first public pension plan around 1880 (I've seen several different years cited for this event!). He set the retirement age at sixty-five. At that time, very few people achieved that milestone, so he didn't anticipate it would cost the state a huge amount.[1] New South Wales passed the *Old Age Pension Act* in 1900. The Australian Commonwealth passed the *Invalid and Old-Age Pensions Act* in 1908. The first American states to allow for retirement followed suit in 1915. They set the retirement age at seventy and had additional stringent conditions.

Yet several factors hindered retirement's widespread enjoyment in these initial stages. The percentage of the population reaching age 65 remained relatively small. Those who did achieve this milestone often suffered from significantly declining health. Many found the pension (and any financial resources they had accumulated) insufficient for their living expenses, which were frequently increased by medical costs. And a level of social stigma often attached to those not working.

The situation changed around the 1950s. Life expectancy increased. Medical services improved. People's financial situation became more secure. The workforce became more youth focused. The social stigma surrounding retirement disappeared. And entrepreneurs introduced a propaganda campaign to encourage retirees to enjoy their leisure.

Further changes occurred by the 1980s. Life expectancy had increased still further, but birth rates had declined. The ratio of those receiving pensions to the size of the workforce grew dramatically. Governments recognized they could no longer afford to sponsor their mushrooming pension expenditures. Thus, in Australia, they legislated for employer-sponsored superannuation schemes and invented other ways to encourage individuals to save for their own retirement.[2]

This very brief (and somewhat simplistic) historical survey demonstrates evolving attitudes toward retirement over a relatively short time frame. Further, at a societal level, pragmatic concerns drove that evolution. The depression years saw a move to get older people out of the workforce to make way for younger ones. Later, superannuation schemes were promoted to prevent governments

from entering bankruptcy. Likewise, the current incremental increases to the retirement age in Australia are meant to reduce the
financial burdens on the government. This pragmatic approach is
unsurprising in a secular society. What is surprising is the apparent lack of theological reflection on the concept.

So, retirement is a relatively recent concept and one that's still
evolving. It's worth pausing to ask: Are there any precursors to
the modern concept of retirement? Did earlier societies have any
comparable practice?

Certainly, examples of an apparently leisured status abound
in history. In ancient Greece, Socrates, Plato, and Aristotle considered manual labor second-rate and harmful to body and soul.
They proposed that the contemplative life was vastly superior. Their
contemplative lifestyle was not mere idleness, but definite mental
activity, which they believed would result in true happiness. Still,
it's unlikely this view was shared by the general populace. Instead,
non-leisured people of the ancient world probably considered work
both necessary and virtuous. Yet, it was the intellectuals such as
Plato and Aristotle who had a marked influence on the development of Western worldviews. Consider, for example, our ongoing distinctions between professionals (often mental activity) and
tradesmen (often manual activity) and the higher status conferred
on the former.[3]

A second example arose within Christian circles. For a wide
assortment of reasons, some Christians abandoned normal occupations for a more ascetic and "holy" lifestyle. This resulted in
various monastic systems where contemplation (*vita contemplativa*)
was prioritized for the purpose of growing in godliness. The issue
was not with manual labor itself—they considered some forms of
manual labor conducive to contemplative activities so that both
could be done concurrently. Yet they attempted to set aside the
"earthly" goods that come from physical work, and placed a higher
value on contemplation. This contributed to what I believe is the
inappropriate division between the sacred and the secular (a view
shared by many of the Reformers). It also tended to downgrade
the overall importance of work and thus may have contributed to
modern preferences for that which is "not work."

Upper-class lifestyles from the past and present provide a third example. Most people envy the status and the accompanying "benefits" of the upper class and hope to make the transition to leisured wealth themselves. Ancient history presents the occasional example of an individual's elevation from relative destitution to successful prominence (for example, the biblical narrative of Joseph), but this was relatively rare. Much later, however, European colonialism and the Industrial Revolution offered increased opportunities for such changes in status. The development of newspapers and increased levels of literacy resulted in both the opportunities and the real-life examples of such rags-to-riches stories being more widely known. The wider distribution of literature (for example, Jane Austen novels) contributed to a greater understanding of and longing for upward mobility. Perhaps membership in the aristocracy was beyond reach for those born "on the wrong side of the tracks," but entry into the middle class was a satisfactory and desirable alternative. And one of the perceived benefits of middle-class status was escape from drudgery into increased leisure.

Now, these examples are still not equivalent to modern retirement. While the ideal seems to date from ancient times, in reality, leisure in antiquity was restricted to a limited group. Most people remained confined in the daily grind of the working classes. True, modern retirement also applies to a limited group: all those who reach the nominated age. The difference is that in Australia *all* who do reach that age are entitled to retire. In other Western countries, not everyone may be entitled to retire, but most older workers do feel the pressure to retire as a sign of status. Those who can't retire at the customary age may feel that they have somehow failed, even though retirement funds can be affected by factors that are out of their control.

Yet I think these examples illustrate attitudes that influence our understanding of work, and hence of retirement. For example, we tend to have:

- a preference for intellectual work over manual labor;
- a preference for self-directed activity over submission to another person;

- a preference for leisure over work;
- a preference to climb the status ladder; and
- a tendency to separate the secular from the sacred.

These sorts of cultural preferences subtly influence how we think. Sometimes they influence and even undermine our interpretation of the biblical material.

THE DEFINITION OF RETIREMENT

I will return to these attitudes and expectations shortly. Before that, I think it is important to come to some understanding of the concept of retirement itself. I grew up and continue to live in a culture where retirement is expected. After my education, I entered the workforce expecting to retire when I turned sixty-five (if not before). Thus, I acquired many of my thoughts and feelings about retirement by something akin to osmosis: they're simply part of the atmosphere in which I exist. They include things such as:

- An extended period of rest following my working life
- A well-earned rest after many years of hard slog
- A life stage to be greatly anticipated
- The cessation of paid work
- Freedom from having to submit to a boss
- A time to catch up on my favorite activities
- A time to travel
- A time to indulge myself as I please
- A time when many constraints are removed

And, if I'm convinced by a recent advertising campaign, it's a time to spend the kids' inheritance!

Do my general impressions provide an accurate definition? During my schooling, I was taught to head to the dictionary to find the meaning of words. *The Concise Macquarie Dictionary* has eight designations for retirement (clearly, it's a busy word!):

1. The act of retiring

2. The state of being retired

3. Removal or retiring from service, office, or business

4. Withdrawal into privacy or seclusion

5. Privacy or seclusion

6. A private or secluded place

7. Retreat of a military force

8. Repurchase of its own securities by a company[4]

The second and third are relevant for my purposes—but they both use the verb to define the noun, which seems a bit circular (and thus somewhat unhelpful) to me!

So, what does the verb mean? The same dictionary defines *retire* in six ways:

1. To withdraw, or go away or apart, to a place of abode, shelter, or seclusion

2. To go to bed

3. To withdraw from office, business, or active life

4. To fall back or retreat, as from battle or danger

5. To withdraw, go away, or remove oneself

6. *Sport.* to leave the field, ring, etc. before completion of the contest, usu. because of injury

Perhaps some may consider that second definition most relevant—whether it's voluntarily or involuntarily, or where "bed" equals "couch in front of the TV" (sorry, couldn't resist that one). But, more realistically, it's the third definition that's pertinent here (as long as withdrawal from active life doesn't mean death—or is that just a form of permanent retirement?).

Based on that definition, the idea of ceasing paid employment—which was my earlier gut feeling about the nature of retirement—is included. People reach a certain stage in life—whether determined by age, health, or inclination—and they either decide or are forced to leave the paid workforce. They retire. They change their status—especially, within my Australian context, as far as Centrelink[5] and the Tax Office are concerned. They now meet their ongoing daily financial needs from superannuation investments and/or government pensions and/or charity.

Yet, is that a comprehensive definition? Think of some of the situations often described with "retirement" language that don't fall within that definition. For example, there are situations where people "retire" without leaving *paid* employment. Some people serve many years in voluntary capacities (that is, "employment" for which they get no payment) and then reach a point where they cease those activities. It's usual to refer to them as "retiring" from their position. They often receive the nonprofit sector's equivalent of "the golden handshake."

A second example is people who officially retire (in the sense of ceasing paid employment) and then engage in voluntary community-service-type roles as a means of both "contributing to the community" and "occupying themselves" during their retirement years—that is, effectively they're still working. Some become so involved they wonder how they ever found sufficient time for paid employment!

A third example is people who begin to draw the age pension and thus are considered "retired" (at least by the relevant governmental authorities) without ever going through the event of "retiring." For example, people (most often women) involved in "full-time home duties" usually don't enter the workforce officially and don't cease such duties on attaining the requisite age, but are entitled to the age pension.

Thus "ceasing paid employment"—while perhaps adequate as a popular working definition—seems somewhat fuzzy around the edges. A significant amount of that fuzziness stems from the separation of the workplace from family and home that resulted from the Industrial Revolution. Rather than working for their livelihood within the family environment (farming and cottage industries), many people began to work in factories and bring their wages home.

That led to a distinction between employment-type work (which also may include community service activities) and maintaining-the-household-type work. In today's society, the former continues to receive preeminence, and is also more likely to be associated with retirement.

I've identified some possible problems with this definition—it doesn't account for people who work without pay, or the fact that they many continue their work long after they have reached the official "retirement age." But there are other problems to note as well: for example, what about people who maintain a very active lifestyle after retiring from their job?

Is it worth pursuing an alternate definition? For example, could retirement be defined in terms of levels of accountability? Those involved in the "workforce" (that is, people in employment-type situations) are accountable to others for various blocks of their time. Employees are responsible to employers to be present during work hours. Volunteers are responsible to supervisors to be present for the tasks they undertake to complete. Even self-employed people have constraints to which they must conform to keep their businesses viable.

Retirement removes those sorts of constraints. It's not that retirees are no longer accountable to anyone—they must, after all, still conform to society's legal requirements. But they're no longer accountable to provide labor within the "workforce." They are legally free from that responsibility. They no longer have to participate in "work-for-the-dole" schemes if they can't find paid employment and wish to avail themselves of pension benefits. Yet this too fails to account for the situation of those involved in "full-time home duties." Their "work" situation and any levels of accountability do not change when the government deems that they have "retired" and begins to pay them the age pension.

Another approach is to consider retirement in terms of the level of expected community responsibility. Under normal circumstances, modern society expects each family unit to fulfill two major functions: to maintain itself (household work) and to contribute to the overall economy (economic work). Within that expectation, each family unit is free to organize itself in terms of how each partner contributes to those two major functions (that is, how they split responsibility for household work and economic work). Retirement involves removing the family unit's ongoing responsibility to contribute economic work. Yet some continue in paid employment or voluntary service even though their "community responsibility" to do so has ceased.

I suspect my education has perfected me in the art of finding exceptions and difficulties. So far, I haven't discovered a fully satisfactory definition of retirement. Part of the problem is that I tend primarily (and incorrectly) to associate work with paid employment (discussed further in chapter 4). But for our purposes, I think "ceasing paid employment" (whether by will or by necessity) will be a workable definition of retirement—as long as we remember the larger issues already noted.

To summarize in slightly different terms: retirement involves a new status. For most, it involves a significant reduction in the amount of work required—but not a cessation of all work (unless, perhaps, one has enough resources to hire sufficient personal servants!). For most, it also involves a significant increase in the amount of discretionary time available.

EXPECTATIONS SURROUNDING RETIREMENT

Thus the prospect of retirement generates significant expectations. Perhaps in the early history of retirement those expectations focused on rest—the long years of physical labor took such an exhaustive toll on the human body that one had little remaining energy or vitality for one's few remaining years. But circumstances have changed. Those few remaining years grew to a couple of decades. And many occupations now require minimal physical exertion, thus reducing the accumulated wear and tear on the human body. And medical science continues to produce important life-improving breakthroughs. The result is that most retirees will enjoy good health for many retirement years. Thus, they now seek a more active lifestyle. The focus has shifted from "retirement from" to "retirement to"; from rest to (active) leisure.

Some sectors of the economy seek to exploit this opportunity. Here is a growing number of "cashed-up" people with large amounts of discretionary time on their hands. They no longer contribute to the overall economy via economic work, but they still have the responsibility to contribute (both to the economy and the bottom line of innovative entrepreneurs) as consumers—or, at least, there is the potential to persuade them that this is their basic community responsibility. They can even access more cash by entering into reverse mortgages!

Thus retirees' expectations—at least as far as they're influenced by popular culture—include things like travel, leisure, hobbies, crafts, good food, exotic drinks, sports, movies, tours, games, social clubs, and the like. They aim to occupy time in interesting ways—perhaps seeking to entertain themselves lest they surrender to boredom. These activities are not sinful in themselves. As I noted in the introduction, one could argue that these are examples of enjoying God's good creation with gratitude and thankfulness. Yet the focus of the overall dream that's presented to us is very much on self: self-direction, self-fulfillment, self-indulgence, self-exploration. After their many years contributing to the community through economic work (though perhaps most would envision this work far more self-centeredly), they are released to pursue their own desires—to put themselves ahead of the community.

At this point, you may wish to ask when any of the good activities mentioned above becomes self-indulgent (whether we're referring to life before or after retirement). Is it okay to spend an hour a day reading a novel, but indulgent if I use more of my God-given time on that activity? Is it okay to spend $50 a week on my hobby, but no more? We like to come up with rules and regulations about such things, but that takes us in the direction of legalism rather than grace. Besides, the Bible warns us that such rules and regulations "lack any value in restraining sensual indulgence" (Colossians 2:16–23). It's certainly not my place to define precisely when any particular activity becomes self-indulgent for any particular person.

Yet I have no doubt that the Western retirement dream promoted by popular culture urges us in the direction of self-indulgence. And so, from a Christian perspective, alarm bells should well and truly be ringing. We claim to follow the Messiah who said:

> If anyone would come after me, he must deny himself and take up his cross and follow me. For whoever wants to save his life will lose it, but whoever loses his life for me and for the gospel will save it. What good is it for a man to gain the whole world, yet forfeit his soul? Or what can a man give in exchange for his soul? (Mark 8:34–37)

How does our culture's self-focused retirement dream fit with Jesus' call to deny self? I think the two are incompatible. What good is it for a retiree to gain the whole gamut of "must-have" leisure experiences on offer and thus achieve the "great retirement dream"? Will this result in a forfeited soul?

Thus it seems to me that, even if I conclude that retirement itself is a biblically or theologically legitimate concept, this self-centered version of retirement remains inappropriate for Christians. Our response to the gospel involves a lifelong commitment to align ourselves with God's purposes and to serve God's will—where "lifelong" includes the remainder of our time in this age and all of our time in the age to come. There is no option for some interim period of retirement from God's kingdom where we await its final consummation. Perhaps that's not quite true—there is such an option, but it involves recommitment to membership of this present evil age that rebels against God. I think the view that retirement is simply heaven's "waiting room"—where we check out of Christian ministry (but not our enjoyment of life) while patiently waiting for our call home—conflicts with the Bible's description of the Christian life.

This is worth thinking through—seriously. Our culture's version of retirement comes with several unhelpful nuances. *You've put in the hard years—you deserve a break. You've done your bit—it's time to relax. Let others pick up the slack. You've looked after others—it's time to look after yourself. You've disciplined yourself to get to this point—now it's time to let your hair down and indulge yourself. You've denied yourself to save for retirement—now you get to spend your hard-earned wealth. You're the boss now—do as you please. You've achieved the magic age—you're entitled to this.*

These subtle messages bombard us throughout life. It's not surprising that they influence us and seep into our mental processes. This is our cultural conditioning. As such, we often don't realize it's going on—it is simply what we accept as normal. As Claude Pepper put it, "That last part of the long journey should be as healthy and as long and as happy as it can be made by a grateful society and grateful families."[6]

But this is where our minds need renewal by the gospel. Much of this cultural thinking reflects humanity's original sin—the choice to establish our own autonomy. Independently of God, we declared our right to determine what was good for ourselves. We chose to define for ourselves what true life is all about. It resulted in death, because we cut ourselves off from the source of true life. It seems to me that so many of the nuances of our culture's version of retirement reassert those same attitudes of autonomy and independence. They reject God's rightful rule over us. Thus, we have a great need to reexamine our ideas about this stage of life in the light of God's word. This is crucial. Even if retirement from paid employment is legitimate, retirement from God's service is not.

Other writers have dealt with this aspect of the issue. For example, John Piper's booklet *Rethinking Retirement* is freely available online.[7] Kel Willis labels retirement as another stage of growth and urges people to finish well in *Interact,* an Australian journal for pastors.[8] In *Purpose and Power in Retirement,* Harold Koenig encourages us to purposefully make the most of the opportunities provided by this last "third" of our lives. Ben Witherington III believes we're given lifelong vocations (note vocation is not the equivalent of a job or paid employment), and that the Bible doesn't support the idea of "retiring" from this service.[9]

OUTLINING THE ISSUES

As I see it, thinking through retirement biblically and theologically raises several interrelated issues. Clearly, since retirement is a modern invention, the Bible doesn't deal with the topic directly. But that doesn't mean it says nothing of relevance to this subject.

For starters, the Bible has plenty to say about the issue of work. In particular, it considers work one of God's good gifts to humanity. As I will argue in chapter 4, I believe the Bible presumes that work is normal for humans: that is, in the Scriptures we find the expectation that humans will work unless there are good reasons to the contrary. Thus I believe the burden of proof is on those who wish to defend the modern practice of retirement. We need to have a very good reason to choose leisure instead of continuing to exercise God's good gift of work.

How might Christians justify withdrawing from work? One possibility is the method of taking "proof texts" from Scripture. I hesitate to use that term because, in some circles, it receives negative press—and with good reason. There are significant dangers. If (or maybe when) Christians look for "proof texts" in Scripture, they may rip passages from their context (both their immediate context and their wider biblical context) and mold them to their personal desires (either intentionally or unintentionally). They may also organize texts of Scripture such that only the passages that support the desired outcome are presented; those that support an alternate viewpoint are simply ignored (again, either intentionally or unintentionally).

But, in the long run, from an evangelical perspective, all our theological assertions rely on the support of biblical passages for their ultimate authority. God's revelation is our final court of appeal. Thus, we strive to present a complete picture that includes all relevant material from the Scriptures considered within its proper context. This will be my primary approach in this book.

Even so, turning to the Scriptures is not the only possible approach to the issue of retirement. An alternate approach might begin at the framework level.[10] Modern retirement is part of a modern economic system. Considering it in isolation from the system has inherent dangers—especially since seeking to alter or abolish it may have repercussions for other elements of the system. Our modern economy is vastly different from and far more complex than the ancient biblical economies. Significant economic developments occurred during the biblical period, both within and outside ancient Israel. Such developments didn't cease with the closure of the canon. This approach involves evaluating ancient Israel's economy as a complete system: how it functioned and what values it sought to promote (especially the values encoded in God's law). Then the issue is how those important values can be promoted within our modern economy and whether retirement fits within them.

For example, according to Israel's written law, the primary means of production within their economy (arable land) was distributed equitably. The Jubilee Year regulations maintained that distribution, even in the face of economic hardship in the intervening years. The Jubilee laws also, in theory, prevented a small minority from accumulating vast estates and becoming land barons in perpetuity. With gleaning laws and the triennial tithe for the poor, God made provision for those who fell through the cracks of the land distribution system (such as widows, orphans, and foreigners). The goal appears to be a community where all enjoyed God's *shalom*—together celebrating life in the land with the blessings God gave them.[11] How do those values translate into our economy? For example, when one applies these biblical values to retirement, framework-level questions arise: Should some permanently stop work to enjoy themselves while others struggle to survive? Should some accumulate resources in superannuation funds while others have inadequate resources for basic necessities? Rather, should they not continue working to provide resources and help for the disadvantaged? On the flip side, if the aged don't permanently stop work, will there be a shortage of jobs for the next generation? Or should we be more innovative about job creation? What can be done to achieve a greater sense of communal celebration that includes all? This is only a small sampling of the complex issues involved at the broader framework level.

I don't deal with those issues in this book—that task remains for a subsequent volume. Yet it's important to remember that perspective. For even if I conclude that the concept of retirement is not justified by what God has revealed to us in the Bible, I might still seek to defend it at this framework level. God allows humanity considerable freedom in the way we structure our economies. God doesn't legislate one economic pattern for all time. For one thing, the legislation he provides has insufficient details to fully define a single economic pattern. Rather, God provides values or ethical norms that he considers important and expects conformity to those values in the systems we construct. The issue then becomes: can we construct an economic system that includes retirement and remains true to God's values?

If the answer is no, then serious thought about appropriate responses will be required. Christians live in secular states—sojourners within this world. Those states enact the laws under which we live, including laws about retirement and superannuation. Are there ways to obey both God and state at the same time? Can we force non-Christians to continue employing us against state legislation? Should we set up our own employment situations? Could we continue to work outside paid employment? And what impact will our actions have on other sectors of the economy? None of these questions have easy answers—I raise them simply to indicate that this too is a complex issue.

On the other hand, if retirement is a legitimate concept, one other big issue that requires exploration is its funding. For example, in Australia, our salary packages are structured to include superannuation. It's obligatory for employers to contribute to their employees' personal superannuation funds. In effect, this is a compulsory savings scheme designed eventually to reduce or eliminate the government's obligation to provide age pensions (which, as we have seen, are a relatively recent self-imposed obligation). Such superannuation schemes could arguably fall within the definition of "storing up treasure on earth" (Matthew 6:19–21). At the very least, it's a question that should be explored within the broader context of what the Bible has to say about money—its purposes, its dangers, the idolatry of greed, the value of contentment, and so on.

Again, the issue of funding retirement could be approached from the framework level (assuming that we believe it's appropriate for individuals to accumulate wealth in superannuation funds). Retirement funds make a significant contribution to modern economies. They provide access to vast amounts of money to be used for investment in diverse projects. Many projects would founder if

these retirement savings did not exist. Yet ethical issues are also involved. First, simply having funds available doesn't justify a project
at the ethical level. Second, the goal of superannuation funds involves maximizing returns for future retirees—and that may result
in investing in unethical projects.[12] Third, maximizing returns may
also result in prioritizing investments toward Western projects—
and that may result in an increasing gap with the majority world.
Again, this short list is not intended to be exhaustive.

In short, I am very conscious that this book only begins to
tackle the issues surrounding the theology of retirement. In the
church circles in which I was raised, there was a desire to justify everything by the Bible. That's a good desire. It demonstrates a longing to submit to God's will and purposes (although I'm unsure why
they never extended that desire to justify our practices by the Bible
to the subject of retirement!). Yet, as noted above, in pursuing that
desire by the proof-text method, it's easy to overlook some parts
of the Bible's teaching—especially matters relating to the broader
context and the overall direction of the Bible's narrative (such as
how to structure an economy). These matters are part of dealing
with the complexities involved in studying issues the Bible doesn't
deal with directly.

Thus, in closing this chapter, I wish to highlight two significant
matters. First, I intend to discuss Scripture passages that could, at
least on the surface, be used to justify the concept of retirement.
Because this is clearly not the purpose of these texts (since retirement was not yet invented when they were written), I wish to take
great care as I draw conclusions on the basis of those texts. Hence,
the desire to be "thorough" in dealing with these texts. Second, I
want to make clear that I'm very conscious that this book is only a
beginning. I think this is the right place to start the discussion—but
I realize that what I write here does not complete the discussion.
I've mentioned a few questions for further study in this introduction, but even this list is not exhaustive. I'm sure you will discover
your own questions along the way.

2

My Cultural and Christian Heritage

Several years ago, I read Craig Blomberg's *Neither Poverty nor Riches*. In the preface, he reflects on factors that influence how he interprets what the Bible says about poverty and riches—such as the tendency to read the Bible so it conforms to his current practices with money and his lack of personal experience of the powerlessness that accompanies poverty. I found this reflection helpful. Not only did he alert me to potential blind spots in his exposition, he also challenged me to be alert to those same potential blind spots in my own thinking. Since then, I've encountered similar introductory comments in other books and likewise found them helpful.

My aim in this chapter is to do that about myself in the hope that you will benefit in a similar way. Of course, the nature of cultural blind spots is that usually we don't recognize them. They're part of what we consider normal. It takes a journey into a "foreign" culture or the challenge of an insightful person for me to realize that not everyone sees "normal" the same way I do. Sometimes those differences are relatively trivial; sometimes they're at the heart of how I view the world. I'm sure I won't cover all of them in this chapter (as cultural blind spots, some of them are still unknown to me!), but hopefully I'll introduce the important ones.

MY CULTURAL BACKGROUND

For the vast majority of my life, I've lived in Australia—a wealthy, Western democracy. Thus, I've enjoyed privileges not readily available in many parts of the world, including a lengthy period of education to further indoctrinate me in Western thought patterns and values. By Australian standards, I'm middle class—which means, by global standards, I'm rich. Yet because of my cultural surroundings, it's very easy to forget the latter and to grumble at my perceived privations—perceptions that are strongly fuelled by the advertising industry. In reality, I've never experienced a time in life when I've lacked life's basic necessities. Rather, my experience is that God has always supplied more than enough for my needs. This is not meant as a boast. Nor is it a result of some level of faith on my part. Nor is it something I've deserved. Nor do I have any desire that God change it (at least, not in a downward direction!). It's simply my assessment of my experience. It's how I see the responsibility God has given me.

Do I understand poverty? Certainly not at the experiential level. Like most people in Western democracies, I've read about it from time to time. Over the years, I've explored several liberation theologies from an academic point of view. On occasion, I've seen poverty firsthand—even ministered alongside it. But I don't delude myself that those brief forays give me an understanding of living it.

Within that context, I recognize that retirement is a rich person's topic. Its widespread availability is limited to wealthy economies that can afford to support large numbers of people not working. In other economies, it is available only to the elite. In some economies, the average lifespan remains below the age at which I expect to retire. For a significant segment of the world's population, retirement is not an option. I think that should influence my thinking about retirement. At the very least, I should recognize that this benefit accrues to me, not because I've earned it, but because of where I was born. Should I simply accept that? Or should I see it as an issue of injustice? And if it is unjust, what should I do about that? Should I continue to cultivate this dream that's unavailable to so many? These are questions I'd rather avoid, but I can't afford to overlook them.

So, how have I viewed this privilege? I entered the workforce expecting to retire at age sixty-five (if not earlier), at which time the Australian government would provide me with the age pension. That was the cultural norm. I didn't think to question it. It didn't occur to me that it was different in other countries. My first employer encouraged me to join their superannuation scheme, and they voluntarily matched my contributions. That too was fairly normal within Australian professional occupations. Over the years of my working life, the government has tweaked that cultural norm. Since I started working, the retirement age has increased, and retirement is no longer compulsory. Most importantly, all employers are now required to offer superannuation funds for their employees.

I suspect that last-mentioned tweak generated the greatest change. It strengthened the "pressure" to save for retirement. The government pension is still available *at present*—but there are hints that may not always be the case. There's a strong rumor (the cynic in me suspects that it is fuelled by financial advisors or some other group with a vested interest) that the pension is not adequate to maintain the Australian lifestyle. And the government, aware of its mushrooming financial burden of paying age pensions, is encouraging people to become self-funded retirees. So I do the patriotic thing and build my own retirement nest egg. But that means I'm less generous in the present, and I'm tempted to find my retirement security in the treasures of this world, rather than in my heavenly Father. This whole scenario could certainly cloud my judgment when considering issues surrounding retirement.

Do I understand what it's like to live in a culture where there's no retirement? It's not a big part of my experience—and not something I was conscious of at the time or discussed at length with those in that culture.[1] It didn't impact me personally since I still intended to retire in Australia. Does that make a difference in this undertaking? At one level, I think not. This book is aimed at people like me. Its purpose is to encourage such people to evaluate what I think is a cultural blind spot. On the other hand, since I do share this cultural blind spot, it would be helpful to hear the perspective of those for whom retirement is not an option. They might well raise issues that haven't even entered my thinking. As you think about the subject of retirement, I encourage you to seek out the perspective of those who don't have that luxury available to them.

What are my own expectations about how I might spend my retirement? I'm aware that, as I've grown older, my attitude toward the things I anticipated about retirement (hobbies, travel, reading) has changed. While I have no doubt I would find pleasure in those things, they seem increasingly trivial in my thinking. I'd like to think that's a good thing, but realize it's quite possible I've simply replaced them with other trivial things that have a more "Christian" flavor, but no real value from a kingdom perspective.

What's the bottom line of all this? I have a vested interest in preserving the concept of retirement. My culture presents it as a highly desirable goal. I can certainly feel its allure—the "greener pastures" beckon. And throughout my working years, I've made financial investments toward achieving this goal. That could certainly skew my judgment when reading the biblical text. Yet I also hope that I continue to grow in realizing I have a vested interest in God's will. In theory, I know that God is good and what he says is best for me. It's just that I often struggle with that in practice—especially when what he says differs from what I want to do (and far too often, what I want is shaped by the materialistic dreams promoted by Australian culture).

On the other hand, I suspect I have ascetic tendencies—not because I think asceticism has value in itself, but because I'm conscious of the vast inequities in our world. On a global scale, I have so much and so many choices. I like to delude myself into thinking it's because I work hard and save even harder, but the reality is that it's primarily because of where I was born. Many people in the world work far harder than I do, and yet struggle to survive. Thus, I seek to live a modest (albeit still very comfortable) lifestyle, so I can use my money for gospel work and the relief of poverty. This also influences my thinking on retirement. How can I sit back and relax while so much gospel work remains undone? How can I indulge myself in endless leisure while so many face poverty and injustice? I think I'm still a long way from allowing that thinking to drive me as much as it should, but it is a significant element.

These are all different ways of highlighting that I live in an affluent culture. It's part of the air I breathe. It's what I so easily take for granted—that this is simply how life's supposed to be. Greed is an art form that's central to the Australian lifestyle. Sometimes I don't even notice that I've adopted it in my own thinking patterns. One generation's privileges become the next generation's rights. Could a government ever announce to the Australian public: "The age pension is bankrupting the country—in order to be economically responsible, we plan to abolish it"? It would be political suicide. Even to suggest that we as a country are living beyond our means, and that everyone needs to tighten their belts, would ensure swift political ruin. We expect our government to increase our living standards. We now even believe that it's our right. That's all part of the environment in which I consider this subject.

To turn now to a second potential blind spot, I'm conscious that Australian culture emphasizes individualism and personal independence. Personally, I find it hard to break out of that mold—even knowing God's desire for his people to exhibit strong communal values. I lived in Papua New Guinea—a strongly communal culture—for five years, but little of that seems to have penetrated my psyche. It was a college situation with several expatriate staff and students coming from many tribal groups, so it wasn't a typical Melanesian community.

I know that my individualistic and independent spirit influences my thoughts about retirement. I tend to focus on securing my personal future, and to place that above both the current needs of others and the overall good of the community. Sure, I can argue that my aim to self-fund my retirement will benefit the community that won't have to support me financially (note my assumption that retirement is the norm)—but I know that, when the time comes, I'll still face the temptation to supplement my self-generated income with the government pension. Greed is part of the cultural air I breathe, and God is still in the process of growing contentment in me.

I think our current notions of retirement are particularly driven by this individualistic spirit—the focus on self-fulfillment and self-indulgence. I wonder what retirement would look like in a more communal culture. Would some community members still be able to withdraw from working for the community's benefit if the community faced significant needs? Would they be able to do so if the community had no resources to support them? I think a very different version of retirement would arise in a communal culture—if it arose at all.

The Australian attitude to work is a third potential blind spot. We affectionately call our country "the land of the long weekend." It may be a way of saying we're lazy, but its primary meaning is that we value leisure above work. We live for the weekend. During the first half of the week, we talk about what we did last weekend. The second half of the week is spent discussing our plans for the coming weekend. The work that happens in between enables us to earn money so we can really enjoy the weekends. This is especially highlighted by the fact we label Wednesday "hump day."

Now, to be fair, work patterns in Australia are changing and becoming far more complex, such that some think we're now the land of the lost weekend. Also, that major focus on leisure is not the only attitude toward work within Australian culture—we have issues with workaholism and people who live for their work as well—but I think leisure remains the predominant, underlying attitude. And that helps fuel the retirement dream. Retirement is the ultimate long weekend. It's leisure forever—well, until your health gives out. It allows you to enjoy the very thing our culture values highly, but without the interruption of work. I need to question that cultural value. Does God value leisure more than work?

I suspect a remnant of Greek culture also underlies this attitude—that something of their aversion to manual labor has broadened into an aversion to all labor. It seems to me that many in Australian culture have a negative attitude toward work itself. It's not something they enjoy; rather, it's a necessary evil they endure both to survive and to fund their leisure activities. It's not a gift from God; rather, it's a curse that cramps their style and hinders them from "real" life. That attitude—though it is perhaps not always put that strongly—permeates Australian thinking at various levels. And that too needs questioning. Is not work one of God's good gifts to us? This issue is discussed further in chapter 4.

Clearly, I also write as a man—a fourth potential blind spot (both genetic and cultural). I lived my formative years in a patriarchal society. I'm aware that my early stereotype of retirement betrayed a male bias—the male breadwinner ceased work at age sixty-five, while the female homemaker continued her tasks till death. That was the cultural norm of that period. The question of retirement from home duties was never raised. Retirement related to paid employment only. In some ways, that stereotype has diminished with increasing female participation in the workforce. Yet I suspect the ongoing "homemaker" tasks following retirement still largely fall to women. This issue remains important in discussions about retirement.

For example, inequality in the workplace—such as the glass ceiling and unequal pay for equal work—does impact retirement savings and result in significant disadvantages for women. Temporary absences from the workforce surrounding the birth of children will also result in lower balances in women's retirement funds compared with men. I don't wish to downplay those important issues. However, these issues focus on how to achieve more equitable retirement models. My present task is to determine whether retirement itself is a legitimate concept.

Ageism is a fifth potential blind spot—one to which I was completely oblivious until recently, when I began to experience it firsthand (though it's only been the proverbial tip of the iceberg). How are older people treated in Australian culture? There is some respect generally, but not as much as was given in previous generations. Many factors contribute to this. First, old age is now relatively common (a version of the familiarity breeds contempt syndrome). Second, much of the old person's previously valued knowledge and wisdom (accumulated through years of experience) is now freely available through books and online. Third, the younger generations of Australians are beginning to resent the aged due to the increasing drain on government resources required to fund the seeming explosion of old people (exacerbated by declining birth rates).

Now, the elderly are simply viewed as people beyond their use-by date. Their knowledge and skills are too outdated for the workplace. Their minds are stuck in a rut and resistant to change. They're isolated from society with age-related activities and in retirement villages. Their deteriorating bodies are suitable only for medical waiting rooms and assisted-care living. Worst of all, they provide poignant reminders of diminishing vitality and everyone's final destination—death.

This summary of ageism is an exaggerated stereotype, but the point remains valid. Our shared cultural understanding of age is problematic. We treat retired people as old. We think they're slow, feeble, confused, doddery, deaf, irrelevant, incompetent, cautious, useless—and treat them accordingly. We sideline them from the main action and leave them to their own devices. And so we're not surprised when our attitude toward the aged becomes a self-fulfilling prophecy.

Australian culture works hard to sugarcoat the pill. With the help of our overseas partners, we've invented a slick, well-oiled retirement industry. It's all about living your retirement years to the fullest and enjoying all those experiences you were too busy for while you worked—as long as you've got enough money. You've done your bit. Now it's time for you to make way for the next generation and enjoy your "golden years." And be assured that your consumption makes a great contribution to the economy—so much so, we'd like you to spend the kids' inheritance. But no one's really interested in you as a person anymore. You've got the time to sit and chat, but no one else does, except people your own age.

This too impacts our thinking about retirement. We have the tendency to view everyone with the same stereotype (after all, using categories is the only way we can make sense of our world). And our stereotype indicates retirement is necessary because old people are worn out. That may be true for some, but I suspect that these days they are a small minority. And the fact that we have few social sanctions against ageism means the stereotypes are widely accepted and even made the subject of humor. While ageism has been explored academically, the results of such studies have made very little impact on mainstream culture.[2]

Now, in what I've written about myself—and my overall approach in this book—I've usually emphasized the fact that I am "Australian" rather than "Western." This is deliberate. I've read books implying that they're written from a general Western perspective that incorrectly assume they're equally applicable to all cultures within the Western world. Sometimes, as I've read, I've thought: "That may be true in England or America, but it's not how things are here in Australia." Usually, I still find those books helpful—I just experience a level of frustration because of their wrong assumptions. I wish to avoid causing you that sort of frustration.

Still, lest you feel that this book is only for Australians, let me also add this: from my limited understanding of other Western cultures gained through the media, I'm reasonably confident that most of what I've observed in my Australian context is also applicable in most other Western contexts. This is a view shared by people from some of those other Western cultures who reviewed the book. However, in the long run, you'll need to decide for yourself whether there are any relevant differences in your own culture.

Enough of my cultural heritage. Looking back on what I've written, I realize I've gone beyond my stated aim. In raising various possible cultural blind spots, I've also strayed into something of a personal confession about the potential pitfalls in examining the subject of retirement. On reflection, I think that's a good thing because it identifies pertinent areas in which others are likely to have similar struggles. The temptations I face are unlikely to be unique to me.

MY THEOLOGICAL CULTURE

Of course, when writing about the Bible, it's not only one's cultural background and viewpoint that are significant, but also one's theological background and viewpoint. So, briefly, what's my religious heritage? I was raised by Christian parents within the Baptist tradition in Sydney. During my university years, I finished Moore College's Certificate in Theology (Anglican) by correspondence. I completed my residential theological study at the Baptist College in Sydney, and most of my postgraduate study was through the same institution. I've ministered in several Baptist churches and one Evangelical (a brand name at this point) church. I've also been involved with several evangelical interdenominational organizations, including five years teaching at a theological college in Papua New Guinea.

My personal theological convictions have developed within that background. These are the communities that have shaped how I read the Bible. I identify myself as evangelical (a label that, unfortunately, is increasingly flexible) and baptistic (a label that also can cover a wide range of viewpoints).

What are the important principles to identify in relation to this study? First, I consider the Bible to be God's authoritative word that trumps any human authority. My aim is to understand what the Bible says and what implications that has for our subject. This is not to say that human authorities are unimportant or that they have nothing to contribute to our understanding of the Bible. As I've just mentioned, the Christian communities I've belonged to have very much influenced my understanding of God's word. While I value that influence and training, my main focus is to understand as accurately as possible what God communicates through the Bible, so as to conform my beliefs and lifestyle to God's will.

Second, I wish to focus on the biblical text that has been handed down to us. For many years now, an important area of critical scholarship has sought to recover the oral and written traditions that are believed to be behind the final form of the biblical text. There is nothing wrong with this in itself. Sometimes the Bible refers to other sources (for example, 1 Kings often refers to "the book of the annals of the kings of Israel"). But such historical studies vary in their results. Part of the reason is their speculative nature. Some, at least, have helped our understanding of the text. Where they're relevant, I'm happy to draw on their insights.

However, it's the final document that the Christian community accepts as authoritative. We don't have "the book of the annals of the kings of Israel" or any other written source alongside the Bible. Even if we established with certainty what was included in the Bible from such a source, we still wouldn't know what was excluded. Nor would it be authoritative for us even if we did have it, since God has not included that document within the canon. Thus, the final form of the text is the focus of my study.

Third, I think it's important to understand the biblical text in its historical and cultural context before applying it in the modern setting. The various books of the Bible originated in specific historical and cultural settings. They relate events that occurred in those settings. While there is a sense in which God communicates a "timeless message" to humanity (in that it's relevant to all humans in all cultures throughout all history), he chose to do so in particular settings. The better we understand those settings—what life was like, how people viewed their world, what the words used meant within their external context—the better we will understand the biblical text.

This will be developed more in the next chapter, but two quick examples will help illustrate what I mean. In my childhood years, the word *gay* meant "happy." I no longer hear it used in that sense. If I read the sentence "I'm gay," its meaning depends on whether the text was written in 1900 or 2000. Similarly, I heard of a relatively new Christian who came across the word *publican* (tax collector) in his New Testament. He quite naturally interpreted the word in terms of his background: he thought publicans oversaw establishments that we in Australia call "pubs." But that's not its meaning in the New Testament text.[3]

Fourth, I believe the Bible presents a unified narrative of God's dealings with humanity. Clearly, many human authors were involved over a lengthy period of time. They wrote with diverse styles and produced a variety of literary genres. They dealt with a vast range of material, both historically and conceptually. Yet one story line brings a basic unity to the overall project. In short, it's the narrative of God's purposes in creation. In order to interpret what God says about specific issues such as work and retirement, we need to understand the broader narrative within which they appear. If we are ignorant of God's original plan or his ultimate goal for this narrative, we are likely to take individual statements about work, age, and rest out of context.

The Bible begins with creation and concludes with the new creation. Both demonstrate life as God intended—humans living in contented harmony with God, each other, and the rest of creation; humans ruling responsibly over creation under God's authority. But in Genesis 3, the story's complication is introduced: humanity choosing to rule independently of God and in defiance of his instructions. The rest of the Bible's narrative is about what God does in response to this rebellion to restore creation to his original purposes and to recreate a people who will submit to those purposes. In other words, it's about what God does to achieve his kingdom.[4] That's the overarching plot—the driving force behind what God communicates to us. Everything else should be considered in the context of that plot. Without that picture of the forest firmly in mind, we're likely to misinterpret the trees.

That's not to say there are no apparent diversions along the way. There are many twists and turns as the Bible's narrative unfolds. And there are elements—such as the wisdom literature—that don't always appear to relate to the main plot. But, as with any piece of communication, we expect a level of coherence. Thus we think it best to interpret the individual sections within the context of the whole. I don't like it when someone doesn't listen to my entire message, or takes part of it out of context. Why should I think I can do this with what God says to me?

This is also not to say there aren't any tensions within the biblical narrative—at least, from our perspective. God is infinite; we humans are finite creatures. God communicates to us within our finitude. We sometimes struggle to hold together all that God tells us. For example, at times I've heard people speak of God's love and God's justice or judgment as if these are two incompatible concepts—as if God acts in love on one occasion and with justice at a different time. Yet God is not schizophrenic; he is a united being who always acts with loving justice (or should that be just love?).

To reiterate: I believe the Bible presents a unified narrative. This is why I consider it essential to establish the comprehensive biblical view of work (the subject of chapter 4). It presents the topic of work in terms of that overall plot—tracing through the major elements of what the Bible says as the plot develops and comes to its conclusion. That's the foundation. It's only within that framework that we can wrestle with the subject of if and when it's legitimate to stop work.

Fifth, I believe the Bible is first and foremost about God. God is the main character in this drama. God creates the setting for the drama. God brings the other actors into that setting. God reveals himself to us through the drama. God acts to rescue a people for himself. God directs history toward his purposes. God is the One who will consummate his kingdom. Sure, the Bible talks about humans as well—indeed, at an important level, it talks about all of us. Yet the spotlight is not primarily on us, except to the extent that we rebelliously keep twisting it in our direction. We are here to conform to God's purposes; God does not exist to conform to our purposes.

We humans often forget that—something that stems from our initial rebellion in the garden. We tend to think we have the right to define work, leisure, and retirement to suit ourselves without reference to God's purposes for us. We often expect God to bless our self-centered plans, instead of following his good plans for us. In a sense, this is another way of saying that I read the Bible to find out God's purposes so I can align my life with them, rather than the other way around. I look for how I can fit into the drama he directs so as to honor him and bring glory to his name.

Sixth, I need to be aware of my own biases when I interpret the Bible. There are the cultural biases I described in the first half of this chapter. These shape the way I read the Bible. There is also the bias arising from my own sinful, self-centered nature. When I read the Bible, I tend to exaggerate the bits I like and ignore the bits I dislike (or think are unreasonable, or find too demanding, or a whole host of other similar excuses). I'm very good at justifying what I want to do. I've had years of practice. Often, I do it without even being aware of it. Thus I need to apply my mind diligently to understanding what the text actually says—not what I want it to say. And I need the enabling of God's Spirit within me both to read the text aright and to help overcome that sinful bias.

Seventh, I believe Jesus is central to the Bible's plot and holds it together. In other words, this narrative is primarily about him. Jesus is the culmination of God's plan to bring rebellious humans into his kingdom. In Jesus' death, God both demonstrates his justice and displays his love. The whole Old Testament prepares for this event. Humanity's history exhibits the disastrous consequences that flow from their original defiance of God's instruction. Even the nation God chose to work through to achieve his purposes showed humanity's inability to truly live in submission to God. It became clear that, if people were to be restored to right relationship with God, he would need to both initiate and enable it. And so God made promises about what he would do. Those promises lead up to and find their fulfillment in Jesus, and then the New Testament and the rest of church history flow forward from the Jesus event.

It involves the proclamation of that event to the ends of the earth, inviting people to enter God's kingdom.

More than that, Jesus not only fulfills what we recognize as prophetic elements from the Old Testament, he also fulfills many of its institutions and other elements. Jesus is true humanity—the One who perfectly displays God's image as Adam was created to do. He is the true Israel—the One who fulfills the task of God's Son. He is the Deliverer. He is the one perfect sacrifice. He is our great High Priest. He is the Temple. He is the true Prophet. He is Wisdom. He is the Word. He is the Messianic King in David's line. He fulfills the Sabbath and brings in the Jubilee. He is God's good Shepherd who truly cares for his flock. The list could go on.

Thus I believe that as we consider the Bible's teaching, we need to understand it in terms of the overall narrative focused by a Christo-centric lens. For example, if I simply studied the Bible's teaching on work isolated from what Jesus has done, I could easily conclude that my own efforts to complete humanity's God-given task of cultivat-ing the earth (discussed further in chapter 4) were the only way to restore my relationship with God. I would seek to justify myself by my work, rather than see that my work flows out of what Jesus has done for me. The focus would be on my achievement rather than God's grace to me in Jesus. But now I've experienced God's grace in Jesus and my relationship with God is restored such that I'm adopted as his child. All of the work I do depends on that foundation. This is stated clearly in Ephesians 2:8–10. It's also apparent from the struc-ture of many of the New Testament letters: the exhortations about how Christians should live always follow from the descriptions of God and the explanations of the salvation he has provided for us.

No doubt other statements could be added to provide a still greater understanding of my theological convictions (some would label them reasoned presuppositions or theological viewpoints). But this is not a book about convictions or presuppositions, and I think these should be sufficient to give a basic understanding of where I'm coming from theologically.

3

ELEMENTS OF THE
BIBLICAL CULTURES

One difficulty we have when reading the Bible is the clash of cultures. Twenty-first-century Australia is very different from Bronze Age Canaan and Roman Galilee. Things we take for granted as part of our everyday life—electricity, banks, printed books, public transportation, and a whole host of other things—simply didn't exist back then. And that, of course, made a difference in the way they approached life. They lived in a different age. The economy was different. The political system was different. Their culture was different. Their life expectations were different. Even their language was different.

We rely on others to solve the language aspect for us. Most of us read the Bible in its various English translations rather than the original Hebrew and Greek. We readily recognize that we need help in that area (although most of us take these translations for granted). But do we as readily recognize our need for help to "translate" the Bible's culture? Not always.

Sometimes we do. We read about four guys digging a hole in a roof so they could lower their paralyzed friend to the feet of Jesus, and we realize they're not dealing with a Colorbond roof. But sometimes, for a variety of reasons, the cultural differences aren't so readily apparent. As noted earlier, most modern translations use *tax collector*, but the old Authorized Version used *publican*—and that caused conceptual issues for at least one person.

And sometimes, at some inner level, we're aware of the differences but we forget to do the translation. We know that the early church had no official buildings, no institutional structure or status, no collected New Testament and perhaps only limited access to the Old Testament, no Christian bookshops—yet how often do we interpret the New Testament references to "the church" in terms of our personal experience? It's especially easy for us to think of *church* as a building and the activities that go on there, but the New Testament church didn't even have buildings.

With some of the material in this book, there's a danger that we'll import our modern culture into our interpretation of the text. Our first goal is to understand the text accurately in its own culture. Only when we've done that will we be in a position to correctly see its implications for our own culture. This is particularly important with the issue of retirement because, as we've noted already, it's a subject the Bible couldn't deal with directly (unless by way of predictive prophecy!).

Many of the cultural differences we encounter in the Bible can be dealt with as they arise in relation to particular texts. However, there are two broad interrelated areas that are worth considering by way of introduction: family and work. The latter is clearly related to our topic; the former appears to be less so within our culture. And that's the point. We tend to separate work and family. Generally, we travel to our place of employment (note the inherent devaluation of work associated with home duties) and return home for family time. We compartmentalize our lives. In ancient Israel, they did walk from their houses to their farmland, but work itself was a family affair, and they brought the produce of their fields back to their houses.

THE FAMILY SITUATION IN
THE OLD TESTAMENT

First, I want to highlight some of the differences between the way families typically lived in the ancient world and our modern family arrangements. During Old Testament times, Israelite children were born into multigenerational households. In Israel, these households could also include servants, foreigners, laborers, and even a Levite. Often, these multigenerational households would reside under one roof—a two-storey structure that archaeologists identify as the four-room or pillar-courtyard house. If the household members became too numerous for the one building, they would spread into a compound of such structures. Thus, children lived not only under the authority of their own parents, but especially under that of the family patriarch—the oldest surviving male household member. This patriarch also exercised significant judicial functions within the household and together with other local patriarchs constituted the "elders in the gate." When the household faced economic difficulties, the patriarch could sell dependents into servitude to clear his debt. Clearly, this varies significantly from Western culture's emphasis on the nuclear (or blended) family. We have a far greater (geographical) distance between generations: children and their parents rarely live in close proximity to their grandparents. In our culture, grandparents exercise virtually no authority in their grandchildren's lives and often don't want to be perceived as interfering.

In the early days of Israel's history, schooling was both unknown and unnecessary. Children's primary education was on-the-job training in the various tasks of subsistence farming and the household chores that accompanied it. This "education" resembled a modern-day apprenticeship, but instead of learning a specific trade, children learned to produce or process the food they ate each day. The amount of knowledge children needed to make their way in life was both limited and specific. In Israel, this was supplemented by instruction in God's law and their covenantal responsibilities. From an early age, they contributed to the household's ongoing survival. This was simply the economic reality in their agrarian environment, where there was no real distinction between workplace and home. Again, this is vastly different from the broad and complex education provided for Western children within schools established for that specific task. Western children are not usually expected to contribute to the household economy apart from a handful of household tasks—and even that practice seems to be diminishing.

When Israelite children reached maturity in their early teenage years, the household arranged a suitable marriage for them. For a man, this meant the introduction of a new woman into his current household; for a woman, this meant her introduction into the household of her husband. For neither did it mean the establishment of a completely new, independent household. Even if the occasion resulted in the erection of a new structure, it remained part of the family compound. The new couple remained under the authority of the household patriarch, continuing to maintain the family land passed down from generation to generation since the conquest of the land. The Israelite monarchy didn't have the option of periodic land releases or expanding the frontier for new households to make a new start. Modern notions of adult independence were basically foreign to their culture.

Women began bearing children as soon as possible after marriage, that is, in their early teens. Sustaining an adequate number of workers was an important component of survival in their subsistence existence. Again, this cultural difference gives a distinctive shape both to the reason for having children and to their place within the family. Further, in those days, infant mortality rates were high and life expectancy was low (estimated at 30 to 40 years[1]). Statistically, normal households would comprise three generations, and four would not be unusual.

It's worth pausing to consider one implication of these cultural differences. In Israelite society, the requirement to honor parents merely reflected the realities of life. As children, like in any culture, they depended on their parents for their survival. Yet as they grew, their main education was also provided by their parents, albeit within the context of the broader family and local village. At this point in their development, the question of "not honoring" would likely not enter their thinking. Respect was simply normal. There were no pressures to rebel against that "normal" within the culture. No one suggested questioning their parents' expertise or their authority. No media existed to provide examples of others questioning their parents' authority. Nor did children come under any competing authority. Sure, their own sinful natures would urge them to disobey from time to time—but the overall atmosphere simply reinforced what everyone considered normal.

Of course, growing in maturity brought increased responsibility. Yet this was characterized by interdependence rather than our notions of independence. As part of their extended families, young Israelites shared the tasks necessary for survival, basically producing everything they required to live. They continued to work alongside their parents (or in-laws) until death intervened. They continued to honor and respect their parents in all aspects of life. The honor given to aged parents by their adult children is the more likely focus of the fifth commandment (as I will note in chapter 12). And even their parents' death did not terminate their obligation. Providing proper burial was an important responsibility. And, despite biblical prohibitions, some scholars maintain that adult children in ancient Israel had ongoing duties to care for their parents' spirits.[2]

These cultural family values remained fairly constant throughout ancient Israel's Old Testament history. In the premonarchical period, the vast majority of Israelites (90–95%) were subsistence farmers living in multigenerational households in small villages. Cities increased in both number and size during the monarchy, but the vast majority of the population still lived within rural households. This situation continued at least into the early post-exilic period.

The rise of Israel's monarchy did add pressure to traditional households. The more centralized state required resources from rural communities. The prophet Samuel warns the people that the proposed king will take their sons for his fields and his army, their daughters for his servants, their fields for his own estate and those of his officials, and their produce in taxes (1 Samuel 8:10–18). Some of this was done in a manner that accommodated the routines of rural households: for example, kings often conducted wars outside peak times on the agricultural calendar, so that soldiers were available to their families for planting and harvest. After all, it was unwise to take too many resources from the mainstay of the country's economy. You can't feed the army if no one's around to plant the crops. But not all of the monarchy's requirements could be so adapted.[3]

THE WORK SITUATION IN
THE OLD TESTAMENT

Second, what was work like in ancient Israel? I hesitate to insert a separate heading here because, for most people in the ancient world (and throughout most of human history), family and work situations overlapped. The modern separation of work from family is largely a product of the Industrial Revolution. Yet work remains a category worth considering because the Israelites' work situation was just so different from our experience and expectations. When I read the expression "subsistence farmers," I tend to skim over it relatively quickly. I think to myself, "That means they provided all their own needs from their own work without using money. I do the same sort of thing by earning and spending money." But the difference is far, far greater. It's a very different approach to work and lifestyle than what I'm used to.

As noted already, for most Israelites, work involved agricultural activity. Joshua, following God's instructions through Moses, divided the land within the community. Each family received their own plot of land—the means of production that enabled them to survive and enjoy life. This land stayed within the same family from generation to generation. If they encountered hard times (crop failures, droughts, wars, accidents that resulted in key workers being incapacitated, insufficient numbers of children reaching maturity), God permitted them to sell their land—but only until the Jubilee Year, which occurred every fifty years). Rather than signing the land away for good, they were effectively selling the crops that the land would produce until the next Jubilee.

So each male child grew expecting to expend his entire working life on his family's plot of land. Female children expected to move to their husband's family's plot of land and spend the rest of their working life there. There was no expectation of exchanging a highland plot for one in a beachside suburb. Nor was there any anticipation of a mid-life change of profession. To us, that sounds quite boring and limiting. We might be amazed by their distinct lack of choice—how did they live with no prospect of developing their various abilities, skills, and gifts to their full potential? To them, this was the only life they knew—and they weren't subject to TV documentaries designed to make them dissatisfied with their current lot!

On their family's plot of land, Israelites experienced a subsistence lifestyle. They produced all that they needed to survive: their food, clothing, shelter, cooking pots, utensils, bedding, furniture, weapons, and whatever else they required were made in the home or nearby. Work included all that was involved in producing and maintaining these things. Clearly, food production was a big part of that, since the alternative was starvation. Some years, they'd have bumper crops. That enabled them to store additional produce for the lean years they knew would come. While we must recognize that they were far less able to store perishable goods than we are (for example, they had no refrigeration), they still had some capability to ready themselves for natural disasters. Archaeologists have found storage pits and the clay jars in which materials were stored.

Although many of the details are patchy, it seems likely that many tasks were divided along gender lines. Building houses, digging pits, the initial preparation of fields, terracing, ploughing, and making tools were generally considered male tasks. Preparing food, collecting water, maintaining the home, and making clothing usually fell within the female domain. Scholars have proposed various rationales for this division of labor: the generally greater strength of men and the need for women who were caring for infants to be closer to the home are the most commonly cited explanations.

Yet this division of labor didn't result in the sorts of distinctions we're used to. All work was considered important. It was all necessary for the household's survival. And there was no real concept of paid work—or that it was somehow superior to unpaid work. All tasks contributed to the family's ongoing life. Each person was responsible to exercise their developed skills for the common good.[4] And some tasks required everyone's involvement—for example, harvesting was a big job and needed to be completed in a short time.

As technology increased, so the possibility for specialization grew. For example, as people invented and developed metal farming implements, it's likely that one of the village's men learned the requisite skills for making and maintaining these implements. Initially, he'd exercise these skills while continuing his own agricultural activities. He may have received assistance with his crops from other households within the village. It's likely that he handed down his specialized skills to one of his sons—and so the line continued down the generations. Eventually, there was sufficient demand for this to become a full-time occupation.

The point is, all this was done in the context of the household. For one person to stop work in order to retire would require the rest of the household to pick up the slack. They would have to take on additional work to facilitate their relative's leisure. Now, this did happen in some circumstances. If one household member was incapacitated (due to age, for example), the others would gladly pitch in to care for that person—and to ensure they experienced *shalom* to the fullest extent possible. The incapacitated family member who could not work in the fields would also likely involve themselves in the household work as much as they could. But to cease work permanently for the sake of personal leisure was unthinkable. It would have been an offense against their community.[5]

FAMILY AND WORK IN NEW TESTAMENT TIMES

When we move to the New Testament, the situation becomes much more complex. There are several reasons for this. First, we move from the nation of Israel in Canaan to God's church scattered throughout the Roman Empire—from *one* Jewish culture to *multiple* cultures over a wider area. Admittedly, those multiple cultures were all molded by both Hellenistic and Roman ideals; yet some local differences remained. And unlike Israel, those cultures had not been shaped directly by God's requirements. The focus was no longer on a Jewish culture, where God's people were to display to the world the magnificence of living under God's rule. God's people still had that goal—but they now attempted that as small clusters of "aliens" living in a variety of foreign cultures that were opposed to God.

Second, in the New Testament, we move to a far more complex and varied economy (although it was much simpler than what we experience today). Many still lived in a rural setting and worked as farmers. Some did this on their own land (similar to Old Testament practices), while others were tenant farmers or slaves working for large landholders. There was a broader range of occupations. Within the New Testament, we meet carpenters, tax collectors, fishermen, sailors, tent makers, metalworkers, silversmiths, cloth dyers, soldiers, merchants, and clergy. There were more opportunities for paid employment. Money was far more common as a medium of exchange than it had been in early Old Testament times. Thus, it was easier both to accumulate wealth and to provide for future contingencies. Yet it was still the norm for children to learn their occupation from their parent of the same gender.

Third, we also move to a more urban focus in the New Testament. It's not that cities are absent from the Old Testament. Nor are rural aspects absent from the New Testament (especially the Gospels). Yet the urban situation is far more prominent in the New Testament. Paul focuses his mission on cities, and his letters (and those of John and Peter) address those in urban settings. It seems likely that Paul anticipated the gospel would spread from the cities into the surrounding rural areas. It's not that he considered the gospel to be only for city dwellers. But it seems he concentrated his efforts on these centers of dense human population as a strategy to reach the greatest number of people in the shortest amount of time.

Because of these factors, it's far more difficult to summarize the cultural background to what the New Testament says about family and work. The situation is more varied. For example, in terms of housing, cities in the Roman Empire accommodated different classes of people. At one end of the spectrum, wealthier families occupied relatively spacious homes (*domus*). These would be occupied by the blood relatives of the head of the household (*paterfamilias*), as well as any dependents—slaves, employees, and clients (those looking for patronage, protection, or advancement). At the other end of the spectrum were those who had no fixed abode and survived as best they could. The majority of the population (perhaps 90 percent) lived in apartment-type complexes (*insula*). These tended to be small, dark, and poorly ventilated. They were often overcrowded and lacked privacy.

The vast majority (if not all) of these cultures were patriarchal. The *paterfamilias* exercised power over his household and was responsible for its well-being. Yet in the writings of both Greeks and Romans (admittedly, this material comes from the educated segment of these cultures and so may not reflect the attitudes of the general populace), marriage was idealized as a partnership. The wife's responsibilities included managing household affairs and supervising servants. In some occupations, she would work alongside her husband. In many places, she could hold property in her own name—including land.

While the extended family remained important, the impression I have is that there was a shift to a greater focus on the nuclear family in at least some regions of the Roman Empire. One reason for this was the tendency for men to marry at an older age, by which time they often were already the *paterfamilias* of their family unit. Again, this custom was perhaps confined to the wealthier educated classes living in an urban environment, and may not have extended to those in rural areas.

Typically, at least in the rural areas, the family household continued to produce most of the basic items they consumed. However, these were supplemented more regularly by the greater variety of items now offered through the increased trade facilitated by the stability of the Roman Empire. The further development of specialized occupations also added to the variety of goods available. Still, most specialized occupations were pursued within the confines of the household.

The fundamental value of many Mediterranean cultures revolved around honor and shame. While this could have an individual element, its main focus was the household group to which one belonged. Each individual had to know their place within the household and demonstrate loyalty to the group. They also needed to know their household's place within the wider community, showing due deference to those of higher rank and appropriate support to the less powerful. Other values, such as honesty, were not as important as maintaining honor.[6]

SUMMARY

I am conscious that the material above fails to do full justice to the topics at hand. A comprehensive coverage of these two broad subject areas is not possible within the space available, particularly given the changes in cultural patterns that occurred over time—not to mention the broader cultural area covered by the New Testament material. Rather, I've attempted to paint with broad brushstrokes to give an overall impression that enables us to gauge something of the differences from our own Western cultures.

In drawing this chapter toward a conclusion, I think it's worth bringing some of those differences together in one place—and noting briefly how they relate to our view of work. Admittedly, some of these differences were also changing by New Testament times.

First, people in ancient Israel had a far more communal approach to life. In many ways, their circumstances dictated that. They needed each other to survive in subsistence conditions. Thus, they made their decisions based on their impact on the household, rather than from considerations of personal preference or advantage.

Second, they generally had no career choice. They grew up expecting to follow in the family business, whether that was farming, fishing, metalworking, or some other trade. That meant if they didn't like their first job, they didn't have the option of an alternate career path. Nor would they likely have the option of a second career following a mid-life crisis.

Third, in Old Testament times, people spent their entire lives living in the same village and working with the same people. The only changes were initiated by births, deaths, and marriages. Workplace issues couldn't be resolved by transferring to another department or searching the classifieds. People didn't change geographical location in search of better employment opportunities (unless they were sold into servitude). By New Testament times more options were available, but for many life remained the way it had been for generations.

Fourth, there was little cultural pressure toward upward mobility on an individual level. Land was distributed equitably and its redistribution was limited. The emphasis was on everyone sharing *shalom* together. In theory, there was no pecking order to climb— that wasn't a cultural norm. In practice, of course, self-centeredness won out. The prophets indicate that people did abuse the system for their own personal advantage.

Fifth, in the early biblical period, there was no entertainment or leisure industry. There was little, if any, time for such activities.

The major interruptions to people's normal routines were provided by the annual festivals, where they celebrated God's goodness to them together. When a class of more wealthy elite emerged, they indulged themselves in leisure activities (for example, Amos 6:1–7). Even with the introduction of Greek and Roman culture, leisure pursuits were likely confined to the upper classes. Overall, work was both valued and necessary. People labored together for the common good of the household.

One final comment is in order. None of this is to say that one culture is better than the other. On the one hand, we don't seek to return to some biblical "ideal" culture. Such a thing doesn't exist. As noted at various points above, culture changed during biblical times, and has continued to change ever since. One big change is that God's people no longer have a national identity. Rather, we're sojourners and aliens scattered throughout all the earth's nations, subject to a variety of cultures. On the other hand, we also don't subscribe to the evolutionary notion that all cultural progress is positive. Thus, we don't idolize modern cultures or choose one as the ideal. Rather, we seek to apply the Bible to all cultures, recognizing that all cultures include good, neutral, and evil aspects.

The point of this chapter is not to idealize some form of biblical culture, but to recognize the differences between biblical cultures and modern cultures. As we grow in our understanding of the biblical cultures, our interpretation of the Bible's instructions will become more accurate, and we will be better able to apply the Bible's values to our own culture and situation.

4

Is Work a Four-Letter Word?

As noted earlier, retirement includes ceasing some aspect of work. Thus the starting point for any theology of retirement must involve an understanding of the theology of work. We need to understand what work is from God's perspective and what its place is in the Christian life. The Bible has lots to say about work, and this short chapter is not the place to cover all the details. Rather, my aim here is to present a relatively short summary of the Bible's teaching about work. In doing so, I've borrowed Tom Wright's concept of a five-act play[1] as a useful framework to outline the Bible's instruction on this subject. I've also added a sixth act—the new creation—which I believe is important in understanding work.

ACT 1: CREATION

The Bible's creation account shows God working. This is quite clear from the way the narrative unfolds in Genesis 1. It's made explicit in Genesis 2:2–3, where it states that God has completed his work of creation. The vital implication of this picture of God working is that work is not bad (or evil) in itself. God involves himself in work. Indeed, Genesis 2:7 pictures God getting his hands dirty, as it were, when he fashions man out of the dust of the earth. It's not beneath his dignity. As the rest of the biblical narrative unfolds, God continues to work in various ways to achieve his purposes in human history.

Genesis 1:26–27 emphasizes God creating humans in his image. This expression continues to generate much discussion. There is a wide variety of opinions on just what it means for humanity to be made in the image of God. In an effort to get a handle on all these different interpretations, Robert Saucy[2] groups them into three major categories:

- The image as substantive or ontological: this view defines the image in terms of characteristics of the human being; for example, volition (the ability to exercise our wills), or rationality (the ability to think).

- The image as relational: this view defines the image in terms of being able to relate with others; first with God, and then also with fellow humans and the rest of creation.

- The image as functional: this view defines the image in terms of the functions God gives humans; the God-given tasks to multiply and fill the earth and to rule over creation.

I suspect that being made in God's image includes elements from all three categories.

Yet I also think some features from the context in Genesis should direct our thinking on this matter. It's fairly basic to the idea of *image* that humans are somehow to display some *likeness* to God. This text appears quite early in the Bible's unfolding revelation. At this point, we haven't been told much about God or what he is like. But one key thing we have been told is that he's a worker. It would not be unreasonable to think that God has created us to copy him in this regard. Further, once God does create humans in his image, what comes next? God gives us a twofold task: to be fruitful and increase in number and fill the earth, and to rule over the earth and subdue it. That is, God gives us work to do. Again, that strongly suggests to me that *work* is at least part of what it means to exist in the image of God.

As I've already noted, I don't think this excludes elements from the other interpretations of the "image." The ability to perform the task God gives humans presupposes certain inherent or *ontological* capabilities that are required to rule. It's difficult, for example, to imagine humans ruling over the rest of creation without possessing rationality and volition. Our God-given task also presupposes *relational* elements, since it cannot be completed independently of God (the ultimate Ruler) and it includes relating to the rest of the created order in an appropriate manner. And further, the task is given to humanity as a whole, not to one individual (beginning with the couple God creates and extending to their future offspring). It's a communal task that assumes relationships with one another to achieve it.

Genesis 2 introduces us to the Garden of Eden—paradise. Again, God gives humanity a task. "The LORD God took the man and put him in the Garden of Eden to work it and take care of it" (Genesis 2:15). How does this relate to the task given in Genesis 1? I think essentially it's the same task. The work described here is what's involved in ruling over the earth. It's not an activity that is abusive to humanity's environment—selfishly exploiting it for humanity's benefit. Humanity is not self-centered at this point—that happens in Genesis 3. Rather, this work means developing the earth positively— caring for it and exercising a benevolent rule. Gardening involves rearranging the environment to produce desired results. It also includes using the environment to meet human needs. In Genesis 2:16, God gives humans permission to eat from every tree in the garden except one. Humans don't just care for this environment; they are also sustained by it. But it's more than that. The task is to expand the garden to fill the earth. And, I believe, the task is to develop the garden—to use God's creation to invent human culture.

In other words, while God completes his creation project, it's deliberately unfinished. God creates humanity to develop his project under his supervision—to take the raw materials and to cultivate, manage, innovate, and develop. The earth isn't fully populated. Nor does the garden cover the whole earth. Nor is the garden necessarily the final ideal. This is the task God gives humanity. This is what we call work. Many also call it the "cultural mandate"—the expectation that humanity would develop a society and build a civilization that glorified God.

Thus, I think work is somehow linked to being created in God's image. I think it's fundamental to what it means to be human. Not everyone would agree with that—especially those who emphasize the distinction between *being* and *doing*. People holding this view define human beings in terms of our essence rather than our actions. And they can present scenarios that suggest we should perhaps remove any thought of a link with work from our definition of what it means for humanity to be created in God's image. For example, one may consider those who have severe disabilities such that they can't work (at least, as we normally understand work—and perhaps this is part of the problem). It would be deeply wrong to suggest that such people are somehow less than human. At this point, I want to affirm two possibly conflicting things: first, those who can't work are truly human; and second, that there's a sense in which the humanity of the severely disabled is damaged (not only functionally, but also relationally and ontologically). We currently live in an imperfect world, damaged in various ways because of humanity's rebellion against God. There's a sense in which our very rebellion against God is a rejection of being made in his image. And so it's not surprising that each one of us fails to fully reflect God's image in us.

As we can see, this matter of humanity being made in God's image raises complex issues. Christians have discussed it at length for centuries. Even though it is difficult to articulate precisely how this image exists in us, I think work (humanity's God-given task) is clearly an important part of what it means to be made in God's image. However, for my current purpose, important conclusions about the nature of work from Genesis 1–2 remain true apart from the *image* language. Work in itself is a good thing. It is a task given to humanity by God. It is a part of God's intentions for humanity. It involves all humanity. And it is part of the harmony of God's creation. I think that Genesis 1–2 demonstrates that work is one of God's gifts to us and is thus good.

To draw that conclusion out further, it's worthwhile to contrast it with other viewpoints from the same era. Other creation narratives from the ancient world (for example, the *Atrahasis Epic*, the *Sumerian Creation,* and *Enki and Ninmah*) describe the gods creating humanity to relieve themselves from the burden of work. The gods didn't want to bother themselves with the mundane tasks involved in providing for their own needs, and so they created humanity to perform those tasks for them. It doesn't follow that work in itself is evil, but these other narratives do imply that work is a burden and that there are more desirable uses of one's time—ideas that are very popular in Australian culture.

The Greek philosophers took the next step and enshrined this attitude toward work in their idea of human nature. They recognized the necessity of human work for life on this earth (after all, the body needs food to survive, and that requires human work), but they tended to despise physical labor. That work was relegated to slaves and the inferior classes. The philosophers followed what they perceived to be the gods' example and gave priority to the contemplative life. They anticipated the soul's release from its bodily imprisonment and their subsequent freedom to contemplate philosophical questions without the distractions imposed by bodily existence.

This is not the Bible's teaching. God pronounces his physical creation *very good*. Bodily existence is part of true humanity, and will continue to be so in the new creation (1 Corinthians 15:35–57). The work that's involved in sustaining our existence (and that of the created order), far from being a necessary burden to be endured, actually expresses God's good intentions toward humanity and exercises one of God's good gifts to us.

It's worth noting three other contrasts with texts from the ancient world. First, for other cultures, part of humanity's task was to provide food for the gods. The Genesis account diverges from this concept by presenting God as lavishly providing food for humanity. Rather than having humans work for his benefit, God works for theirs in creating the environment in which he places humanity. This theme of God's gracious disposition toward humanity is developed throughout the biblical narrative. Sure, God gives humans the task of cultivating their environment—but this is not to feed or benefit God; rather, it's for humanity's own benefit.

Second, other texts from the ancient world refer to *kings* being made in the gods' image. They represented the gods to their subjects. The gods were thought to authorize kings to carry out the divine functions of ruling and administering justice. The kings exercised these attributes of the gods and did so on behalf of the gods. The Bible democratizes this picture. It presents humanity as a whole, rather than an individual human leader, communally ruling the created order as divine representatives. All are involved in demonstrating God's qualities and completing his work.

Third, in the ancient world, many important cultural advances were attributed to the gods. For example, in Mesopotamian tradition, the gifts of civilization, writing, crafts, music, and arts are given to the earliest kings through semi-divine figures.[3] While God is not averse to giving humanity gifts (for example, he later gives Israel his law), Genesis strongly implies that many cultural advances will result from humanity's work rather than specific divine intervention (remembering that the abilities that enable this are also from God). Genesis 4:17–22 shows this happening. Humans take up that aspect of their God-given task.

ACT 2: THE FALL

So, if work is God's good gift, why don't we always enjoy it as an exhilarating and uplifting experience? Genesis 3 provides the answer. The overall positive picture is clouded by humanity's choice to rebel against God's rule. Humans chose autonomy rather than submission. They chose to determine their own lives rather than submit to God's purposes for them. In response, God pronounced judgment. This judgment impacts the twofold nature of humanity's God-given task: the pain to be experienced by the woman in childbirth (3:16); and the curse on the ground that increases the difficulty of humanity's rule (3:17–19). While both aspects cause significant difficulty for humanity, neither negates the original task given by God. Nor do they change or undermine the essential goodness of that task.

The content of humanity's work doesn't change, but its manner of exercise does. With respect to their rule over the rest of creation, humans now find a creation that resists that rule. The rebels are themselves confronted by rebellion. With respect to tending the earth for the production of food, humans now find an earth that produces such food reluctantly. The earth will still produce the necessary food for them, but it now produces less useful plants more abundantly. And with respect to their duty to exercise the rule communally, people now feel threatened by one another. They compete with each other. They experience disharmony with each other. They still rule the earth, but they do so in a divided way, and this adds its own friction to the accomplishment of their God-given task. In short, the good work humanity was created to do now becomes something associated with toil, drudgery, exhaustion, and fatigue, and is even considered detestable.

Further, because humans rejected God's rule, we fail to fully comprehend God's purposes for the created order. Thus our attempts at dominion or rule, as expressed through technological advances, often fall short of God's intentions and creative purposes. Further, our technological advances often result in additional difficulties, such as the various ecological crises our planet faces.

Yet human rebellion also impacts work at another level. Sin often carries with it a built-in "judgment." This is evidenced at the level of our relationships. Humans chose autonomy. Humans chose not to trust God. We now doubt God's good intentions. Instead of viewing work as God's good gift, we see it as an imposition on our personal freedom. This appears in various attitudes: living for the weekend, prioritizing leisure, seeking early retirement, and so on. We tend to link leisure with personal autonomy. And that self-centered attitude contributes to the tedium, discontent, and resentment we have toward work. It feeds our desire to be the ones calling the shots. It goes to the very heart of what sin is. Contrary to God's intentions, we think life would be improved if we could reduce or eliminate work. This underlying perspective adds to the toilsome nature of work.

It's difficult for us to escape this perspective, for we have only experienced life after the fall. I want to explore this with a couple of analogies. First, consider the highly positive attitude you have toward your most anticipated leisure activity. Imagine having that same attitude toward work. How would that transform your work? Wouldn't work become a constant delight? Some people occasionally find that delight in their work. Was that what work was like in the garden? If work was like that for you, would you just want to do more and more? Would you truly see it as a delightful gift? Yet, for us today, what's the underlying basis of that attitude? It contains the seeds of self-centeredness—and that was absent from the garden. And so the analogy is not perfect.

Consider a second analogy. For us, work brings weariness. That weariness can be understood in different ways. For example, at times I'd describe the weariness work brings quite negatively: a level of mind-numbing repetition, maybe a feeling of boredom, or even a genuine dislike for what I'm doing, and a desire to do something more exciting. On those occasions, work is a burden I want to discard. Yet, at other times I'd describe the weariness more positively: a level of tiredness that slows my progress, fatigue from sustained mental effort, or the exhaustion that comes at the completion of a lengthy project. On those occasions, work still feels like a burden—but not one I wish to discard. Rather, I wish to deal with the weariness so I can get back to work. This type of weariness comes with the satisfaction of accomplishment. Was there weariness in the garden? This is pure speculation. It seems to me that the negative type of weariness stems from the fall—it's a result of our self-centered and rebellious natures. But I suspect the positive type of weariness was still present in the garden—for God created us as finite beings who tire and need sleep.

Why have I spent so much time on this? My Australian culture presents a complex agglomeration of twisted attitudes toward work. We seek to define our identity and justify ourselves by our work. We seek the meaning of life in our work. Meanwhile, we work at things God says are evil, or we seek to work in ungodly ways. We seek to avoid work, or we work to indulge ourselves. We use work to avoid other God-given priorities.

The net result of these conflicting and self-centered ideas tends to be a negative attitude toward work—an attitude that conflicts with Genesis 1 and 2. As already noted, that negative attitude helps fuel a very positive attitude toward leisure and retirement. We need to recognize that our culturally shaped attitudes need scrutiny in light of the biblical text. It seems to me that, while the Bible acknowledges that work is difficult as a result of the fall, it does not share any element of our aversion to work. Rather, the biblical expectation is that humans will work and rejoice in this good gift from God.

ACT 3: ISRAEL

This expectation is affirmed in various places throughout the Old Testament. Both before and after Israel's formation as a nation, there are many incidental references to human work. The

various biblical writers present a picture of the growing diversi-
fication of human activity and increasing complexity of human
culture and economy. The primary purpose of these texts is not to
present evidence for humanity's attempt to fulfill their God-given
task. Arguably, humanity acts in its own interests, rather than consciously doing what God desires. Nor do the biblical writers directly
assess humanity's progress in this regard. They merely provide descriptive evidence for some aspects of how work was progressively
attempted. While many insights pertinent to a theology of work
may be gleaned from these numerous references, our current purpose has a more narrow focus.

Thus for now I'll focus on God's expectations for Israel as his
people. What did God expect from them in terms of work? What
attitudes toward work did God encourage them to develop? The
ideal is presented as *rest* in the land God gives them (Deuteronomy
3:18–20). This includes rest from their enemies so they may live in
safety (Deuteronomy 12:8–10). It also includes enjoying the land's
good and abundant produce in humble and obedient dependence
on God (Deuteronomy 8:6–18; 11:8–21). Yet this rest in the land
doesn't exclude work. As in the Garden of Eden, God's people didn't
have to establish the infrastructure in Canaan. God provided them
a land with cities, houses, wells, vineyards, and orchards. Others
(on this occasion humans, rather than God directly) had done that
hard work for them (Deuteronomy 6:10–12). But the Israelites still
had to maintain and develop the infrastructure, and they needed to
labor to produce their own food. In the wilderness, God sustained
them with manna from heaven. All they had to do was collect and
cook it (and yes, that's still work, but it's fairly minor when compared with normal agricultural labor). That stopped once they entered the land. From that point, *rest* in the land that God provided
included work as a normal part of life.

That reality is reflected in various aspects of the Mosaic law.
Many of the statutes cover issues related to work. For example,
some laws protect the means of production (for example, laws pro-
hibiting the moving of boundary markers and laws requiring the
care of stray animals), and others protect the rights of workers (for
example, laws about the treatment of slaves and laws requiring the

timely payment of wages). Still other laws provide for the disadvantaged (for example, laws establishing the practice of gleaning and laws instituting the tithe for the poor). Even the laws commanding the temporary cessation of work—the Sabbath and the festivals—assume labor is the normal status in life.

Likewise, within the Old Testament wisdom literature, the book of Proverbs encourages a diligent attitude toward work. The wise person fears God—that is, he or she honors God by living according to his instruction. That involves developing godly character and God-honoring attitudes in all aspects of life, including work. The proverbs aren't a foolproof magic formula for worldly success, nor do they encourage the pursuit of riches at all costs. Rather, they demonstrate what God values and encourage the reader to live in conformity with those values.

With respect to work, the most prominent theme in Proverbs is encouragement to be industrious. Hard work puts food on the table. Laziness leads to an empty stomach. Wise people plan their work in proper order (21:5; 24:27), prepare and work their fields (12:11), gather crops at the appropriate time (6:6–8; 10:4–5), care properly for their animals (12:10; 27:23–27), provide for unforeseen circumstances (21:20; 30:25), and have their needs satisfied (13:4; 28:19). The book concludes by celebrating the success of the hardworking "wife of noble character" (31:10–31). In contrast, the sluggard goes hungry (19:15; 20:4) and ends in poverty (6:6–11; 14:23; 20:13; 21:25–26; 24:30–34) and slave labor (12:24).

Proverbs' instructions were common sense in an agricultural economy. You needed to know the seasons. You needed to adequately prepare your fields. You couldn't put the work off because you didn't feel like it that day. You couldn't approach harvest halfheartedly, or your food supply would rot in the field. Industriousness was especially important in a subsistence economy where there were no government handouts to fall back on. Sure, under the law, gleaning was an option—but even that was hard work, requiring you to harvest your own grain, remove the husks, and then prepare your food.

There is other work-related material in Proverbs. Aspects of the law are reinforced, such as the importance of honest scales (11:1; 16:11; 20:10, 23) and not moving boundary markers (22:28;

23:10). There is a similar concern about being generous to the disadvantaged (11:24–26; 14:21, 31; 19:17; 21:13; 22:9; 28:27). In addition, Proverbs stresses the importance of children paying attention to instruction from their parents. Indeed, we should remember that Proverbs anticipates that all of its instruction is handed down from one generation to the next within the family work environment. This is the context for its counsel about seeking advice, heeding commands, and accepting rebuke. This is a dimension we're apt to overlook because of our different cultural background. Yet so important is this that, to preserve the viability of the family inheritance, a father would give precedence to a wise servant over a foolish son (17:2; cf. 19:13). After all, the family's ongoing survival is at stake.

Ecclesiastes provides an important balance in our understanding of work. Like the rest of the Old Testament, the Teacher affirms the value of work: it provides for our physical needs and helps occupy our time (4:5; 6:7; 9:10). Thus, it keeps us alive. But he refuses to overvalue work. He warns of the dangers of overwork (4:8). He notes the vagaries of life that sometimes undermine our work (2:17–21; 3:1–8; 9:11; 11:1–6). He speaks of working from wrong motives, such as envy of others (4:4). He encourages a balance between work and enjoying the fruit of our work (2:24–25; 3:9–13, 22; 5:18–20; 8:15). Above all, he counsels that the meaning of life is not to be found in work (1:12–14; 2:11, 26; 8:17). Yet, even within that counterbalancing aspect, the Teacher does not undermine the overall expectation that we should work.

ACT 4: JESUS

Jesus enters history as a Jew—that is, within a nation that values God's Old Testament revelation, including what God has taught about work. He is known as the carpenter's son (Matthew 13:55).[4] And, as was normal in that culture, he entered the family business (Mark 6:3) by learning the trade from his father. This wasn't an agricultural occupation whereby he produced his own food. The economy had developed greater specialization by New Testament times. Yet, Jesus conformed to the pattern that work was expected from all members of the community.

But then, he abandoned the family business in favor of an itinerant ministry of teaching and healing. He no longer produced any physical goods—either food itself (well, I guess he fed a couple of large crowds—but you get the idea) or goods that could be exchanged for food. His physical needs were met through the generosity of others (Luke 8:1–3). Yet, it's quite clear he still considered his ministry to be work. In John 5:17, in response to Jewish complaints about healing on the Sabbath, he claims: "My Father is always at his work to this very day, and I, too, am working." This is part of a broader pattern in John's Gospel, where Jesus repeatedly speaks of completing the work given to him by the Father.

So, what is the nature of Jesus' work? At the beginning of his ministry, Jesus announces the nearness of God's kingdom (Matthew 4:17; Mark 1:15). In Luke 4:18–19, he also provides a programmatic statement of his ministry at the synagogue in Nazareth, quoting from Isaiah 61:

> The Spirit of the Lord is on me,
>> because he has anointed me
>> to preach good news to the poor.
> He has sent me to proclaim freedom for the prisoners
>> and recovery of sight for the blind,
> to release the oppressed,
>> to proclaim the year of the Lord's favor.

These were both ways of arousing Jewish expectations of God's intervention in their affairs.

God made promises to his people from the time of Abraham on. Those promises were reiterated and expanded throughout their history. There were also significant setbacks that seemed to threaten the fulfillment of God's promises. Despite God's generous goodness to them, the Israelites demonstrated their disloyalty to God again and again. That disloyalty became so pervasive that eventually God removed the Israelites from the land and sent them into exile. Yet even then, God reaffirmed his promises to them. Indeed, the promises seemed to get even bigger and better. As well as promising to bring them back to the land he'd given them, God promised to deal with the underlying problem of their rebellious hearts. God did bring them back to the land, but the bigger promises remained largely unfulfilled. In many ways, the people remained in exile. And then Jesus entered their world and announced that he was about to do the work of fulfilling God's promises.

So, what does his work look like? The overall New Testament presentation can be summarized in three elements.

- Teaching about God's kingdom—what it is like; what its values are; how to enter it; how it grows in the world.

- Demonstrating the nature of God's kingdom—healing the sick; freeing the demon-possessed; feeding the hungry; protecting people from the destructive forces of nature.

- Providing the means for others to participate in God's kingdom—bearing the punishment for human rebellion; giving the new birth; giving the indwelling Holy Spirit.

This is a unique work executed by God's King.

What implications does this have for our work? At one level, our work continues as normal. Jesus doesn't take his followers out of the world. Nor does he provide daily manna from heaven (the feeding of the five thousand is not a paradigm for life in the church!). None of his teaching undermines the expectation that his followers will work to produce their daily food (though, as the Lord's Prayer reminds us, this remains God's gift to us). Indeed, many of his parables and sermon illustrations are drawn from normal first-century working life. Like the writer of Ecclesiastes, Jesus warns against idolizing work or treating it as the source of our security (Matthew 6:19–34), but he also doesn't remove it from our daily agenda.

At another level, we have additional work. During his ministry, Jesus sent his followers on short-term missions where they replicated elements of his own work (Luke 9:1–6; 10:1–20). After his resurrection, Jesus authorized his apostles to make disciples of all nations (Matthew 28:18–20)—a mission that was taken up by the whole church. How does this work relate to the task God gave humanity at creation? On the one hand, it doesn't directly produce any "goods" to sustain or enhance our physical life on earth. On the other hand, it does extend the dominion of the Man who is truly God's image. It does contribute to the development of godly culture. And it enables people to ingest "spiritual" food that sustains life with God (for example, John 6:25–59).

Further, the concept of mission work is not totally foreign to the Old Testament. Following the fall, God established his people, the nation of Israel. They were to live under God's rule and exercise dominion over their own land in accordance with the instruction and values God gave them. But they weren't an end in themselves. God's vision included blessing the nations through them (Genesis 12:1–3). And so he gave Israel work to do. The way in which they were separated for God's purposes and exercised their dominion in Canaan was supposed to give clear evidence of God's rule over them and thus provide a model for the world. That, I take it, is what it means to be a "priestly kingdom" (Exodus 19:5–6). They were like a display home—demonstrating the blessings of belonging to God. Israel's "mission" was to live in a way that drew people to them.[5]

The big difference with Jesus is that he sends his followers out to do their mission. They are still to live in an attractive way—lives that demonstrate the goodness and desirability of God's rule (for example, 1 Peter 2:11–12). But added to that is the work of proclaiming the message that Jesus is God's true King, and challenging people to submit to him.

ACT 5: THE CHURCH

When we move to the period of the church in the New Testament, we find an ongoing expectation that humans will work. The clearest expression of this is Paul's words to the Thessalonian church:

> For even when we were with you, we gave you this rule: "If a man will not work, he shall not eat." We hear that some among you are idle. They are not busy; they are busybodies. Such people we command and urge in the Lord Jesus Christ to settle down and earn the bread they eat. (2 Thessalonians 3:10–12)

In other words, the event that's at the center of biblical revelation—Jesus' death, resurrection, and enthronement—has not abrogated the requirement to work. Nor has the addition of mission work overturned or somehow superseded this original task for all Christians (though provision is made for some Christians to receive support from others so they can devote themselves more fully to this mission work). The New Testament gives us several reasons to work:

1. To provide for our own physical needs (2 Thessalonians 3:10–12).

2. To provide for the needs of our families (1 Timothy 5:4, 8).

3. To win the respect of non-Christians (1 Thessalonians 4:12)—or, to turn it around, so non-Christians don't think we're lazy good-for-nothings.

4. To have something to share with those in need (Ephesians 4:28).

5. To support people in Christian ministry (1 Corinthians 9:7–12; Galatians 6:6).

They're not novel reasons. They're all anticipated in the Old Testament in some form.

For some Christians, there remains a distinction between what we might call creation work (work that fulfills the task given at creation or the "cultural mandate") and mission work (work that fulfills Jesus' command in Matthew 28).[6] For example, Paul speaks of his own practice of mission work in 1 Corinthians 9. He certainly believes he's entitled to financial support to enable him to do this task unhindered (verses 3–14). We know from his other letters that he was pleased to accept financial support for his mission work on other occasions (Philippians 4:10–19). But in Corinth he refused to exercise this entitlement, so that he could preach the gospel to them free of any financial obligation on their part (verses 15–19). Instead, he supported himself, presumably through the "creation work" of tentmaking (Acts 18:3). And when he did the same thing at Thessalonica, he held it up as a model for the Christians there to follow (2 Thessalonians 3:8–9).

Should we give priority to mission work? Certainly, it's an important God-given task—people's eternal relationship with God is involved. It certainly depends on us. Those outside the church aren't interested in completing this work—nor can they without the Spirit's intervention in their own lives. And the mission task is urgent.

But several other factors must also be considered. First, creation work is also an important God-given task. As such, it has value. The fall may have tarnished the task, as noted above. And, as with God's other gifts, we have abused the task for our own purposes, resulting in damage to both ourselves and our environment. But that doesn't change the underlying task. The world needs those who have submitted to God's King to demonstrate what creation work should look like and the God-centered attitude with which it should be approached—and perhaps that in itself would provide opportunities for mission work.

Second, since creation work is given to humanity as a whole, it would seem unjust for Christians to shirk their responsibilities in this area. Indeed, in the spirit of the gospel, should we perhaps be willing to sacrificially do more than our "fair share" on others' behalf, for their benefit, and out of love for them? This, it seems to me, would be a means for winning the respect of non-Christians—and perhaps also provide opportunities for mission work.

Third, what is actually involved in giving priority to mission work? The temptation is to think in terms of full-time mission workers—that our effectiveness in this work is proportional to the number of mission workers we can financially support. If we succumb to that temptation, I think we devalue our mission work. The true priority of mission work is reflected in all Christians being involved. It's not an either/or situation. It involves all Christians consciously living the totality of their lives to honor King Jesus. Involvement in creation work doesn't exclude full involvement in mission work, because the latter ultimately stems from an attitude that seeks to live in submission to Jesus—in both word and deed. Sure, mission work needs to be done sensitively—after all, your boss doesn't employ you as an evangelist—but our very lifestyle should be an advertisement for the gospel (1 Peter 2:11–12). Perhaps the problem is that too many of our lifestyles are an advertisement for Western culture.

One of my concerns in this discussion of "creation" and "mission" work is our tendency to divide the sacred and the secular. It's a church tradition that goes back many centuries. It's sprung up in all sorts of ways, and some of them are still familiar today: for example, the view that the life of devotion is more valuable than the active life, or that performing certain religious rituals will get you closer to God, or that pastors are more important than the laity, and so it goes on. I've battled this tendency in my own thinking since my university days, but I still catch myself thinking this way on occasion (which leaves me worried that it's still slipping under my radar in other areas). The Bible doesn't support that sacred/secular distinction. All of life is to be lived under God's rule and for his purposes. And so I want to avoid any suggestion that our everyday tasks are "only" creation work or that those doing "secular" jobs are second-class Christians.

ACT 6: THE NEW CREATION

Christians anticipate the new creation—the new heavens and the new earth. At that time, God's people will live together under his rule in perfect harmony. All rebellion against God will be excluded from his kingdom. All the results of rebellion against God will also have been removed (Revelation 21:1–4). It's described as an unending period of rest or *shalom*.

Two issues related to work in the new creation are important for our discussion—both of them disputed. The first is more incidental to our present purpose and so I'll only mention it in passing: This is the issue of whether any current human work lasts into eternity. On the one hand, some suggest only conversions and character will survive God's judgment and enter the final state. This view may lead to prioritizing mission work and valuing creation work only insofar as it provides opportunities for evangelism and character development. On the other hand, some suggest that the final state is not a return to the Garden of Eden but the descent of the new Garden

City to earth. When God renews his creation at the end, he will incorporate elements of transformed human work into the new City. This adds an element of value to our creation work in the present.[7]

The second issue is whether humans will continue to work in God's new creation. What will we do for eternity? Is work part of God's ultimate plan for us? Will we be required to work? At the popular level, many Christians anticipate an eternal spiritual existence. One oft-parodied vision of our final state has half-embodied souls sitting on fluffy clouds and strumming harps—an ethereal existence characterized by contented near-inactivity or blissful rest. Other similar caricatures exist. These conform more to Greek ideas of the immortality of the soul (often connected with a belief that physicality is essentially evil) than to biblical revelation.

The Bible corrects this view in three important ways. First, the New Testament strongly affirms that our final state is a bodily one (1 Corinthians 15:35–37; 2 Corinthians 5:1–10. This conforms to the Jewish understanding that being human involves a bodily existence—that's how we're created. Jesus has a resurrection body. In his post-resurrection appearances, he assures his followers of his physical existence. The Gospel writers indicate that there is some degree of discontinuity with his pre-resurrection body—this body could enter locked rooms (John 20:19–31). And perhaps there are hints that this body had not completed its resurrection transformation (John 20:17). Yet, Jesus is not a disembodied soul: he is alive today in his resurrected and ascended body. The New Testament affirms that he is the prototype (the firstfruits) for our future resurrection. We too will have transformed bodies (1 Corinthians 15:35–57).

Second, there are significant indications that our transformed bodies will inhabit the new earth. Much of the biblical imagery for the future state points in this direction. We read in Revelation of the new Jerusalem coming down to earth (Revelation 21:1–2) and the kings of the earth bringing their treasures into Jerusalem (Revelation 21:26–27). The Old Testament uses agricultural language to describe the future, including the image of each person sitting under their own vine (Micah 4:1–5; Zechariah 3:10). There remains need for caution.[8] Descriptions of the future state are images. The biblical writers seek to explain that which is beyond our current experience in analogies related to that experience. That is their only option. Perhaps they describe a non-earthly existence in earthly terms. Yet the imagery remains strongly suggestive.

Third, God originally created humans for an earthly existence. That's his design. While it appears he established a probationary period in the garden to establish our commitment to his will, there is no suggestion of a similar trial period concerning our earthly existence—that if we successfully negotiate the trial, we'll be promoted to a heavenly, immaterial existence. Thus, it seems reasonable to suggest the future state will likewise be an earthly one.[9]

Even though our final state is a bodily existence, however, that does not demonstrate that we'll work in eternity. After all, we tend to associate rest, not work, with our eternal state. But what does living in "God's rest" in the new creation involve? Expanding the common popular-level caricature mentioned above, many Christians think of the future existence as an eternal church service. God's people, it is proposed, will forever participate in corporate worship (often pictured as playing harps and singing). Many secretly dread the potential boredom of this prospect (especially if a sermon is also anticipated) and wonder if perhaps "the other place" is preferable. Many ridicule such caricatures—and rightly so. But what underlies them? First, in this current age, many believers connect "rest" and "worship"—possibly since the Christian day of worship (Sunday) has also traditionally fulfilled the function of the Sabbath. It seems natural to continue that in the age to come. Second, many consider "worship" to be the prime or ultimate expression of the Christian's relationship with God. In the eyes of many, John's vision of God's throne room in Revelation 4 adds support to this view.

I note two things in response. First, we must be careful when interpreting the symbol-laden language of Revelation. The vision in Revelation 4 speaks of honoring God, acknowledging God as God, and submitting fully to him. It is not a church service. It is a complete acknowledgement of and submission to God's absolute sovereignty. God is worshipped here in the holistic sense of everything being done in conformity to his will.

Second, we must again consider the concept of *rest* in this context.[10] We are normally inclined to think of *rest* in terms of inactivity and ceasing work. On that basis, many anticipate the final state as a time of extended—even eternal—leisure (for Australians, a perpetual long weekend). How is such a lifestyle thought to be enabled? It is simply God's generous provision. Our role is to sit back and enjoy it—and perhaps to *worship* the God who so graciously provides in such abundance. While that certainly acknowledges God and his role, I suspect it betrays our anthropocentric bias.

I think the Bible's vision of *rest* focuses on *shalom*. Its pictures of the final state stress a lifestyle of justice and righteousness resulting in abundance, contentment, and community. They also stress the absence of certain things: sin, sorrow, suffering, and death. The biblical authors envision perfect harmony: fellowship between God and human, human and human, and human and creation. They picture life as God intended. They assure us we will fully experience life as God intended.

What was God's intention for us at creation? Certainly it included enjoyment of his magnificent creation. God is good and desires good for his creatures, including humans. And it clearly included enjoyment of fellowship with God himself. Although there's no suggestion that God needed humanity or was somehow compelled to create, the Bible constantly refers to God's desire to be in right relationship with his people. But the original intention with which we were created also included work.

The biblical material includes a series of passages that seem to indicate that God's people will be involved in some form of rule in the age to come. Daniel 7:27 refers to the sovereignty of the kingdoms under heaven being given to the saints. In Luke 19:11–27, Jesus tells a parable about servants entrusted with their master's money. At the time they're called to account—a time that seems to correspond with Jesus' return—the faithful servants are "rewarded" with further work (Luke 19:17, 19). Paul affirms that those who endure will also reign with Jesus (2 Timothy 2:12; perhaps also Romans 5:17). Revelation also contains a couple of references to humans reigning in the future state (3:21; 5:10; 22:5).

Does this "reign" in the age to come include work? We readily associate rule with power and privilege, and think those exercising such authority have servants to do their work for them. But within

God's kingdom, Jesus affirms that authority is given for the sake of serving others (Mark 10:42–45). And, from a biblical perspective, isn't it better to see this future rule as a return to God's original intention? As noted above, at the beginning, humanity was told to rule over the earth and subdue it—not in self-centered exploitation of the environment, but by proper cultivation of the earth. And that involved work. Is it not likely that this future rule will involve similar work in fulfillment of that original command—and perhaps additional work that we cannot yet envisage?

And then, how does Isaiah picture the new creation?[11] Among other things, he writes in 65:21–23:

> They will build houses and dwell in them;
>   they will plant vineyards and eat their fruit.
> No longer will they build houses and others live in them,
>   or plant and others eat.
> For as the days of a tree,
>   so will be the days of my people;
> my chosen ones will long enjoy
>   the works of their hands.
> They will not toil in vain
>   or bear children doomed to misfortune;
> for they will be a people blessed by the LORD,
>   they and their descendants with them.

It's certainly a picture of *shalom*—and the *shalom* envisaged here involves human work.[12]

SUMMARY

Thus, it seems to me that the Bible teaches us that work is part of our humanity, both now and in the final kingdom. Work is one of God's good gifts to us, to be exercised and enjoyed in submission to him. The question that then faces us in relation to the issue of retirement is: Can we justify ceasing work? Is it ever right for us to lay aside God's gift? That is the question that will occupy us in the remainder of this study.

5

GOD'S REST AND HUMAN REST

We turn now to the concept of *rest*. In one sense, this would have been a logical place to start our investigations. After all, retirement is a form of rest. Sure, it involves *stopping* work. But that's to define it in negative terms—what it isn't. Why not start with what it is? Why not just look at the positive things the Bible says about rest and fit retirement into that category, so we can rejoice in this great opportunity we have to rest?

I think it's important to consider the topic of rest within the context of the Bible's positive attitude toward work. Yes, the Bible does also highlight some negative aspects of our work, as we've noted. But it traces those back to the results of human rebellion. Work itself was one of God's good gifts to humanity—and it remains so despite the fall and its consequences.

In my culture, I think it's important to reaffirm that. While my culture certainly doesn't have a totally negative attitude toward work, it definitely has a strong bias toward nonwork and leisure (to such an extent that the latter is often idolized). I don't think this leisure that Australians crave is the same as what the Bible means by *rest* (as I'll explain below), but it's what my mind gravitates to when I see the word *rest* in the Bible. Thus, I think people in my culture and other Western cultures need to overcome their inherent bias when dealing with this subject. We need to remind ourselves that, along with rest, work is also good and desirable.

Admittedly, in the ancient world most people didn't have the opportunities for leisure that I have. The ruling classes were the exception. The ordinary person's lifestyle was much closer to subsistence conditions—as is still the case in many parts of the world today. The rest that stems from the finiteness of their bodies was a necessity; additional rest was a luxury they could rarely afford if they wished to survive.

Now, it would be easy for me to interpret the Bible on the basis of my different circumstances: to claim that in modern Australia, economic conditions justify a rebalancing of the time we allocate to work and rest. There may even be truth in such a claim. As I noted in chapter 1, I think that requires further investigation. Perhaps retirement could be justified on the basis of our God-given freedom to develop suitable economic structures.

The point here is that I can't simply assume that. I need to be aware of my inherent cultural (and perhaps sinful) bias in that regard. The Bible affirms work as one of God's good gifts to us. Thus, it seems to me, I require good reasons if I'm to stop enjoying that gift. The Bible also speaks of *rest* in very positive terms. This at least raises the possibility that its teaching about rest may provide the required good reason to stop enjoying God's good gift of work— that rest may somehow be a better gift and thus justify some form of retirement. I therefore now propose to explore what the Bible teaches about rest and its relationship with work.

By way of warning, I think *rest* is a complex issue. It presents us with several minefields to negotiate.

GOD'S REST IN GENESIS 2:1–3

Rest appears quite early in the Bible. We read in Genesis 2:1–3,

> Thus the heavens and the earth were completed in all their vast array. By the seventh day God had finished the work he had been doing; so on the seventh day he rested from all his work. And God blessed the seventh day and made it holy, because on it he rested from all the work of creating that he had done.

At this point, I wish to attempt a difficult task: to pretend that this is the first time I've read this passage and to pretend also that the only other portion of the entire Bible that I've read is Genesis 1. How would I interpret these verses?

Initial Impressions

The first thing I'd notice is that several words are repeated:

- "Completed"/"finished"—twice (while the NIV uses two different words in its translation, the same Hebrew word is used in verses 1 and 2)
- "The seventh day"—three times (compare this with the single identification of each of the previous six days)
- "Work"—three times
- "Rested"—twice (note that the Hebrew word used can also mean *cease* or *stop*)

The Hebrew verb meaning *to do* or *to make* is also used three times. It's not as easy to spot in the NIV, which uses a different expression each time—"he had been doing," "all his work," and "he had done." It's crystal clear in the ESV, which uses "he had done" on all three occasions. That's quite a lot of repetition in three fairly short verses.

The second thing I'd notice is the connection to Genesis 1. *The heavens and the earth* in verse 1 repeats a phrase from Genesis 1:1. The threefold reference to *work* summarizes all that God did in Genesis 1. And the reference to *creating* also takes us back to Genesis 1:1. While our Bibles have a chapter division at this point (and remember that the chapter and verse divisions aren't part of the original text), I can conceive of no logical reason for its existence. These verses clearly conclude the Bible's opening scene and belong with it. This indicates there's a reasonable chance this is the climax of God's creation.

The third thing I'd note is that this seventh day lacks the concluding formula of the previous six days. Genesis 1 contains a refrain that completes each section: *God saw that it was good, and there was evening, and there was morning,* and a reference to the number of the day just described. The fact that this formula is omitted here appears significant. It signals there's something different about this day.

The fourth thing I'd observe—if I snuck a look at Genesis 2:4— is that there's no eighth day. While seven days correspond to one of our weeks, in this case there's no second week. God doesn't have a day off and then get back to work. When the text says *completed*, it indicates some finality to what God's done.

The fifth thing I'd notice is that this is not the first time God has *blessed* something. The first blessing happens on day five, when God blesses the sea creatures and birds: "God blessed them and said, 'Be fruitful and increase in number and fill the water in the seas, and let the birds increase on the earth'" (Genesis 1:22). The second blessing is on day six, when God blesses humans:

> God blessed them and said to them, "Be fruitful and increase in number; fill the earth and subdue it. Rule over the fish of the sea and the birds of the air and over every living creature that moves on the ground." (Genesis 1:28)

On both of those occasions, the content of the blessing appears to be defined by the words God speaks—namely, the idea of *increasing*. No words accompany the blessing of the seventh day—at least, none that are recorded in the text. How are we to understand this blessing? Do we import the idea of *increasing* from the earlier occasions of blessing? Or is the blessing defined by the seventh day being *made holy*?

That leads directly to the sixth observation: God *sanctifies* or *consecrates* or *makes holy* this seventh day? What does that mean? The word often has the idea of something being *set aside* for God or for use in God's service. It's not immediately clear how that applies here, since the whole passage (1:1–2:3) refers *only* to God's activities—this is what God did when he made the world and brought that activity to its completion. In what sense can it be said that he's *setting aside* this particular day? The word also has the idea of *different* or *distinct*. That certainly describes the status of this seventh day of creation. It's distinct because God does no new creative work on this day. Is God simply drawing our attention to that fact? I think the second half of the verse points in that direction. Or does God here make a positive declaration that achieves his purpose of making this seventh day holy? Perhaps it has a forward-looking reference—this is how future seventh days will be treated.

But that's not how this Hebrew construction is usually understood, and there's no reference to future seventh days in the text (in fact, there's no hint of future weekly cycles). Unless it's simply stating the obvious (that this seventh day is different)—and I think that's a distinct possibility—this text doesn't supply the answer.

The final thing is a question: What does it mean that God *rested?*

- Is he tired? Does all this strenuous creative activity result in a state of exhaustion for God? Does he need to recuperate? That's not the impression provided by Genesis 1.
- Is it total rest from all activity? Does he do absolutely nothing?
- Would it be better to use the word *ceased* (the NIV's alternate translation)? This would remove from the passage any concept of *rest.*

Or is this about enjoying the fruit of one's labor? The work of the creative project is finished; now it's time for the "work" of relishing in its use.

The Purpose of Focusing on Initial Impressions

Why have I gone through that "pretend" task? So often we read into this passage our understanding of other parts of the Bible—in particular, the Fourth Word (or, to use the more usual terminology, the fourth commandment), in which God instructed his people to rest on the Sabbath. Within the context of the biblical narrative, the Decalogue (transliterating a Greek word meaning "ten words") is listed on two separate occasions.[1] I think there are some advantages in thinking of them as "Ten Words" and I plan to use that terminology. This is not to say they aren't commands—clearly they are. As someone once quipped, they're not called the "Ten Suggestions." Yet, for us, I think the word *commandment* brings with it some unnecessary negative connotations—a bit like the word *work.* Think of the introduction to these Words: "I am the LORD your God, who brought you out of Egypt, out of the land of slavery" (Exodus 20:2). God graciously rescued these people from

Egypt. God graciously chose these people for special relationship with himself (Exodus 19:5-6). God graciously gives them these Ten Words (and the other laws that follow) because this is what true life looks like, this is the way to *shalom*. Rather than see these Words as unfair and unreasonable impositions on our freedom, we should think of them as good wisdom and kind instruction to guide us to what's desirable.

It's quite understandable that we read the Fourth Word into Genesis 2:1–3 because the Fourth Word itself appears to encourage us in that direction.

> Remember the Sabbath day by keeping it holy. Six days you shall labor and do all your work, but the seventh day is a Sabbath to the LORD your God. . . . For in six days the LORD made the heavens and the earth, the sea, and all that is in them, but he rested on the seventh day. Therefore the LORD blessed the Sabbath day and made it holy. (Exodus 20:8–11)

We're so familiar with that passage that we naturally read it—or our understanding of it—into Genesis 2. We may even argue that it's desirable, based on the principle of using Scripture to interpret Scripture. However, the danger is that we may import all of the concepts that we usually associate with the weekly Sabbath into our interpretation of God's rest on the seventh day.

Even as I tried to confine myself solely to Genesis 1:1–2:3 in writing out my initial impressions about the seventh day, when I came to the question of God's "blessing" I started to write:

> Are we perhaps to infer that it too is to be increased—that we are somehow to multiply the seventh day in comparison to the previous six and to work (if you'll excuse the pun) at expanding our rest days into more than one each week? Are we to have the goal of reducing work and increasing leisure?

Nothing in the text supports that idea. Nothing in the text even refers to humans stopping work on *this* seventh day—let alone *every* seventh day. Humans are in existence by this point, but they aren't the focus of Genesis 2:1–3. It's only because I'm used to reading this text in terms of Exodus 20 and the weekly Sabbath that I think in terms of human work and human rest.

But should the influence go that way? Clearly Exodus 20 makes use of the distinctiveness of creation's seventh day. Equally clearly, it tells the Israelites to also make that day distinctive, and thus sets up a weekly cycle for them. But does it necessarily follow that God's "rest" in Genesis 2 sets up a weekly Sabbath?

Let me illustrate by an unrelated example. In 1 Corinthians 9:9, Paul quotes a law found in Deuteronomy 25:4. "Do not muzzle an ox while it is treading out the grain." Paul applies that law to himself and the other apostles. For apostles, he claims the right to financial support from churches as they do the work of apostolic ministry. He compares the situations of oxen and apostles and concludes that both have the right to eat on the basis of their work. Paul notes that the two situations aren't exactly parallel. For example, he writes in 1 Corinthians 9:11, "If we have sown spiritual seed among you, is it too much if we reap a material harvest from you?" It's unlikely he thinks there's anything particularly *spiritual* about an ox treading grain. But there is a sufficient parallel for the conclusion he asserts.

So, knowing what Paul writes in 1 Corinthians 9, do you now automatically interpret Deuteronomy 25:4 on that basis? If the discussion in Deuteronomy 25 were about supporting people involved in full-time mission work (rather than creation work), then it would be appropriate to interpret it that way. But if the discussion were about the creation work of farming (as it is), why would you wish to import this later application of the Deuteronomy 25 principle and suggest that's the real meaning of that earlier passage?

Genesis 2 doesn't use the word *Sabbath*. That word is first used in Exodus 16. Genesis 2 does contain concepts that are later associated with the Sabbath—the seventh day, the cessation of work, the idea of *holiness*, and perhaps the concept of rest. That's why it's so easy for us to read Genesis 2 as if it is talking about the Sabbath. And it may be that Exodus 20 actually intends to define what Genesis 2 is about—after all, *God* is the one who gives the Fourth Word and connects it in some way to his "rest" in Genesis 2. But it is still possible that the biblical concept of rest, as it is introduced in Genesis 2, goes deeper than the Sabbath regulations given to Israel and the particular view of human work and rest that we tend to associate with the Sabbath.

Considering the Biblical Trajectory

Now, I know for many that's a big step to take. Perhaps you've found plenty of reasons why the ox/apostle example doesn't work for you. So, allow me to try a second example.

In Exodus 25–30, God gives instructions for the construction of the tabernacle and its furnishings and associated paraphernalia. In Exodus 36–39, many of those details are repeated as Israel obediently proceeds to construct the tabernacle. Later, David decides to upgrade the tabernacle to a temple (2 Samuel 7)—although Stephen hints this was a downgrade (Acts 7:44–53). The temple is constructed by David's son, Solomon (1 Kings 7–9). Yet, in the New Testament, both the tabernacle and the temple are tied to Jesus.

- The Word became flesh and made his dwelling [literally "tabernacled"] among us. (John 1:14)

- "Destroy this temple and I will raise it again in three days." . . . But the temple he had spoken of was His body. (John 2:19–22)

The New Testament presents Jesus as the fulfillment of the tabernacle/temple and all that happened therein. Does that mean we now read these Old Testament passages about the tabernacle and temple as if they're defined by Jesus? Here I want to answer both "yes" and "no." On the one hand, we continue to read these Old Testament passages as they were written to Israel. The tabernacle and temple are specific institutions that were part of Israel's history. They functioned in particular ways within that history. They taught Israel, and us, enduring truths about how God relates to his people. Yet on the other hand, as Christians we recognize Jesus has fulfilled these things. We don't have a temple today. We don't offer blood sacrifices on the altar in that temple. Yes, God did teach Israel important truths through these institutions. Yet God also set up these institutions with the purpose of preparing for the coming of Jesus.[2] They teach us who he is and what he has done.

This example is of a different nature from the one about oxen. It sets up a trajectory in the biblical narrative that reaches its goal in Jesus. The trajectory helps us understand Jesus. And Jesus defines the true meaning of the trajectory.

At this point, you may think I've backed myself into a corner about the Sabbath. Surely the Sabbath is part of the trajectory that begins in Genesis 2. Surely this example justifies the idea of reading a later definition into an earlier text. I agree. But the real issue is: which later definition? I think that by the time we get to the Sabbath in Exodus 16 and 20, the biblical narrative has already established a trajectory of the concept of rest. Certainly, the Sabbath is included within that trajectory—but I don't think it defines it. Rather than fitting our concept of rest into our understanding of the Sabbath, I think we need to fit our concept of the Sabbath into our understanding of rest.[3]

GOD'S REST IN GENESIS 2:4–25

So, what is that understanding of rest? For that, we must turn back to the first part of the biblical narrative. Our English translations don't use the word *rest* in this next section of the biblical narrative. However, I contend that this passage provides important clues that help us understand what it mean for humans to enter God's rest.

Scholars have long discussed the relationship between what some have called the two "creation accounts": Genesis 1:1–2:3 and Genesis 2:4–25. Personally, I find that description distinctly unhelpful. I agree the first is a creation account: it portrays the majestic sweep of God's creative activity. But the second is much more confined: it provides further details of only a small portion of the events outlined in Genesis 1. Its focus is different; it's about the place of humans within God's creation.

This is not the place to survey all the suggestions scholars have made about how the two narratives relate, most of which are compatible with my purpose. I think one of the purposes of Genesis 2:4–25 is to describe what it looks like for humanity to live in God's rest. Now, I should warn you that I don't remember having read that anywhere else. I can't list a string of scholars who agree with me. That doesn't mean such scholars don't exist—just that I haven't come across them. Nor does it mean that they would disagree with me. But I thought it important to point that out to you so that you read what follows with appropriate caution.

Rather than the language of rest, it's more common to speak of the harmony God establishes in his creation. Genesis 1 describes that harmony with broad brush strokes. God brings order out of the primeval chaos. He separates things and puts them in their place. He establishes an ordered environment. He populates that environment with appropriate and varied creatures. And he repeatedly pronounces the results of his creative work to be good. The overall result is a well-ordered world that conforms to God's purposes. The component parts each have their place so that they serve their appropriate functions in the overall system. It's a broad canvas of coherence and harmony. Even more than that, as Walter Brueggemann notes, the narrative "proclaims that creation is a source of rejoicing and delight for creator and creature"[4]—an inspiring picture of goodness and harmony.

I think Genesis 2:4–25 describes that harmony particularly as it relates to humanity. In this narrative, God establishes a delightful garden. He provisions the garden abundantly. He gives humanity the task of caring for and extending the garden. And he deals with the problem of the man's aloneness by instituting the pleasures of the marriage relationship. Again, the text provides a picture of coherence, goodness, and delight. God doesn't place people in a harsh, barren landscape and force them to eke out a bare existence from scarce and inadequate resources. Rather, in his generosity and goodness, God provides a pleasant, enjoyable environment with abundant provisions that cater to humanity's needs. The strong implication is that God desires humanity to benefit from and enjoy the fruit of his creative labor.

The events of Genesis 3 shatter the harmony established in these two opening narratives. Adam and Eve fail to trust God's word; that is, they introduce disharmony into how they relate with the God who was so generous to them. Instead of trusting his assessment of how they should live in his garden, they choose to assert their own, independent assessment of what they think is good for themselves. They choose to be masters of their own destiny; they (mere creatures) see themselves as equal with God (the one and only Creator). In a fairly brief narrative, the impact of the disharmony they introduce is evidenced in several ways. When they hear God walking in the garden, they hide from his presence. When God questions them concerning their actions, they look to blame others—the serpent, one another, even God. God's pronouncements speak of further disharmony: enmity between the humans and the serpent, a striving against each other in marriage, a struggle to produce food from the land, and the introduction of human death. God expels them from the pleasurable setting of the garden into the more difficult environment of the world beyond. They now experience disharmony in their relationship with God, their relationship with one another, and their relationship with their environment. The ongoing narrative demonstrates the extent of that disharmony.

I think there is little doubt that the latter is life "outside God's rest." I will argue that the former can be described as life "within God's rest." As I indicated earlier, that's a description I don't remember having read anywhere else, but I think the text deliberately shows us this clear contrast. While Genesis 2:4–25 shows us life as it was intended to be, Genesis 3 shows us life as it actually is now. As will be shown, this association of the whole harmony of creation with rest is supported by the biblical trajectory of the concept of God's rest.

Why is this important for our discussion of retirement? It's important because the description of harmonious life in Genesis 2:4–25 includes human work. Part of living within the harmony of God's creation is work. "The LORD God took the man and put him in the Garden of Eden to work it and take care of it" (Genesis 2:15). That is, I wish to suggest the Bible's concept of rest doesn't necessarily exclude work.

Now, I realize I'm a long way from proving that at this point. First of all, it goes against our normal understanding of what *rest* is. We normally see *work* and *rest* as opposites. We may sometimes struggle with definitions. For example, in times past when my body was significantly younger, I classified playing sports as part of my *rest*. At one level, it was a long way from *rest*. It was the most physically strenuous part of my week. It could also be the most stressful part of my week—depending on the decisions officials made during the game and my attitude toward them. The fact that it was competitive sport (and I have a strong bias toward winning) also added an element of stress. Yet for me it was an important break. It was very different from my normal work, which largely involved mental activity sitting at a desk—both before and after I became a pastor. The strenuous activity of competing on a sporting field was a welcome change. Usually, I found it *restful* and *re-creational*. But I suspect if I were a professional sportsperson that would be different. Still, despite such gray areas, we normally see work and rest as opposites.

Second, Genesis 2:1–3 seems to confirm our gut sense that rest and work are opposites. It uses the verb *rest* in the context of God having finished his creative work, and it appears to do so by way of contrast. God completed his creative work in six days, *so* on the seventh he rested. God blessed and sanctified the seventh day *because* he rested from his work of creating.

Third, it doesn't look as though rest is the theme of Genesis 2:4–25. If I surveyed a hundred people and asked them what they thought was the main theme of this passage, I reckon there's a good chance that none of them would answer *rest*. The NIV doesn't even use the word in this passage. The closest it comes is when God puts Adam to sleep while he does some creative surgery and forms Eve (2:21–22). In the discussion above, I've used the word *harmony* and then jumped to the word *rest*; but while there is some overlap between the two words, one would hardly say they're synonyms. So isn't it a bit of a long shot for me to suggest this passage describes what it means for humanity to live in God's rest?

Having seemingly torpedoed my theory, let's see if I can salvage anything. The word *rest* has a range of meanings. George Guthrie identifies several "thematic categories" for how the word is used in the Bible:[5]

1. To rest on someone or something
2. An emotional state of peace
3. Physical rest: ceasing work or travel, laziness, sleep, and death
4. Rest from war
5. Rest from wandering in the wilderness
6. Eschatological rest

It's likely that list does not cover all the ways we use the word today. In Genesis 2:1–3, the idea of ceasing work (in this case, God's creative project) is what initially comes to mind. In terms of our current discussion, I think a broader concept of rest is in view (defined more fully below). For now, it is enough to note that the broader trajectory of rest in the Bible includes much more than merely ceasing activity.

Other elements of that trajectory can also inform how we interpret Genesis 2:4–25. In particular, Hebrews 3:7–4:11 refers to *God's rest*. It uses the description as if the readers should be familiar with this concept. The closest the passage comes to defining it is in 4:3–5.

> Now we who have believed enter that rest, just as God has said,
>
> > "So I declared on oath in my anger,
> > 'They shall never enter my rest.'"
>
> And yet his work has been finished since the creation of the world. For somewhere he has spoken about the seventh day in these words: "And on the seventh day God rested from all his work." And again in the passage above he says, "They shall never enter my rest."

Clearly, the writer of Hebrews connects *God's rest* with Genesis 2:1–3. And, like that passage, he describes it as the seventh day rather than the Sabbath.

A cursory reading of the passage may suggest that last statement is incorrect. After all, Hebrews 4:9–10 states: "There remains, then, a Sabbath-rest for the people of God; for anyone who enters God's rest also rests from his own work." However, the writer of Hebrews doesn't use the usual Greek word for Sabbath. Instead, he uses the word *sabbatismos*. Some scholars believe he coined this word.[6] Certainly, it's the only place the word is used in the New Testament. And so there's some level of uncertainty about the writer's exact meaning: for example, the NKJV simply uses "rest" and William Lane suggests "Sabbath celebration."[7] Scholars have argued about this passage at some length, and many of their conclusions are based on their presuppositions. This is natural because there isn't much in the text itself to define the writer's exact meaning, but I think it's clear that the focus remains on God's seventh day rest. The *sabbatismos* is directly connected with God's seventh day rest in verse 10.

It's also clear that the writer of Hebrews believes it's possible for humans to *enter* God's rest. The passage highlights four groups who were invited to enter this rest: first, the generation of Israelites that refused to enter Canaan because of the spies' report (they failed to enter God's rest because of their rebellion and unbelief); second, the generation of Israelites that entered the land under Joshua's leadership (they also failed to enjoy God's rest, although the reason is not specified); third, the Israelites living in the land during David's reign; and fourth, the people to whom Hebrews is addressed (who are encouraged not to fall away from God's promise).

So, what does it mean to *enter* God's rest? What would it have meant for Adam and Eve? If I go to my usual default position of importing the Sabbath into Genesis 2:1–3, I'll think in terms of Adam and Eve taking a break from work every seventh day so they could recuperate for their next six days of labor. But how does that fit with God's "rest"? We know that God doesn't need to recuperate. Instead, his rest appears to be final: he does not resume his creative work (at least, not in terms of what he does on the first six days). The passage itself doesn't establish a weekly cycle. And the text doesn't specify the ending of the seventh day.

Rather, I think *God's rest* (and notice that Genesis 2:1–3 uses a verb rather than a noun) relates to his enjoyment of the fruits of his creation. Consider an analogy. Suppose a keen sailor decides to build her own boat. She's not a boat-builder by trade; this is simply a one-off project for her own benefit. She labors diligently in the construction. She is meticulous over the details. Finally, she finishes. She ceases to build the boat. But she didn't build the boat simply for the satisfaction of adding that skill to her CV. She built it to sail. And so the completion of the construction signals the beginning of a new relationship with the boat. The "creative" work is ended, but the ongoing work of sailing continues. The project is satisfactorily finished and now is the time to enjoy it.

I think it's like that when God *ceased* (remember that the NIV gives that as an alternate translation to *rested*) his creative work. It's the time when he sits back to enjoy the fruits of his labor. That's why there's no ending to the seventh day and no beginning of the eighth day. In terms of human existence there must have been an eighth day. The seventh day ticked over into the eighth day and the millions of days that subsequently followed. But there's no end to God's enjoyment of the fruits of his labor.

God invited Adam and Eve to join him in that enjoyment—not by having one day off every seven (there's no mention of this in Genesis 2), but by living within the pleasurable garden he established and partaking of his bounteous provision. In other words, Adam and Eve enter God's rest by living in the harmonious creation described in Genesis 2:4–25—and that includes the work of caring for and extending the garden (one of God's good gifts).

Unfortunately, Adam and Eve chose to reject God's rest. They rebelled against God, introduced unrest and disharmony, and were expelled from the garden. But that doesn't mean God's rest disappeared or that it was no longer available to humans. Hebrews 3:7–4:11 indicates God offered the possibility of entering his rest to others.

GOD'S REST FOR ISRAEL

In discussing this, the writer of Hebrews introduces us to three generations of Israelites (as noted above). I think it's fairly clear that the writer believes entering God's rest involved those ancient Israelites living in the land of God's promise. This was the land God first promised to Abraham, the man to whom all Israelites traced their ancestry.

This promise to Abraham well and truly predates any mention of the Sabbath. The first time the promise appears is Genesis 12:1–3, while Abram is living in Haran.

> The LORD had said to Abram, "Leave your country, your people and your father's household and go to the land I will show you.
>
> "I will make you into a great nation
> and I will bless you;
> I will make your name great,
> and you will be a blessing.
> I will bless those who bless you,
> and whoever curses you I will curse;
> and all peoples on earth
> will be blessed through you."

Once Abram arrives in the land, God affirms: "To your offspring I will give this land" (12:7). The promise is repeated several times throughout the narrative of Abraham's life. Different aspects are emphasized according to the occasion that gives rise to the promise's reaffirmation. But there is little elaboration on what life in the land will be like.

It's not until Genesis 22:17–18, after Abraham demonstrates his willingness to sacrifice Isaac (the son of the promise), that a new detail is added.

> I will surely bless you and make your descendants as numerous as the stars in the sky and as the sand on the seashore. Your descendants will take possession of the cities of their enemies, and through your offspring all nations on earth will be blessed, because you have obeyed me.

For Abraham's descendants, living in the land included the dispossession of their enemies. This hints at a level of stability and security.

The next new element is added when God confronts Moses at the bush that burns without being consumed. Abraham's descendants are now slaves in Egypt. Moses himself fled the country forty years earlier. In Exodus 3:8, God tells Moses:

"So I have come down to rescue them from the hand of the Egyptians and to bring them up out of that land into a good and spacious land, a land flowing with milk and honey—the home of the Canaanites, Hittites, Amorites, Perizzites, Hivites and Jebusites."

This expression—a land flowing with milk and honey—is repeated at regular intervals in the narrative that follows. It's a way of describing the bounty of the land God will give them.

All of this is promised before we get to the first mention of the Sabbath in Exodus 16 and the Fourth Word about the Sabbath in Exodus 20. Admittedly, these early promises give only a bare outline of what life in the land—what the author of Hebrews identifies as entering God's rest—will be like. Forty years after the exodus, Moses provides fuller details. Moses tells the Israelites that the promised land is a place where the hard work of establishing the basic infrastructure was done by others (Deuteronomy 6:10–12). It's a land where God will remove their enemies and allow them to live in security (Deuteronomy 6:18–19; 7:1–2, 17–26; 11:22–25). There they can dwell with God in their midst and serve him as his chosen people, secure in their knowledge of his love toward them (Deuteronomy 7:6–11). It's also a land where they can experience the abundance of God's provision and blessing if they pay attention to God's instructions (Deuteronomy 7:12–16; 8:6–9; 11:13–15). It's like they're being put back in the garden—only now it's a bigger version and God's people number far more than two.

The picture is comparable with Genesis 2:4–25. It's a place of harmony, abundance, peace, security, and blessing. It's a place where they can live in right relationship with God, with one another, and with their environment. It's a picture of *shalom*—of what God always intended for people living in his world. It's an image of God and his people together enjoying the fruits of God's creative labor.

And that picture includes human work. While they're not required to establish the initial infrastructure in Canaan, they do have to maintain, utilize and improve it. They're expected to plant and harvest crops, to tend and prune orchards, and to pasture and care for their flocks and herds. In the wilderness, God provided manna each day, but that ceased once they entered the land (Joshua 5:12).

Just as in the garden, entering God's rest includes ongoing human labor. In other words, in the Bible, there's a trajectory of *rest* that includes human work.

GOD'S REST FOR ADAM?

Earlier, I noted that the NIV doesn't use the word *rest* in Genesis 2:4–25. However, the idea may be present in the original Hebrew. Verse 15 echoes verse 8—the statement that God put the man in the garden—but two different Hebrew verbs are used. The verb used in verse 8 means *to put* or *to set* or *to place*. There's nothing particularly unusual about it. But the verb used in verse 15 may have the underlying meaning of *to rest*. The text uses a causative form that "could be rendered literally 'caused to rest.'"[8] The name *Noah* comes from the same verbal root—and Gordon Wenham notes that his name literally means *rest*.[9] The word translated *rest* in Psalm 95:11 (on which the exposition of Hebrews 3:7–4:11 is based) also comes from the same verbal root. John Sailhamer suggests the following implications:

> Unlike v. 8, where a common term for "put" is used, in v. 15 the author uses a term . . . that he elsewhere has reserved for two special uses: God's "rest" or "safety," which he gives to man in the land (e.g., Gen 19:16; Deut 3:20; 12:10; 25:19), and the "dedication" of something in the presence of the Lord (Exod 16:33–34; Lev 16:23; Num 17:4; Deut 26:4, 10). Both senses of the term appear to lie behind the author's use of the word in v. 15. Man was "put" into the garden where he could "rest" and be "safe," and man was "put" into the garden "in God's presence" where he could have fellowship with God (3:8).[10]

Now, before I begin to wax eloquent about the support this provides for my theory of rest, I should highlight two potential weaknesses. First, the Hebrew verb with the connotation of *rest* in verse 15 is different from the Hebrew verb used in verses 2 and 3 to describe what God does. However, there is good reason for this. The verb used in that concluding paragraph of the creation narrative highlights the change in God's activity: he was working; now he has *ceased*. That nuance is absent from the verb used in verse 15. There is no report of Adam doing anything before verse 15—and so there is nothing for him to *cease*. Nor does it make sense to infer that God causes Adam to cease something when he "places" him in the garden.

Second, the Hebrew verb in verse 15 has a wider range of meanings than *rest*. My Hebrew lexicon provides several nuances: *set, put, settle, leave, let stay*.[11] You can understand why our English translations choose one of these rather than: "The LORD God took the man and 'rested him' or 'caused him to rest' in the Garden of Eden to work it and take care of it." So the NIV translation is not incorrect. Yet it seems to me that it omits a significant element of what the narrative wishes to communicate. It does use a different verb when compared with the same expression in verse 8. God *settles* Adam in the garden. This is not a place where Adam restlessly wanders or feels insecure. I think it has many of the connotations we'd associate with the concept of *home*. In other words, I think—to use the Bible's later terminology—God places Adam within the ambit of his rest.

Moreover, the narrative appears to draw a connection between this verb and the following two verbs: God *settles* Adam in the garden for the purpose of *working* it and *taking care* of it. Now, this latter part of verse 15 has generated considerable discussion among scholars:

- What is the nature of the garden? A paradise? A royal garden attached to the palace? A temple?
- What exactly do the two verbs mean? Pastoral work? Agricultural work? Service of the creation? Priestly service? Obedience to God?
- To what does the pronoun "it" refer? In Hebrew, it's not the same gender as the word for "garden."

These are important exegetical issues, but they are beyond our current purpose. For while they may supply varying nuances and a range of helpful insights into the nature of human work in the garden (many of which are not mutually exclusive), they all agree on the one central point: God blessed humans by gifting them with work. I would simply add this: that notion of work is here connected with the idea of *rest* as *shalom*—something I've already noted within the broader context of this passage.

JESUS' REST FOR HIS FOLLOWERS

I think Jesus also points us in this same direction. In Matthew 11:28–30, Jesus offers people *rest*.

> "Come to me, all you who are weary and burdened, and I will give you rest. Take my yoke upon you and learn from me, for I am gentle and humble in heart, and you will find rest for your souls.[12] For my yoke is easy and my burden is light."

What would people understand by this offer? What is this *rest* that Jesus offers? At first glance, these verses appear to be a huge shift in subject matter from the immediately preceding verses. Indeed, some scholars suggest Matthew has simply lumped together several isolated sayings of Jesus at this point—as if he had a few juicy morsels from the lips of Jesus that he very much wanted to include in his Gospel but didn't quite know where best to fit them in. I disagree.

I think we have some clues in the broader context. Matthew 11 opens with a new location. It also opens with a question from John the Baptizer: "Are you the One who was to come?" Jesus' response to that question points John to Isaiah 35—a passage which promises restoration for a people who have been oppressed and exiled from their land. While the passage doesn't use the specific terminology, the image Isaiah paints holds out the possibility that God's people will again have the opportunity to enter into God's rest. After John's messengers leave, Jesus instructs the crowd about John's position in history and the dawning kingdom of heaven. He affirms the importance of the present. All the Prophets and Law point to what unfolds in Jesus' ministry. This is the climax of God's plan to remove the disharmony introduced by human rebellion in the garden and to restore God's good rule and *shalom* and true *rest*. Jesus' miracles demonstrate God's presence among the people and provide a foretaste of God's future kingdom as he reverses the curses of the fall. Jesus calls for repentance. There is both the threat of judgment and the offer of *rest* for those who come to Jesus and accept his yoke.

Two things stand out. First, *rest* is not directly mentioned earlier in this chapter. Yet what the chapter does speak about points to the eschatological rest promised by God in line with his original intentions at creation: the fulfillment of Isaiah 35, the culmination of the Law and Prophets, and the threat of impending judgment on those who reject Jesus. That is, if I may import the terminology of Hebrews 3:7–4:11, we are to construe Jesus' offer in terms of the possibility of *entering God's rest.*

I think Matthew intends his readers to interpret Jesus' offer on the basis of the Bible's overall plot. God's original purpose is for humans to enjoy "his rest." Adam and Eve rejected God's purpose and thus he excluded them from "his rest." In some sense, God offers Israel "rest" in Canaan—but their experience demonstrates their failure to trust God fully and thus participate in "his rest." Solomon builds God's temple and again introduces the concept of "God's rest" (2 Chronicles 6:41–42). Yet as is apparent upon Solomon's death, this comes at the cost of deep dissatisfaction among God's people (2 Chronicles 10). From there it's basically downhill, culminating in the exile and exclusion from "rest" in the Promised Land. With that overall background, Jesus presents this claim to make rest available.

Two further factors support this interpretation. First, Jesus here quotes from Jeremiah 6:16.

This is what the LORD says:

"Stand at the crossroads and look;
　　ask for the ancient paths,
ask where the good way is, and walk in it,
　　and you will find rest for your souls.
　　But you said, 'We will not walk in it.'"

Jeremiah warns the people concerning their wickedness. He indicates that pursuing such evil will result in a distinct lack of rest because of God's impending judgment. And so he calls them to consider the good path: the path God showed them long ago; the path that will lead to harmony and *shalom*; the path that will result in *rest*.

Second, in the following text, Matthew reports two Sabbath controversies (12:1–14). The weekly Sabbath remains a controversial subject in the church today. Although I've already touched on it in the discussion of rest in Genesis, we'll consider it in its own right in the next chapter. For the moment, suffice it to say that very few of the combatants in the Sabbath wars deny that it's related to the topic of *rest*. The Sabbath controversies provide a fitting context for Jesus' teaching about the rest he offers.

The second thing that stands out about this teaching is the surface incongruity of Jesus' offer. Accepting a yoke doesn't sound like *rest*. Putting the yoke on an animal was the prelude to the animal's work. Although Jesus doesn't intend a literal yoke, it's difficult to escape the idea that he summons those accepting his offer to shoulder some form of responsibility. For not only does he wish to *yoke* respondents, he also wants to provide them with a *burden* (albeit a light one).

How are we to deal with this incongruity? Your answer to that will likely depend on which parts of the Old Testament readily spring to mind. I think there's little doubt that Jesus here offers God's eschatological rest. As I've indicated already, I think there's sufficient context to support that interpretation. Besides, it's difficult to construct a plausible alternative. That in itself points us to a wide variety of images that the Old Testament uses to picture the perfection of God's rule.

Where does *the burden* fit into those images? Donald Hagner notes that yoke "is a common metaphor for the law, both in Judaism . . . and in the NT (Acts 15:10; Gal 5:1)." He suggests that Jesus invites people "to follow his own teaching as the definitive interpretation of the law."[13] Yet, as Hagner points out, that doesn't solve the problem. Jesus later (Matthew 23:2–4) refers to the heavy burden the Jewish religious leaders placed on people with all the traditions they added to God's law (though that is no guarantee that he refers to that in Matthew 11[14]). Yet in terms of obedience to the law, the way Jesus interprets it in the Sermon on the Mount (Matthew 5:21–47) is exponentially more difficult than anything the religious leaders required. How can that be said to be *easy* and *light*?

Moreover, the two New Testament references Hagner cites both speak of humans' inability to keep God's law. In Acts 15, Peter notes that it's inappropriate to require Gentile converts to submit to the yoke of the law—something the Jews had been unable to achieve themselves. In Galatians 5, Paul urges the church to stand firm in their freedom in Christ rather than being burdened again by the law's yoke of slavery.

In addition, it's worth asking: Why should God's law be considered a burden at all? Surely it reveals the perfection of God's rule. It's a good thing that explains to us how to live rightly and points us toward the experience of *shalom*. The psalmist, for example, expresses his delight in God's law (for example, Psalms 19 and 119). How can something as excellent as God's law be thought of as a burden?

And yet the reality is that we do experience God's law as a burden. We wish to reject it and substitute our own desires. That was Israel's experience. She experienced God's judgment—and also God's promise. It may be that Jesus' offer of rest echoes the words of Jeremiah 31:25: "I will refresh the weary and satisfy the faint." Those words introduce God's promise of a new covenant—one where God will put his law in people's minds and write it on their hearts (Jeremiah 31:33). Ezekiel puts it in terms of heart surgery—removing people's hearts of stone and replacing them with hearts of flesh so that people will have the ability to keep his laws (Ezekiel 36:26–27).

I think Jesus' offer is along these lines. It can hardly be an offer to relax the constraints of God's rule—as if God would somehow relax his righteous standards so that some elements of human sinfulness were now permitted. That would defeat his purpose of achieving true *shalom*. No, the change is not to God's standards. Rather, the change must occur in those who accept Jesus' offer. They are given new hearts such that they rejoice in God's goodness and his will. Their desires are changed so that they now conform to his purposes. And that means they delight to serve under his direction.

Jesus' offer has a present aspect to it. Even now, his followers can begin to experience something of this eschatological rest as they are restored to right relationship with God. Yet as we are only too well aware, we still fail to perfectly desire God's will. That awaits Jesus' return. At that point, this trajectory of God's rest will be brought to completion. God's kingdom will indeed be a place where his people dwell in harmony and security and contentment and *shalom*.

But it won't be inactivity. We will rejoice to serve God and one another within the purposes God sets. I think that's hinted at here with the language of *yoke* and *burden*. In terms of Jesus offering present rest, I think that's clear: his followers are called to the work he gives them. But in terms of the offer of eschatological rest, I don't think I can prove that it definitely involves work from the language of this text. Rather, I admit that I import it from my overall understanding of the Bible's trajectory in its teaching about God's rest.

SUMMARY

A full theology of rest is beyond the scope of this chapter. That would require an exploration of several other passages we haven't covered. Hopefully, I've provided sufficient evidence to at least convince you of the basic plausibility of my theory that rest and work are not always opposites in Bible. I will examine some of those passages when we explore the Sabbath legislation and its possible implications for the concept of retirement in the next chapter.

The purpose of this chapter is to demonstrate that entering God's rest most likely includes ongoing work. The kingdom for which we long does not involve a state of inactivity. That's not the goal. Nor will it be an unending round of activities that we currently classify as leisure. The goal will be ongoing service of God according to his purposes. It seems to me that if the concept of voluntary retirement includes ceasing to contribute to the kingdom's purposes, it is inconsistent with that goal.

The other implication of this biblical trajectory of rest for our current lives is that our goal should be to find God's rest in our daily work (and in our lives in general). Rather than thinking of work and rest as opposites, we should seek to understand how to experience God's rest as part of God's gift of work.

Finally, I should note that this doesn't negate the need for physi-cal rest. We remain finite creatures. We are to serve God within the confines of the strength he supplies. For example, we cannot survive without sleep. Our physical and mental capacities have their individual limits for which we are responsible as stewards. And God encourages us to enjoy his creation. That too is part of *shalom*—true rest. As such, it's to be enjoyed with regard for the common good—not self-indulgently and not with disregard for my fellow humans and our environment.[15]

6

A SABBATH REST?

Having considered the overall concept of rest, it's now time to return to the subject of the Sabbath. In the last chapter, I claimed that we needed to fit our concept of the Sabbath into our understanding of rest rather than the other way round. How does that work? Where does the Sabbath legislation fit within the Bible's teaching about work and rest, particularly the trajectory of rest that I've described? And is it possible that the requirement of resting every seventh day somehow suggests that we should give priority to rest? Is our goal to expand the quantity of our rest? Does this Old Testament command have potential to justify a concept of retirement?

On its face, the weekly Sabbath doesn't seem to have any direct connections to the idea of enjoying a period of leisure at the end of one's life. After all, no one expects to retire for only one day each week. But it's possible that this Word about the Sabbath may broaden our understanding of the biblical trajectory of rest discussed in the previous chapter, such that it could incorporate a concept of retirement. In this chapter, I will first examine several issues concerning the interpretation of the Fourth Word and then proceed to examine how the Sabbath relates to the biblical trajectory of rest.

THE GENERAL TERRAIN

Thus, before answering the question as to whether the Sabbath legislation may have the potential to justify a concept of retirement, we need to consider the overall "lay of the land." As I intimated earlier, the Sabbath is a rather controversial topic among Christians. The 2011 book *Perspectives on the Sabbath: Four Views* identifies four major views held by different Christian groups today.[1]

1. *The Seventh-day View*: The Fourth Word is one of God's moral laws and is not abrogated. Further, it's a creation ordinance (that is, something God "ordained" as part of the structure of creation and that is therefore binding on all humanity). It clearly specifies the seventh day (Saturday). It remains the day of rest and worship for Christians.

2. *The Christian Sabbath View*: The creation ordinance establishes the principle of resting one day in seven. The Fourth Word specified this as the seventh day for God's Old Testament people. Since the resurrection of Jesus, this has been transferred to the first day of the week.

3. *The Lutheran View*: The Word concerning the Sabbath was given to the Jews alone and, as such, is not relevant for Christians. Yet the creation account gives general principles regarding both rest and worship. These remain important for Christians, but are not tied to a particular day.

4. *The Fulfillment View*: Jesus fulfills the Old Testament. The way in which he fulfills the weekly Sabbath is by providing true rest for his followers. Thus, the Old Testament commands about the Sabbath are no longer binding on Christians.

I recognize that those are very brief and (in many respects) inadequate summaries of these four positions. Yet they're sufficient to provide an initial indication of where the major divisions lie in issues concerning the Sabbath.

Is the Sabbath a creation ordinance? That is, did God build it into the very fabric of creation and thus make it a natural requirement for all humanity?

Is the Sabbath part of the enduring "moral" law, which would make it relevant for all humanity? Or should it perhaps be classified as "ceremonial" law and thus be viewed as relevant only for Israel (and possibly also for the new Israel, the church)?

Are all the details of the Fourth Word equally binding? Or does it affirm an essential principle (rest one day in seven) and provide details of how this operated during one period of God's dealings with humanity?

The Ten Words do not contain all the Torah teaches concerning the Sabbath (for example, Numbers 15:32-36 provides the death penalty for a man collecting wood on the Sabbath). Should we treat these additional details with the same level of seriousness as the Fourth Word?

Is worship part of the Word about the Sabbath?

What difference does Jesus make? Does he leave the Mosaic Sabbath (as opposed to the various traditions that had accumulated by New Testament times) unchanged? Does he transform only some details of the Sabbath? Does he transform it completely? Does he fulfill it? If the latter, then how does this impact its ongoing relevance?

I think it's fairly clear that how you answer some of those questions will significantly influence your answers to others. They form an interconnected web of issues that threatens to overwhelm us with its complexity.

In this short chapter, I can't pretend to deal with all the issues raised in a four-hundred-page book. And even more than that, the book itself indicates it doesn't cover all the possible perspectives available.[2] All that is to say: this is a complex issue. I wanted you to get something of a feel for its complexity before we address what it has to tell us about retirement.

OUR VIEW OF THE TERRAIN

And, to add to that feeling of complexity, let me throw another proverbial spanner into the works. I think the real debate is not about the texts themselves (although it often looks like that's what's happening), but about the presuppositions we bring to the texts (the sorts of things I discussed in chapter 2). Craig Blomberg highlights this in his contribution to the *Perspectives* book. For example, he highlights four general approaches Christians have when it comes to applying "the Old Testament law in the New Testament age."

1. Dispensationalism: "Nothing in the OT law applies to Christian living unless the NT repeats and endorses it."

2. Covenant Theology: "Everything in the OT carries over to the NT age unless the NT explicitly rescinds it."

3. Moral, Civil and Ceremonial Laws: "The *moral* parts of the OT laws remain in force for believers, but the *civil* and *ceremonial* (or ritual) portion of the laws do not."

4. Privileging the "Big Ten": "Elevates the Ten Commandments above all the others."

He then identifies his own approach as contributing a fifth position—Fulfillment: "Every portion of the law remains an inspired, relevant authority for believers; but none of it may be applied properly until one understands how the new covenant has fulfilled that particular law or part of the law."[3]

Perhaps it's best explained by example. You may think the Fourth Word represents God's perfect moral will that's binding on all people for all time (that could be based on the third or fourth approach in Blomberg's list). That's a presupposition, because the text doesn't actually say that. Let me hasten to add that it may be a correct presupposition. You may have sound, logical reasons that support that presupposition. You may even be able to find other texts that seem to support that presupposition. You may feel that your presupposition enables you to best interpret the Bible as a whole. But I don't think you can find a text that categorically states this claim.

How does that presupposition impact your exegesis? You will come to a text like Colossians 2:16–17.

> Therefore do not let anyone judge you by what you eat or drink, or with regard to a religious festival, a New Moon celebration or a Sabbath day. These are a shadow of the things that were to come; the reality, however, is found in Christ.

And your presupposition will guide your exegesis. Before you start, you already know this can't mean that the Sabbath of the Fourth Word is somehow abrogated. That's God's perfect moral will that's binding on all people for all time. And so you find a way to interpret that New Testament passage that is consistent with your presupposition. You might notice that Colossians talks about "a" Sabbath rather than "the" Sabbath. It connects it with other religious festivals that weren't part of God's moral law. It also connects it with food and drink. And so it must refer to some sabbath-like celebration that's not the seventh-day Sabbath.

I won't bore you by going through the same process with the other approaches Blomberg lists because I'm sure you've got the idea by now. But it's important to note that the same sort of thing can be demonstrated for each of those approaches.

What are we to do? Should we discard all presuppositions? No. In the first place, it's unlikely we could identify them all. But more importantly, presuppositions usually aren't random. They're built up over our lifetime. All sorts of things shape and influence and contribute to them: our communities, our worldview, our overall understanding of the Bible, various books we read and sermons we hear, interactions with those outside our communities, and so on. In essence, they form our current understanding. It's natural that we interpret new information in line with what we currently think.

But we should make the effort to interpret new information with as much "objectivity" as possible. So, to return to the example above, when you read Colossians 2:16–17, you should at least recognize that, on the surface, this conflicts with your presupposition. And so, three things are possible: Your surface reading of Colossians 2:16–17 is inaccurate (the typical default position highlighted above); or your presupposition is wrong; or both your surface reading and presupposition are wrong (the option we're least likely to consider!). It seems to me that there's no point in reading the text if we're unwilling to allow that reading to challenge and change our presuppositions.

The second important lesson is to recognize that we don't all share the same presuppositions. This is crucial when it comes to dealing with our disagreements—at least some of them. It's so easy to find ourselves arguing about the meaning of the text of Scripture—and to think that's the heart of our disagreement—when our real difference concerns the presuppositions on which we interpret the text. To go back to the example, if I bring a "fulfillment" presupposition to Colossians 2, it becomes very obvious to me that Paul encourages me to discard the shadows of the Sabbath for the reality I now have in Jesus. But if I bring a "moral law" presupposition to that passage, it will be just as obvious to me that Paul doesn't mean that. And so if that's the heart of our disagreement, we're more likely to make progress if we identify and focus on the presuppositions.

It seems to me that the two key areas of presupposition that influence our understanding of the Sabbath are first, whether it's a creation ordinance, and second, the relationship between the Old and New Testaments. And, in terms of our current discussion, it's the former area that is more significant.

MY JOURNEY OVER THE TERRAIN

We'll come back to that soon. First, I want to share something of my personal struggle with the whole topic of the Sabbath over many years. I do this because it will help you understand my presuppositions—both my former and current ones.

My childhood Christian community emphasized Sunday as a day of rest (which included gathering for corporate worship). That rest wasn't defined as strictly as it was in some other communities of which I later became aware, but there were still certain activities that my community discouraged. At this time, Sundays also stood out as different in the wider community—it was an era when there was little Sunday trading or sport. In terms of the four views identified above, it was a form of the Christian Sabbath view—although, being Baptist and thus placing little emphasis on creeds and confessions, the theological rationale was probably a bit different from that outlined in the *Perspectives* book.

During my teenage years, I remember making bargains with God: if I honored him by observing his rest day, he was duty-bound to reward me with good academic results. It seemed to work pretty well at the time, although I now realize the unmitigated evil that attitude expresses—that I, a mere creature, should have the audacity to attempt to manipulate God for my own purposes. Within that context, like those whom Jesus opposed during his ministry, I wrestled with what was permissible on the rest day (that is, what constituted work).

Those wrestlings escalated when I became a pastor. My college lecturers and fellow pastors encouraged me to have a "day off" each week—but what exactly did that mean? Since I was reading and studying the Bible on the other six days, did that mean my Bible should remain closed? Should I also have a "day off" from prayer? I assumed pastoral emergencies were permissible because of the exceptional circumstances—but I soon discovered I had a different definition of *emergency* from many people in the congregation. Since much of my regular work involved sitting at my computer, did vigorous activity like sports and mowing the lawn count as rest? Were computer games taboo because my equipment needed the "day off" too? I could go on, but I suspect you've got the general drift.

Over the years, I found it more and more difficult to continue with my original presuppositions—and the interpretations of the texts given to support those presuppositions. Initially, this centered on the Sabbath-conflict narratives in the gospels. I realized that Jesus didn't confine himself to emergencies in the healings he did on the Sabbath. And there's no indication that he stopped his work as an itinerant teacher one day a week—certainly not on the Sabbath (and yes, that's an argument from silence that one could hardly count as positive proof). I also became less convinced of the usual explanation given for why Jesus' disciples weren't "working" on the Sabbath in Mark 2:23–28—namely, because harvesting didn't fall within their normal job description. The Fourth Word doesn't seem to admit any exceptions, nor does that rationale form part of Jesus' response. I puzzled over Jesus' use of the example of the priests working on the Sabbath (Matthew 12:6) and wondered whether that implied pastors shouldn't be having a "day off."

But there were wider issues as well. First, I was never comfortable with the distinction people make between moral, ceremonial, and civil laws in the Old Testament (which is a bit unusual for me because I like having everything neatly classified). I didn't find it specified in the text. Nor did the text observe such distinctions when it presented the various laws. And, if God *commands* a ceremonial action, doesn't that bring a moral component into it anyway? Besides, if the distinction was valid, it seemed to me that the Fourth Word fitted within the ceremonial—not moral—law.

Second, over the years, I became more convinced of a "fulfillment" approach to relating the two testaments (based on passages like Matthew 5:17–20; Luke 24:25–27, 44–49; 2 Corinthians 1:20, as well as the way the New Testament applies the Old Testament).

Third, I also developed an aversion to divisions between the so-called *sacred* and the so-called *secular*—something about which I still struggle to be consistent (possibly because I like to distinguish and classify). Now, on any interpretation, clearly God distinguished the Sabbath for at least the nation of Israel. But he did that within the context of a raft of legislation that was designed to teach them that all of life belonged to him. I investigated ways to affirm both.

Eventually I got around to reading a book that had sat on my shelf for years: *From Sabbath to Lord's Day.*[4] Harold Dressler's chapter on "The Sabbath in the Old Testament" challenged my presupposition that the Sabbath was a creation ordinance. For me, that opened up several possibilities. It enabled the possibility of a different link between Exodus 20 and Genesis 2, which I've explored in the previous chapter. It meant I could see the Sabbath as a pointer to something else rather than an end in itself, providing an opportunity to see Jesus as the fulfillment of the Sabbath. It challenged me to explore the biblical concept of rest first and to see how the Sabbath fitted into that (rather than the other way around). I now realize that, without knowing the terminology at the time, I was looking for a new set of presuppositions that would help me make sense of the whole.

That remains an ongoing process. For example, in preparing this chapter, I looked at Greg Beale's *A New Testament Biblical Theology*—especially the chapter entitled "Sabbath Observance as a New-Creational Mark."[5] He notes that "it is possible that God 'blessed the seventh day and set it apart' in order to celebrate his own resting, and it has nothing to do with humans resting."[6] However, he proceeds to argue strongly that the Sabbath is a creation ordinance. I found myself agreeing with many of his arguments, but wanting to take them in a different direction. Because of this, I now wonder if I can affirm *entering God's rest* as a creation ordinance, but not the concept of resting every seventh day.

As I understand it, Beale presents four arguments to support his contention. The first builds on a conclusion he reaches earlier in the book: being created in God's image involves reflecting God's activity. That includes both ruling the earth and filling it. He now adds that humanity is also "expected to reflect God's goal of resting at the end of the creative process."[7] I agree. But, as I asked in the last chapter: What does Genesis 2 mean by God's "rest"? Does God "down tools" every seventh day so he can share the day with humanity, strolling together in the garden? As I argued then, I think God's rest has more to do with the ongoing enjoyment of the fruits of his labor—an enjoyment in which he expected humanity to participate.

Beale's second argument explores the meaning of the *blessing* of the seventh day. He claims the Hebrew word used here "is normally restricted to living beings in the OT and typically does not apply to something being blessed or sanctified only for God's sake."[8] I haven't explored the Hebrew terminology or the references he cites, but I'm happy to accept his conclusion (probably because it doesn't challenge my presuppositions!). Where I part company with him is in the next sentence: "Accordingly, Gen. 2:3 appears to be directed to humanity as a creational ordinance to regard the seventh day of each week to be 'blessed and set apart' by God."[9] I think the phrase "of each week" is not present in the context, but imported from either the cultural existence of weeks (an integral part of our lives) or the Fourth Word. I think the "creational ordinance" of entering into God's seventh day (that is, God's rest) is quite different from observing a weekly rest-day—as explained in the last chapter.

Beale's third argument relates to the word *sanctify* or *set apart* (the NIV's *made it holy*). After presenting the evidence, he states: "outside of Gen. 2:3, all other sacred days include humans and, at least implicitly, God, in their purview."[10] And so he infers the same is the case for Genesis 2:3. Again, I'm happy to agree with his analysis. But what is being *made holy* in Genesis 2:3? The text refers to the *seventh day*—but it's the seventh day that's the culmination of the creation "week," not a weekly seventh day. Now, it's not an unreasonable inference to see that as the prototype for a weekly seventh day— Exodus 20 makes that connection (discussed further below). But it's not a necessary inference. And I suggest there's another inference in the context—that God establishes his unending rest of enjoying his completed work and invites humanity to enter into that rest.

His fourth argument relates to God establishing "a temporal structure within which humans were to live" (Genesis 1:14). He suggests the word *seasons* is better translated as *festivals* and *cultic seasons*—and that "the seventh day in Gen. 2:3 is one of those festival days included in Gen. 1:14, which is part of the temporal divisions within which Gen. 1:14 says humans are to live."[11] I agree that God creates a temporal structure for humanity. But I struggle to see *festivals* being included in that. Certainly, God later gives Israel festivals. And God does tie them to the temporal structure he created. But, apart from harvest festivals, they don't arise naturally from that temporal structure—for example, Passover is tied to an historical event that now marks the new year for Israel, but the movements of the celestial bodies don't in themselves establish that particular month as the new year.

And so, while I could affirm *entering God's rest* as a "creation ordinance," it would not be in the traditional sense in which *the weekly seventh day (Sabbath)* is considered a creation ordinance. I struggle with this traditional interpretation for several reasons. First, Genesis 1:1–2:3 doesn't establish a weekly pattern. It presents one week only. There is no second week. Nor do we find any corresponding suggestion that God again rests on day fourteen. Genesis 2:1–3 presents a unique "day" to conclude God's creative activity—it lacks the formula that's a distinct part of the other six days. That points to the distinctness of this "day" (which is further highlighted by the terminology of blessing and sanctifying). I think at least part of that distinctness is that God's rest in terms of the seventh day is unending.

Associated with that, God's work is completed at this point such that he doesn't take up this work of creation again—at least, not until the new creation. Much of our human work is not like that. While we accomplish a good deal during our six work days, we rarely finish a big project, and we never fully complete our work. For me, this also undermines the idea of a pattern we're to copy.

Third, Genesis 1:1–2:3 contains no command to humans to rest every seventh day (the closest it comes is the use of the "sanctify" terminology). In addition, the "creation ordinance" view also seems to assume that God told the human couple the details of Genesis 1:1–2:3. That may well be the case, but it's not affirmed in the text. Further, the biblical narrative doesn't provide any evidence of humans observing a seventh day rest before God commands it in

Exodus 16 (nor is there any evidence of other cultures observing a weekly rest day). There's no mention of Genesis 2 at that point, and it seems to be a new practice—since some of the Israelites initially ignore God's instructions not to gather manna on the seventh day (Exodus 16:27–30). To be fair, it's also possible that it's the re-establishment of a practice long-forgotten during their decades of slavery—but we have no definitive evidence that this is the case.

Fourth, God's rest is not inactivity. Admittedly, this is not in the text of Genesis 2:1–3. It's a theological conclusion imported from other parts of Scripture (such as Jesus' comments in John 5:16–17 that the Father is always at work).

And just as God does not need a day to rest, it seems to me that it's not obvious from creation itself that *we* need a weekly rest. Other aspects of the temporal structure are obvious: the twenty-four-hour cycle of night and day, the twenty-nine-and a-half-day cycle of lunar months, and the rhythms of the annual seasons. Some of these demonstrate a need for rest. Each part of the animate creation exhibits a need for daily rest. In many parts of the world (but not the tropics), the onset of winter brings a reduction (even a cessation) of growth in some species. But as far as I'm aware, nothing similar indicates a weekly cycle. Plants don't stop growing. Cows still need milking. The day seems to be like any other day—except for the way humans structure their activities (some of which relates to God's Fourth Word).

And so, my current reasoned[12] presupposition, or rather, my conclusion, is that *the weekly Sabbath* is not a creation ordinance. Further, I think the goal of the creation narrative is not rest in terms of inactivity, but rest in terms of enjoyment and harmony and *shalom*. And, as I've indicated previously, for humanity, I think that enjoyment includes (but is not confined to) work—that we can find an experience of enjoyment and harmony and *shalom* in our work.

OTHERS' UNDERSTANDING
OF THE TERRAIN

Now, I recognize not everyone shares my presupposition. After all, I began this chapter by noting the different Christian views identified in *Perspectives on the Sabbath*. And since those scholars were unable to convince each other of their own particular view, I know it's likely some of my readers will remain unconvinced by the above brief outline of my view. What difference does that make in terms of our current study? If your presuppositions have led you to grow increasingly frustrated as you've read the above material—if you're starting to think my views on rest and the Sabbath are so far out in left field that I can't possibly have anything useful to say to you—now is the time to pay attention again.

For those who think God does establish a creation ordinance (as that is usually understood—a weekly Sabbath) in Genesis 2:1–3, there remain several options for how that impacts our thoughts about retirement.

The first option is that God establishes this principle of resting every seventh day as a permanent ordinance that will continue into the new creation—that is, in the eternal kingdom, humans will continue to work six days and then rest on the seventh. As this option affirms the ongoing goodness of God's gift of work (something I also affirm) such that it will continue within the new creation, I think it undermines any notion of retirement. It views stopping work as a temporary measure only. Work is always resumed after the seventh day ends. In my opinion, to voluntarily stop work altogether is inconsistent with the final vision this option offers—for it does not value rest (in the sense of ceasing work) above work.

The second option is that God establishes this principle of resting every seventh day as a permanent ordinance only within this creation. The Sabbath rest in this life is a shadow—it points to the eschatological rest in God's eternal kingdom. The issue then becomes: What's the nature of that eschatological rest? Within this option, it seems to me there are two main camps.

The first thinks the eschatological rest involves the end of all work. This camp essentially contrasts work and rest and gives priority to rest. Rest (in the sense of ceasing work) is the ultimate goal. This is our final destination. This should be our desire. And so, to reach this destination early—in the form of retirement—appears a desirable outcome. Why should we object to importing a touch of heaven into our earthly lives? To those of this persuasion, I refer to my earlier discussion of rest—and that my understanding of the eternal kingdom includes ongoing human work—for that is the real level at which we disagree.

But I would add that even if I'm wrong about my understanding of life in God's kingdom and inactivity is our "task" in the new creation, it doesn't necessarily follow that ceasing work is God's purpose for us in the present creation. We would still need to find reasons to justify bringing that final state into our present existence. God gives us humans a task (the creation mandate) during our earthly lives. Our responsibility to God is to continue that task according to the strength and ability he provides.

The second camp's view of eschatological rest is similar to my own. They see it as a time of enjoying God's good creation in harmony with God, one another and our environment. They think ongoing work will be part of that—and that such work is a good gift from God that's not inconsistent with living in God's rest. Thus, retiring from work in this present life isn't something to be voluntarily undertaken.

FITTING THE SABBATH
INTO THE TERRAIN

Up to this point, I've said little about the Sabbath itself. Most of what I've written has distanced the Sabbath from the seventh day of creation. That's because there's a sense in which I see the Sabbath (at least, the way it's often discussed) as a bit of a distraction from the main game. But the Sabbath is a biblical topic and features significantly in the Gospels. And Exodus 20 does link it with Genesis 2. So, it seems natural to ask: What do I think is the significance of that link? Doesn't it undermine my presuppositions? Do God's instructions about the Sabbath require us to modify our understanding of the biblical trajectory of rest?

The main instruction of the Fourth Word is in Exodus 20:8: "Remember the Sabbath day by keeping it holy." Or, as the ESV translates it: "Remember the Sabbath day, to keep it holy." It contains three key terms.

In terms of the biblical narrative, it's the second passage to refer to *the Sabbath*; the first is a few chapters earlier in Exodus 16:21–30. Scholars still debate the origins of this word; yet it likely belongs to the same semantic field as the verb used in Genesis 2:2 and 2:3—meaning *cease* or *stop* or *rest*. Thus, the Sabbath is the "stopping day" or the "resting day."[13]

The Hebrew verb translated *remember* has a range of nuances. Lawrence Richards groups them into three categories:

1. The mental acts themselves, such as remembering, meditating on, paying attention to, and thinking about.

2. The mental acts and the behavior appropriate to these acts (thus to "remember the covenant" is to act in accordance with covenant stipulations).

3. Speaking to invoke memory or to recite from memory.[14]

The focus here is most likely on the second sense, *keep*—that is, don't forget to stop each Sabbath. This is the sense Moses gives when he repeats these Ten Words to the next generation in Deuteronomy 5. There he uses a different verb—one that the NIV translates *observe*. That is, the focus of the instruction part of the Fourth Word is forward-looking (this is what you're to do in the future), rather than backward-looking (you are to think back to an "original" Sabbath or to the institution of Sabbath legislation).

The third term is to *keep holy* or *sanctify*. Genesis 2:3 uses the same verb when it informs us that God *sanctified* the seventh day. Israel is now to treat this day as different from the other six days. More than that, I think it also contains the idea of the day being consecrated to God. There's a sense in which this day belongs to him—yet, I would hasten to add (on the basis of my presuppositions and aversion to distinguishing between the sacred and the secular), not in a way that suggests the other six days don't belong to God.

The manner in which the day is to be different is specified in the next two verses:

> Six days you shall labor and do all your work, but the seventh day is a Sabbath to the LORD your God. On it you shall not do any work, neither you, nor your son or daughter, nor your manservant or maidservant, nor your animals, nor the alien within your gates. (Exodus 20:9–10)

The Deuteronomy version is much the same. It adds ox and donkey to the list of animals that aren't to work. It also adds an explanation: "so that your manservant and maidservant may rest, as you do."

The way in which the Sabbath is to be different is that the Israelites are to cease work. That seems fairly straightforward—until you try to define what's meant by *work*. By Jesus' day, the Jews had developed many regulations to help prevent them inadvertently doing something that could be considered work. People today still struggle with this issue. For example, it's not uncommon to hear Christians talk about ceasing "normal" work—that if my normal job is cooking, it's okay for me to plant my fields on my "stopping day." It seems to me that the text doesn't make that distinction.

Apart from that slight hiccup of definition (which perhaps reflects our inbuilt desire to find loopholes when it comes to God's instructions), it's clear that they're to stop work on the Sabbath. What's not clear is whether there are any positive requirements—whether there's anything they have to do (if we can define *do* in a way that doesn't involve *work*). So far, the text hasn't answered that question.

The final part of the Fourth Word provides what appears to be a rationale for stopping.

> For in six days the LORD made the heavens and the earth, the sea, and all that is in them, but he rested on the seventh day. Therefore the LORD blessed the Sabbath day and made it holy. (Exodus 20:11)

The connection with Genesis 2:1–3 is clear. Yet, there are two notable differences. The first is that a different Hebrew word is used for *cease/rest* (compared with Genesis 2:1–3). It's the same verb used in Genesis 2:15—for when God *puts* or *settles* and *rests* Adam in the garden. The second is that the word *Sabbath* is substituted for *seventh* toward the end of the verse.[15] In Genesis, God blesses and sanctifies the *seventh day*; here that seventh day is identified with the *Sabbath*.

At first glance, I admit that both those changes seem to push one in the direction of viewing the Sabbath as a creation ordinance (as usually defined). It looks like this text identifies the seventh day of Genesis 2 as the first Sabbath.

I indicated above why I struggle to make that identification. Because of this, my current presuppositions cause me to ask: Is there another way of interpreting this text? It seems to me that the crucial issue is how the two halves of the text connect—how we understand the sense of the word the NIV translates *therefore*. Is it along the lines of: "Because God ordained this pattern of the Sabbath back at creation—for that reason you are to observe this same pattern as a weekly cycle"? That's in line with viewing the weekly Sabbath as a creation ordinance. Or is it along the lines of: "God now commands you to stop every seventh day. This is like what God himself did when he created the world: he worked six days and then he stopped"? This views the connection as an analogy. What God did then is like what God now commands. As he blessed and sanctified the seventh day at creation, so he now blesses and sanctifies your Sabbath days.

In other words, does Exodus 20 define what was happening in Genesis 2 or does it simply use Genesis 2 as an illustrative example of what it now commands?

Support for the latter interpretation is found in the account of this Fourth Word in Deuteronomy 5. On that occasion, Moses provides a different rationale. Verse 15:

> Remember that you were slaves in Egypt and that the Lord your God brought you out of there with a mighty hand and an outstretched arm. Therefore the Lord your God has commanded you to observe the Sabbath day.

The structure of this verse is similar to Exodus 20:11. And the word the NIV here translates as *therefore* is the same Hebrew word that's used in Exodus 20:11. How do the two halves of this verse connect? I'd suggest it's more difficult to interpret the connection in this verse in terms of the "ordinance" view rather than the "analogy" view.

Now, it may be that the two rationales operate at different levels. That's certainly possible. But I think one also has to admit the possibility that the two rationales function in much the same way—that they're both used as analogies. That is, the two rationales provide complementary insights into God's reason for instructing Israel to observe this weekly Sabbath. And, as I mentioned in the last chapter, that alters the direction of the influence. Instead of understanding Genesis 2 in terms of how Exodus 20 defines the Sabbath, I think we should seek to understand Genesis 2 in terms of *God's rest* and ask what that means for what God is teaching Israel by now instituting a weekly Sabbath.

As we've worked our way through Exodus 20:8–11, I hope it's become apparent that very little is said in terms of the purpose of this day. The text defines the day negatively: what God's people are not to do. There's little by way of positive definition (what they are to do). That hasn't stopped others filling in that gap. As I've read Christian books commending Sabbath practices, I'm amazed at the variety of purposes that people suggest. I told myself to make a list of them—but that list hasn't progressed beyond a place on my "to do" list. Most of them sound good to me. Most of them seem sensible. And so, at one level, I don't want to reject them. But I don't think they're actually based in the text itself.

One common suggestion is that God establishes the Sabbath as the day for corporate worship. And you can find some support for this in the text. After all, it's a *holy* day and it's a Sabbath *to the* LORD *your God*. In the Old Testament, usually when something is *sanctified* (a word related to *holy*) to God it indicates that "something" is to be used exclusively for God—most often in a cultic setting. And so it seems natural to think that a day *sanctified* to God would be spent in cultic activities. But what may seem a *natural* conclusion isn't a *necessary* conclusion. God could have said: "Remember the Sabbath by keeping it different. The seventh day is a Sabbath to your God. You shall do no work. Instead, you shall participate in athletic contests."[16] A day is *sanctified* for God by doing on that day whatever it is God tells you to do. The terminology in itself doesn't necessarily include a cultic requirement.

At this point, I think it fair to remind you of one of my biases— for I recognize that it influences my interpretation of the text at this point. I have an aversion to the so-called sacred/secular divide. And so, when I read that it's a *Sabbath to the* LORD *your God*, I want to interpret that in a way that does *not* imply that the other six days are somehow ours to do with what we please. Since serving God is a whole-of-life proposition, those other six days are also to be used as God directs. And thus, I want to affirm that what these ancient Israelites did on those other six days was just as important in terms of their obedience to their God as what they did (or did not do) on the Sabbath—just as it remains so for us.

In fairness, there is other evidence within the Torah that may suggest one purpose of the Sabbath was corporate worship. Leviticus 23:3, in the context of a list of God's appointed feasts for Israel, refers to the Sabbath as *a day of sacred assembly*.[17] In the Exodus narrative, both the conclusion of the instructions for constructing the Tabernacle (31:12–16) and the introduction to its actual construction (35:1–3) contain reminders about the Sabbath—thus implying a connection between the cultus and the Sabbath. So one may construct a reasonable case for treating the Sabbath as a day of worship. Even so, as Craig Blomberg notes, "If all we had were the Hebrew Scriptures we might never guess that a day of rest eventually also became a day for worship."[18]

But let's return to the two rationales/analogies. Do they tell us anything about the Sabbath's purpose? First, what's the link between God ceasing his creative work and the Sabbath? Those arguing for a creation ordinance often focus on the requirement for rest in the sense of recuperation. While it's true that our finite bodies do need that sort of rest, I don't think that's the focus here. Certainly, God didn't require that sort of rest after his creative work.

Rather, I think the link is to God's rest in the sense of having completed his creative work and now enjoying the fruits of his labor and inviting humanity to enter into the pleasure of the environment he created. Yes, by the time of Exodus 20, humanity was well and truly excluded from the garden. But even then, God said that was not the final word. God would not abandon his purposes for humanity to enjoy the true benefits of his creation. God now does a new thing with this rescued people. And he offers them a new beginning in the land flowing with milk and honey—the offer, as Hebrews puts it, of *entering his rest*. he gives them the Sabbath as a sign of his covenant with them (Exodus 31:12–17)—a sign that points to the possibility of humans truly enjoying God's rest.[19] Often throughout their history, Jewish people have welcomed the Sabbath and treated it as a special day, feasting on the good food God provides.

Second, what's the link between the rescue from slavery and the Sabbath? One could argue that slavery prevents rest at the physical level. The text refers to the Egyptians dealing harshly with the Israelites. The narrative in Exodus 5 implies they had lengthy work-hours each day even before they had to gather their own straw. And there's no indication they had weekly rest days (nor, for that matter, that the Egyptians themselves had such days). God freed the Israelites from that slavery. The weekly Sabbath could serve as a reminder of their freedom to rest at that physical level.

But I think it's more than that. Their slavery also demonstrated disharmony in the world. One group of humans oppressed another group. One group of humans enjoyed their lifestyle at the expense of that other group. That's a far cry from God's original intentions for humanity. It's not *shalom*. The exodus reminds them that God intervened in their history to rectify that situation of oppression.

Thus I think both rationales point in the same direction. They point Israel back to God's rest at creation (the harmony of perfect relationships within a perfect environment) and their current non-experience of fully entering into that rest. They fail to fully trust God. They fail to fully live according to God's purposes. And those failures lead to various experiences of disharmony in their relationships with one another and their environment. The Sabbath reminds them of that—though not in a negative way. It's a call to celebrate the goodness of God's creation—to experience something of God's rest. It also calls them to work against oppression and for *shalom* that others too may experience God's rest (something that will become clearer in the next chapter).

SUMMARY

Much more could be written concerning the Sabbath. There are many other Sabbath references in the Old Testament. There are also the Sabbath conflict narratives in the Gospels. I think these fit comfortably within the trajectory of rest I have outlined so far. But this is not the place to explore that further.

My purpose in this chapter has been twofold. The subsidiary purpose has been to demonstrate a way of viewing the Sabbath legislation within what I think is the more important biblical theme: the theme of *God's rest*. Within the larger trajectory of what the Bible's narrative teaches us about entering God's rest, God gave the Sabbath to Israel as a picture[20] both of his original intentions and of his ultimate goal for humanity and his creation. That goal can be summarized in various ways: *shalom*, peace, harmony, eternal life, rest. As indicated in the last chapter, Jesus offers the fulfillment of that picture and, in some sense, makes that available to his followers now—although there's also a very real sense in which its ultimate fulfillment awaits Jesus' return.

The primary purpose of this chapter has been to demonstrate that the Sabbath legislation does not provide support for a concept of retirement. I hope I've demonstrated that remains the case even if you disagree with my overall understanding of how the Sabbath fits within the Bible's larger narrative.

I should also add that what I've written should not be used to deny our human finiteness. God doesn't intend us to work 24/7. At the very least, our bodies need sleep. And I believe it's also appropriate for us to build periods of nonwork into our weekly routines. Further, God knows the limitations of those who have a reduced capacity for work and doesn't expect them to function beyond those limitations. For each of us, within the limits of our personal finiteness, all is to be done according to God's will and for his glory. All is to be done in a spirit of humble service.

7

Sabbaticals and Jubilees

Less well known than the weekly Sabbath are the laws concerning the seventh (Sabbatical) and fiftieth (Jubilee) years in the land of God's promise. Indeed, during my church upbringing, I can't remember these being mentioned. Looking back, I find that rather curious. I was encouraged to observe a weekly rest-day, but there was no similar encouragement to observe the seventh or fiftieth year. Of course, part of the reason for this might be obvious—a fiftieth year didn't occur during my childhood or youth. But no one suggested I take a sabbatical from school. Nor were my parents instructed to take a year off from work every seven years. As far as I can tell, the seventh year was simply ignored.

In the law, the Sabbatical Year's connection to the Sabbath is quite clear.

> When you enter the land I am going to give you, the land itself must observe a sabbath to the LORD. For six years sow your fields, and for six years prune your vineyards and gather their crops. But in the seventh year the land is to have a sabbath of rest, a sabbath to the LORD. (Leviticus 25:2–4)

It's the same sort of terminology that's used in the Fourth Word. The legislation for the Year of Jubilee follows directly afterwards. It too is introduced by Sabbath terminology in Leviticus 25:8. "Count off seven sabbaths of years—seven times seven years—so that the seven sabbaths of years amount to a period of forty-nine years." It too is to be a year in which the fields aren't sown.

Why was this aspect of that Word ignored in the church in which I was taught the ongoing importance of observing the Fourth Word? It wasn't discussed—at least, not while I was present—so I don't know. Perhaps since the law specifies that it is for "the land," people considered it rural legislation and not applicable to us city slickers. Maybe they somehow managed to categorize it as merely civil legislation from a different era—though I can't envisage how one can do that and consistently affirm the weekly rest day as moral law. Perhaps they took a "Big Ten" approach and somehow didn't see this as being included. Or maybe they realized these laws don't actually instruct humans to stop all work for the year.

THE PURPOSE OF THIS CHAPTER

Why include this chapter after the lengthy discussion of the Sabbath in the previous chapter? The surface answer is that the Sabbatical and Jubilee years appear to constitute extended rest periods. Each seventh year, life was different. There was a sense (to be clarified shortly) in which people had a "year off." Then, when they experienced the seventh of these in the forty-ninth year, they immediately got another "year off" the following year. We've noted that the Sabbath doesn't justify a concept of retirement—the weekly rest-day was always followed by more work once it concluded. Perhaps the fact that these rest periods are lengthier could justify incorporating an even lengthier "rest period" (retirement) toward the end of one's life.

Right up front, let me outline two reasons why I think the answer is no. The first simply extends what I said about the Sabbath: these years were always followed by more work. They're not indefinite breaks with the option of not returning to work. The only way you didn't resume work in the eighth year was if you died—and that's not a very practical option in terms of a retired lifestyle!

I hinted at the second reason above: there's no instruction to stop work for the year. The land gets a rest. That means they don't plow their fields and sow their seed and harvest their crops. They get a break from that sort of work for the year. But they can continue with their other work. They can work on their infrastructure—building terraces, mending fences, clearing rocks. They can repair their houses and other buildings. Domestic chores will continue as normal. They still tend to their herds and flocks. The year won't disappear in idleness.

And for those who aren't farmers (admittedly a minority of the population in ancient Israel), there's nothing to suggest that life wouldn't continue as normal. Merchants (except perhaps those who dealt in agricultural produce) could continue trading and travelling on business ventures. Those working at trades aren't told to curtail their activities. The unemployed landless poor (one group to benefit from this legislation) essentially still do the same work—gleaning in fields not their own.

The short answer is that I don't think you can justify the concept of retirement on the basis of either the Sabbatical years or the Jubilee years. I could go into more detail, but I think that's fairly straightforward. While these two years may look like an attractive way to justify retirement on the surface, it only requires a little thought to see that they're untenable.

I also think we can gain further value from these laws in terms of the bigger picture of what the Bible teaches concerning the concept of rest. Now, strictly speaking, the rest of this chapter won't deal directly with the issue of retirement. What I'll argue in the rest of this chapter is that the legislation surrounding the Sabbatical and Jubilee years contributes to and supports the understanding of rest that I've outlined in the last two chapters: namely, that God's rest is about harmony and *shalom* rather than inactivity. Thus, in this current, sinful world, where the perfection of God's rest remains a future hope, entering God's rest involves both enjoying the goodness of his creation and working toward having others also share that enjoyment (however imperfectly that will happen before Jesus' return).

THE PURPOSE OF THESE YEARS

The legislation for the Sabbatical years is found in Leviticus 25:2–7. Other passages that are usually considered relevant to this year are: Exodus 21:1–6; 23:10–11; Deuteronomy 15:1–18; 31:10–13. Likewise, the legislation for the Year of Jubilee is found in Leviticus 25:8–55 (although some of this also relates to Sabbatical years). I can't cover all the details of those passages here. Nor can I deal here with the difficulties of how those passages interrelate. For an introduction to those issues, I recommend the articles by Chris Wright in the *Anchor Bible Dictionary.*[1]

Instead, I wish to focus on the main aspects of the laws for these two years and their intended purpose.

First, in both the Sabbatical and Jubilee years, the land is to lie fallow for the year—that is, it's to be uncultivated. As noted above in relation to the Sabbatical Year, this command is linked directly to the Fourth Word—the land itself is to have *a sabbath of rest* and this is identified as *a sabbath to the* Lord. This Sabbath terminology is not repeated in the regulations for the Jubilee Year, but the instructions concerning the land for that year are the same: it is not to be sown or reaped. Thus, given also that this command directly follows the Sabbatical Year legislation, it seems reasonable to assume the same underlying rationale. This strongly implies a connection between these three institutions: the weekly Sabbath, the Sabbatical Year and the Year of Jubilee. For me, that connection is caught up in the concept of entering God's rest.

I think the other rationale the text provides for leaving the land fallow supports this idea.

> "Whatever the land yields during the sabbath year will be food for you—for yourself, your manservant and maidservant, and the hired worker and temporary resident who live among you, as well as for your livestock and the wild animals in your land. Whatever the land produces may be eaten." (Leviticus 25:6–7)

Or, as the earlier passage (Exodus 23:11) puts it: it's one of the means by which Israel's law provides food for the poor. In other words, a significant part of the purpose of Sabbatical years is to encourage communal well-being. In the fallow year, I am entitled to use the land's produce for my own survival. With thankfulness to God, I may meet my daily needs and those of my family. But I'm not to use that produce for my own profit. I'm to recognize the needs of others. I'm to realize that the land belongs to Yahweh and I'm only a tenant. As he is generous in allowing me to use the land, so I'm to be generous to others and to allow them likewise to benefit from God's good provision. Observing these fallow years not only reminds me of my God-given obligations to help others enjoy God's good creation, it also forces me to adopt a lifestyle (not cultivating my fields) that facilitates that. It legislates generous actions toward those in need—though, of course, it can't legislate the generous spirit that would make those actions automatic.

Second, in the Sabbatical Year (and possibly also the Jubilee Year), people are to be released from debts and pledges. The regulations for this are found primarily in Deuteronomy 15 (there is some overlap with the material on debt in the latter part of Leviticus 25). Scholars debate the exact extent of the "release" envisaged. Some claim it was a complete cancellation—all debts were annulled and all pledges to secure debts were returned to their owners. Others interpret it as a release from any repayments during the seventh year only—effectively, the debt was frozen at the end of the sixth year and thawed out again when the eighth year ticked over. Still others claim that all pledges were returned during the seventh year—that mortgaged land or indentured dependents were returned to the debtor for that year. There are several variations and combinations of the various possibilities.[2]

For our purposes, we don't need to decide which is more likely (a luxury not enjoyed by ancient Israelite debtors!). All the interpretations point in the same direction: namely, relief is given to the indebted (that is, to the poor). Again, these laws promote the values of communal well-being. They recognize that people encounter hard times. Sometimes that's because of their own foolish decisions or actions; more often it results from circumstances beyond their control. This text doesn't make that distinction. It doesn't legislate release from debts and pledges only for hard-working, sensible Israelites. Rather, it encourages those who haven't encountered such difficulties (and especially those benefiting from others' misfortunes—that is, creditors) to give relief to these struggling families. Indeed, Moses strongly urges the Israelites not only to act generously, but to develop a generous spirit that is to be expressed in the financial transactions they have with each other (Deuteronomy 15:7–11).

Third, in the Sabbatical Year, during the Feast of Tabernacles, the people hear the law read to them. Deuteronomy 31:12–13 provides the purpose of this particular instruction:

So they can listen and learn to fear the LORD your God and follow carefully all the words of this law. Their children, who do not know this law, must hear it and learn to fear the LORD your God as long as you live in the land you are crossing the Jordan to possess.

What does that achieve? Probably several things. I wish to suggest that one relates to the concept of God's rest.

When Moses gives the Israelites these instructions, they're still outside the land. They still anticipate inheriting this land God has promised to them—a land described in garden-like terms. As Hebrews later expresses it, they still anticipate entering God's rest. They still anticipate the time when they will live in harmony as God's community in God's land. Admittedly, given their track record in the wilderness, they'd surely have to wonder if they could ever fully trust God and live together in harmony. Yet this is the vision that's set before them. And this law that they're to read every seven years provides them with God's instructions on what it means to live in harmony with himself and with one another. One way of putting that is that this shows them what God's rest looks like.

You may think I'm stretching it a bit here and that I'm simply finding ways to discover God's rest under every rock I turn over— and you may be right. But it's important to remember that several biblical themes are tied together with the covenant between God and Israel—including God's promises and God's laws. As Peter Craigie notes, this reading of the law every seven years is not a covenant renewal ceremony; rather, it's a commemoration of the covenant.[3] And since God's promises have the ultimate purpose of gathering a people within the ambit of his rest, I don't think it's unreasonable to suggest that's part of what may be achieved by a "commemoration of the covenant." The nation is thus reminded of the goal and what it looks like—and thus encouraged to work toward implementing that in their lives.

Fourth, in the Jubilee Year, all land returns to the family to whom it was originally distributed (Leviticus 25:10). Land was important in ancient Israel. In economic terms, it was the basic means of production. The original allocation in Joshua's time ensured an equitable distribution for each family. Each family owned

the means for prospering. In an ideal world, that would be sufficient. But ancient Israel's world, like ours, was less than ideal. The
exigencies of life resulted in inequities. Some families prospered,
others struggled. Some struggled to the extent that they needed to
sell their land—the source of their annual "income."

The regulations for the Jubilee Year ensured that the family's
future generations weren't impoverished indefinitely. In effect, they
banned the outright sale of land. A household patriarch could only
sell the potential crops until the next Jubilee Year (Leviticus 25:14–
17). It's designed, over time, to maintain the equitable distribution
of the means of production.

And once again, this regulation also promotes the values of
communal well-being. It pushes the community in the direction of
equality. It recognizes that, over time, imbalances will arise for all
sorts of reasons—some sinful, some not. But if those imbalances
aren't addressed, they will likely result in unhelpful polarities in the
community: some will accumulate large landholdings, while others
will likely be reduced to slavery. That's not what God envisages in
his ideal of *shalom*. Personal prosperity is not to be pursued either
at the expense of or with indifference toward others. This regulation
seeks to restore a measure of balance. It protects future generations
from endemic poverty and it prevents the long-term accumulation
of large landholdings by any family.

Fifth, slaves are to be given the option of freedom. This is clear
for the Jubilee Year: "Consecrate the fiftieth year and proclaim lib-
erty throughout the land to all its inhabitants" (Leviticus 25:10).
Leviticus 25:39–43 provides some further details. This aspect isn't
included directly in the Sabbatical Year regulations. Instead, the law
provides for slaves to be released after six years' actual service—that
is, the clock starts ticking at the commencement of their service
and isn't related to the timing of Sabbatical years (Exodus 21:2–6;
Deuteronomy 15:12–18). Still, because the opportunity for release
comes at the end of six years, these laws may be said to exhibit a
"sabbatical" flavor.

For Old Testament Israelites, God rescuing them from slavery
to the Egyptians was the prelude to experiencing God's rest in the
land. In the previous chapter we noted the way Deuteronomy 5

links that to Sabbath observance. The same rationale supports the
command to free slaves.

> "Remember that you were slaves in Egypt and the LORD your
> God redeemed you. That is why I give you this command today."
> (Deuteronomy 15:15)

Generally, slavery is considered inconsistent with the ideal of *shalom*. And so providing for release from slavery has the aim of increasing overall community well-being.

Moreover, the law also encouraged those releasing slaves to be
generous.

> "And when you release him, do not send him away empty-handed.
> Supply him liberally from your flock, your threshing floor and
> your winepress. Give to him as the LORD your God has blessed you."
> (Deuteronomy 15:13)

In other words, this fellow Hebrew served you for the last six years.
Most likely this wasn't his or her first preference. Desperate circumstances forced this person to sell himself or herself to you. If you
send this person out empty-handed, he or she will most likely face
those same desperate circumstances very quickly. So it's your responsibility to ensure that doesn't happen. Give your former slaves
the resources to enable them to stand on their own two feet. Try to
ensure their future *shalom*.

There is one slight hiccup with this fifth aspect, the release of
slaves: the slaves could choose to remain in service and even to
do so for life (Exodus 21:5–6; Deuteronomy 15:16–17). The natural
question is: why would they do that? Why would they choose to
remain in circumstances that appear contrary to the goal of *shalom*?
The reason given in both passages is *love of master*. It's clear that
we're not talking here about the harsh bondage they experienced
in Egypt. When Hebrews served their fellow Hebrews (as "slaves"),
they basically joined their master's household. The ideal was that
they were treated like any other household member—that is, with
justice and respect. In modern terms, it was closer to an employment contract than slavery: the master received the labor and, in

turn, provided for all the slave's basic needs. So it's feasible that over the period of six years the "slave" could become quite attached to this other household.

I don't think the concept of *love of master* excludes self-interest. The "slaves" may wish to avoid the responsibilities that accompany self-employment. Their conditions in this household may be significantly better than in their family home. If their master has no heir, the "slaves" may be hoping for a prominent place in his will. The point is they freely choose to remain in this situation because they think it provides greater opportunity for them to experience *shalom*.[4] Thus, while it's a slight hiccup, I don't think it undermines the overall thrust of this law.

THE NATURE OF GOD'S REST

That provides a very brief overview of the main regulations for both the Sabbatical and Jubilee years. I haven't mentioned all the areas of scholarly debate surrounding these institutions. Even where I have mentioned that debate, I certainly haven't dealt with it fully. That's because the outcome of those debates won't alter the overall direction of these laws.

These regulations promote communal harmony and *shalom*—the qualities that I think are identified with God's rest. This is not rest in terms of human inactivity. The land itself gets a rest from human work (although it still actually produces), but the humans don't cease their other work. Rather, it seems to me that the year focuses people's attention toward the ideal of God's restful *shalom*. Not only are they to remember God's rest and the fact that they currently fail to experience its perfection in their lives, but they're actually to work toward restoring *shalom* in the community of God's people, especially in terms of their relationships with one another.

Moreover, they are to work at this even at the expense of individual prosperity. It's not that individual prosperity is discouraged or condemned. Rather, it's subservient to a higher value—the prosperity and well-being of the community. While it's true that overall communal well-being can't be achieved without also promoting individual well-being, the reverse does not follow. It's very easy to pursue individual well-being in a way that's detrimental to communal well-being. I know there's a self-centered bias within me that pushes me in that very direction. And the Bible tells me I'm not alone in that bias. Despite the fact that our modern emphasis on individualism had not infected their ancient culture, the Bible also illustrates that same bias at work in ancient Israel. The prophets regularly rebuke the rich for the way they defraud, abuse, and mistreat the poor. These laws counteract that bias.

I think it's worth pausing to consider some of the attitudes encouraged by these regulations—and how the lack of these attitudes or the promotion of their opposites will work against the achievement of true *shalom*.

They're to see the land as belonging to God and their use of it as God's generous gift to them. It's stated rather bluntly in Leviticus 25:23–24:

> "The land must not be sold permanently, because the land is mine and you are but aliens and my tenants. Throughout the country that you hold as a possession, you must provide for the redemption of the land."

This strongly implies that the land's produce is also God's gift. The Israelites are to enjoy that produce with thankfulness. But they're also to enjoy it within the context of God's generosity to them and their obligation to be generous to those around them—especially the poor. We noted above the repeated encouragement to generosity.

So, what attitudes fight against developing a generous spirit? Let me express this in terms of the ones I struggle with.

First, I think I deserve the rewards of my labor. I worked hard to get qualifications. I worked hard to earn my wages. I worked hard and sacrificed immediate gratification to accumulate savings. Surely I deserve to benefit from all that hard work. I fail to remember the gift aspect—that it's God's gift that I was born in Australia (the lucky country!) and enjoyed a middle-class upbringing; that it's God's gift that I have the abilities that allow me to take advantage of opportunities provided by my culture; that it's God's gift that I had sufficient resources not to start from a position of endemic poverty; that it's God's gift—the list is fairly lengthy.

Second, I'm tempted to think that others don't deserve the rewards of my labor—especially the poor. Clearly, they haven't put in the hard work like me—otherwise they'd be in my position. They weren't disciplined enough to get the qualifications. They weren't disciplined enough to forego instant gratification. They don't work hard in their jobs. Why should I be generous to them? I fail to remember exactly the same things I listed above. I also fail to remember that people face tragedies totally beyond their control—and that very few of those tragedies have entered my life.

Third, I worry that I need to provide for the future—in case those tragedies do enter my life; in case an unforeseen opportunity arises; in order to replace deteriorating assets (like cars and refrigerators); in order to acquire more assets (like a bigger home entertainment system); in order to retire comfortably(!). That's simply exercising wisdom in how I use the resources God entrusts to me—isn't it? I fail to remember that my stewardship also includes responsibility for others and working for the common good and helping them enjoy God's *shalom*. God generously gives to me that I may demonstrate his generosity to others. One of the reasons for working is to provide for others' needs (Ephesians 4:28).

Fourth, I like to hoard—it's part of my personality. I collect things. I don't know why. Perhaps it gives me a sense of importance or achievement. I don't like throwing things out. My experience is that I always find a need for something a week after getting rid of it.

I've put that in modern terms, but I don't think the underlying sentiments I've expressed would have been foreign to the ancient Israelites. There is some truth in each of those attitudes—just enough to make them sound plausible if I don't think about them too much. But each of those attitudes fights against generosity. Each of those attitudes is content to sacrifice communal well-being for the sake of my individual well-being. What's the antidote? That's found in the law itself.

"Follow my decrees and be careful to obey my laws, and you will live safely in the land. Then the land will yield its fruit, and you will eat your fill and live there in safety. You may ask, 'What will we eat in the seventh year if we do not plant or harvest our crops?' I will send you such a blessing in the sixth year that the land will yield enough for three years. While you plant during the eighth year, you will eat from the old crop and will continue to eat from it until the harvest of the ninth year comes in." (Leviticus 25:18–22)

God asks them to trust him—and to trust his provision for them.

CONFIRMATION OF THE TRAJECTORY

There's one other thing to consider in relation to these Sabbatical and Jubilee years—and that's their trajectory. Within the Old Testament, the language used to describe them also provides the vision for the future. Chris Wright puts it this way:

> At the very least the sabbatical year and the jubilee gave the poorer section of Israelite society something to look forward to—a hope, in a purely economic sense. But beyond that, concepts like rest, release, and (from the jubilee) return and restoration could easily fit metaphorically into the vocabulary of the hoped-for new age of God's unhindered blessing on a perfectly obedient people. Thus we find that future hope in the prophets sometimes draws allusively from the sabbatical milieu (e.g., Isaiah 35, 58, 61).[5]

Admittedly, not everyone agrees with that. For example, in relation to the Isaiah passages Wright cites, some argue these deal with the issue of release from exile (rather than Sabbath or Jubilee). I think there's little doubt that the issue of release from exile is a major theme in Isaiah's overall message—including these chapters. He intends to comfort those suffering captivity and encourage them that God will end their exile and return them to their land. But I don't think it's necessary to view these two interpretations as competing options. After all, both point in the same direction. The return from exile is not a return to the same conditions that prevailed before God sent his people into captivity. Rather, God promises them new hearts that will desire to live according to his purposes and will. In other words, Isaiah reaffirms the original vision of experiencing God's rest in the land. Likewise, the Sabbath and Jubilee language used in Isaiah 58 and 61, in line with what I've outlined above, also points to entering God's rest—the experience of *shalom*.

While Cyrus ended Israel's physical exile when he conquered the Babylonian Empire, one could hardly say God's promises were fulfilled at that time. Only a remnant returned. They struggled to survive. Their rebuilding program was slow and second-rate. They remained under foreign rule. Perhaps they could point to improvements in keeping some aspects of God's law, but complete renewal was still far distant. Thus, in a very real sense, the exile persisted.

And within that context, at the beginning of his ministry, Jesus (quoting from Isaiah 61 and 58) announces:

> "The Spirit of the Lord is on me,
>   because he has anointed me
>   to preach good news to the poor.
> He has sent me to proclaim freedom for the prisoners
>   and recovery of sight for the blind,
> to release the oppressed,
>   to proclaim the year of the Lord's favor."

He concludes by saying: "Today this scripture is fulfilled in your hearing" (Luke 4:18–21).

As with the Isaiah passages (and often based on their interpretation of those passages), scholars debate exactly what Jesus claims here. Does he see himself as the eschatological prophet? Does he think he is the Messiah? Does he identify himself with the Suffering Servant?[6] In the long run, Jesus is all three—and more. More importantly for our purposes, in this programmatic announcement about his future ministry, what does Jesus promise to do?

I assume that Luke explains Jesus' promise by what he records in the rest of his Gospel. His record of Jesus' deeds and teaching demonstrates how Jesus fulfills this programmatic announcement. If this were not the case, I'd expect Luke to draw attention to any inconsistency.

So what confronts us in the rest of the gospel? Immediately following this episode in the synagogue, Jesus releases a man from demonic bondage (4:31–37), heals a woman's fever and all manner of unspecified physical sicknesses (4:38–41), and astonishes fishermen by telling them where to find fish and demonstrating abundant provision (5:1–11). Luke provides additional examples throughout his gospel.

Luke also tells us of Jesus' clashes with the Jewish religious leaders that further highlight what Jesus sees as his mission. Jesus claims to forgive sins (5:17–26). He speaks of calling sinners to repentance—rather than focusing on the "righteous" (5:27–32). He asserts a new era is dawning around himself such that it's time for rejoicing rather than fasting (5:33–39). And he claims to be Lord of the Sabbath and demonstrates that the Sabbath is an appropriate day to work for good and wholeness and true life (6:1–11).

Luke provides a snippet of Jesus' teaching about the kingdom of God (6:20–49). He speaks of great reversals: relief for the oppressed and judgment for their oppressors. He describes a new ethic where people desire to work for the good of others—even their enemies. He calls for a generosity of spirit that reflects God's own merciful nature. He encourages people to obey his words and warns of dire consequences for those who fail to heed his warning.

Another healing (7:1–10) and the raising of a widow's son (7:11–17) lead into the question from John the Baptizer: "Are you the one who was to come, or should we expect someone else?" (7:20). Jesus answers in terms that remind us of how he initially described his program:

> "Go back and report to John what you have seen and heard: The blind receive sight, the lame walk, those who have leprosy are cured, the deaf hear, the dead are raised, and the good news is preached to the poor. Blessed is the man who does not fall away on account of me." (7:22–23)

However, this passage is closer to Isaiah 35 than Isaiah 61.

Many read all this and see a foretaste of God's kingdom. Jesus comes as the King (the Messiah) and exhibits what his rule is like— and, given the "not yet" aspect of his first coming, what it will be like when it is fulfilled at his return. He demonstrates his power over his creation and his ability to provide. He reverses the results of human rebellion. He explains what true goodness looks like— something that goes beyond the letter of the law. He offers release for those who recognize their bondage to sin and its effects. He brings the fulfillment of all that God has promised.

And don't all those things also point to the culmination of this trajectory of rest? Is this not the direction to which that vision points? Isn't this what the true Sabbath is about? Doesn't this fulfill the Jubilee? And can't this also be described as entering God's rest?

What I wish to suggest is that the three concepts of Sabbath, the Sabbatical Year, and the Year of Jubilee are part of one broader model. All three are part of this trajectory of God's rest. From the beginning, God intended humanity to enjoy his rest with him. Humans refused, choosing instead to follow what they thought was an independent path. But God didn't abandon his original intention. For his people, he provided images of that intention—to remind them both of what had been forfeited and of what remained their true hope. Jesus fulfills these images. He offers true rest to those who submit to his rule.

ONE POTENTIAL PROBLEM AREA

Now, if you read the Isaiah passages, you may have noticed one potential problem for my overall theory. It's not a problem in terms of how the passages can be understood under the broader theme of God's rest. Rather, it's a problem for how I've defined that rest. Isaiah 61:5 reads:

> Aliens will shepherd your flocks;
>   foreigners will work your fields and vineyards.

At first glance, it would be easy to conclude three things: foreigners get the "dirty," menial jobs; foreigners work as slaves; and God's people get to do nothing. From the broader context, it's tempting to interpret this passage as if the circumstances of the exile are now reversed: the enslaved have become the new masters.

However, several factors should cause us to pause before setting those conclusions in concrete. First, does the Bible support the concept of "menial jobs"? As I've noted throughout this study, the Bible presents work as one of God's good gifts to humanity. And when it refers to work, it's not talking about what we might identify as some cushy office job; its primary reference is to the tasks mentioned here—working the land and caring for God's creation. We must resist reading our values into the text.

Second, the text itself doesn't mention slavery. Nor does it indicate forced service. We draw those implications from the references to *your* flocks and *your* fields. That's not the only possible way of reading the text. They may offer themselves as voluntary employees.

Further, Israel's history includes the exodus—her own release from slavery. Israel's law drew several implications from that liberation for the way they treated others. While the law didn't explicitly abolish slavery (as noted previously), it did legislate against oppressive measures. God did not rescue Israel so that she could become the new superpower and copy the Egyptian example of enslaving other nations. Rather, her role was to be a visual example of the benefits of serving God—a model that attracted others to worship God with them.

Third, the immediate context contains something of that vision for Israel. Verse 6 refers to Israel as a whole as *priests of the* LORD. Presumably, Israel's ministry is directed both to these foreigners now in her midst and to those remaining outside her borders. This ministry would hardly be effective if it were based on oppressive practices. How would that attract the nations by demonstrating the glory of God's gracious rule? Within this situation, God's people are not inactive or simply enjoying leisure while others work. Rather, they fulfill a different role.

Fourth, this is not the first reference to foreigners in Isaiah. For example, Isaiah 56:1–8 refers to foreigners who participate in God's covenant with Israel by binding themselves to God. This is a voluntary action on their part. Thus, it's quite feasible that the services described in Isaiah 61:5 are also voluntary.

I know that doesn't answer all the issues involved in this passage. For example, while this passage clearly has an eschatological thrust—and, I think, uses Sabbath and Jubilee language to support that thrust—some elements suggest we're still not at the final state. Still, I hope I've provided enough to indicate there are reasonable ways of interpreting this text that are not inconsistent with my overall position. Overall, I think we're pointed to the restoration of God's original vision for his creation—and that includes human work.

SUMMARY

In these last three chapters I've tried to present an overall vision of God's rest. That vision differs from the one I picked up during my church upbringing (which may not be identical with the one I was intended to acquire!). I now see God's rest not as inactivity, but as *shalom*—the idea that everything is as God intended it should be and that all are together enjoying the goodness of God's creation within the context of God's perfect rule. I now also see our participation in God's rest as including human work—that work in itself, as one of God's good gifts to us within his creation, is not inconsistent with the idea of enjoying God's rest.

I've also tried to demonstrate how the institutions of the Sabbath, the Sabbatical Year, and the Year of Jubilee fit within that framework and how Jesus fulfills them. I believe they too are primarily about the pursuit of *shalom*. They remind us of God's original intentions and call us to work toward those intentions in our lives. That includes working in a way that enables others to join us in the celebration and enjoyment of God's good creation.

Willard Swartley notes some of the implications of this interpretation of the Sabbath legislation:

> He declared himself Lord of the Sabbath, calling people to live all of life for the well-being of others. The true purpose of the Sabbath found its clear expression in the life and death of Jesus, a man for others; Jesus extended God's jubilean grace to all people.

> By fulfilling the humanitarian purpose of the Sabbath, rest and equality for the servants, Jesus inaugurated a continuous practice of Sabbath, sabbatical, and jubilean ethics.[7]

Within that context, I believe that the Sabbath principles can't be used to justify a concept of retirement, especially the self-indulgent version currently encouraged by our Western culture. The latter promotes the pursuit of personal leisure experiences rather than a desire to contribute to the community's well-being. It promotes a carefree focus on fulfilling my own wants rather than accepting the responsibility of serving others. As in the garden, it offers me the opportunity to rule my own kingdom—it asks me to substitute that paltry self-centered dream for God's glorious vision of *shalom*.

Swartley rightly claims that the sabbatical vision calls us to live for the well-being of others. That vision doesn't change when people reach a certain age. The way we act on that vision varies with our life circumstances at any particular time: our abilities, our training, our family situations, our circumstances, the opportunities that present themselves to us, and so on. And, yes, the aging process does impact that with the result that our opportunities may change. We'll discuss some of the specifics of this in the final chapter, but the overall vision remains the same throughout. That vision remains just as relevant after we reach some government-defined retirement age.

8

ECCLESIASTES—WORK AND PLEASURE

In my discussion of the Bible's positive attitude toward work in chapter 4, I referred briefly to the book of Ecclesiastes. Because work is a major topic within that book, we need to return to it in more detail. Taken at face value, this book makes both positive and negative statements about work and its benefits. For example, Ecclesiastes 2:24 states: "A man can do nothing better than to eat and drink and find satisfaction in his work." Yet just before that, the writer laments:

> What does a man get for all the toil and anxious striving with which he labors under the sun? All his days his work is pain and grief; even at night his mind does not rest. This too is meaningless. (2:22–23)

Clearly, there's some tension here. It's a tension we noted when exploring the theology of work in chapter 4. I suspect it's a tension that has been felt by most workers throughout the centuries. It's a tension many Westerners today may hope to resolve through retirement. Perhaps something in these negative statements could be used to justify such a resolution. Thus we return to Ecclesiastes and its perspective on the human experience after the fall.

THE TENSION OF ECCLESIASTES

With such surface contradictions in Qohelet's[1] statements, it's fairly evident that context will be important in thinking about what Ecclesiastes may contribute to our understanding about work and retirement. It seems logical to search for some grasp of the writer's overall purpose and to see how the various, apparently contradictory, statements fit with that. That's fairly standard procedure. We assume that writers present a coherent message. Thus, when we come across part of a document that appears to contradict the overall message, we look for a logical explanation—some way to clear up the apparent contradiction.

To be fair, not everyone takes this approach with Ecclesiastes. Some consider it a series of wise sayings, life observations, and proverbial nuggets thrown together in a relatively random order with no need to fashion them into a coherent whole. We are intended to weigh up each piece of sage advice and apply the embedded wisdom where it's appropriate. The fact that bits of wisdom contradict each other doesn't matter. That just reflects the vagaries of life. After all, in our culture, we affirm both "Look before you leap" and "He who hesitates is lost." Both proverbs teach important truths—even though they contradict each other. Some take that sort of approach with Ecclesiastes.

Clearly, there is an element of truth in that when it's applied to individual pieces of wisdom. I, however, believe Qohelet does present a more coherent argument. I think there is order to the document (though not the type of order that conforms readily to the framework of Western logic) and that the tension between these statements is part of the way the writer unfolds his message. He goes back and forth between the poles of the contradictions as he narrates his experiences of life. He knows there is truth in traditional wisdom, but he also knows that traditional wisdom doesn't provide answers to all the contradictions in life. He leads us to struggle with these contradictions and thus to recognize the limitations of our own wisdom.[2]

So, what's Qohelet's overall purpose in writing Ecclesiastes? Unfortunately, there's widespread disagreement about that among commentators. Craig Bartholomew opens his commentary on Ecclesiastes with these words:

> As far back as we go in the history of the interpretation of Ecclesiastes, this book has provoked controversy. And it still does, with contemporary commentators polarized as to how to read it, whether as a positive book affirming life or as deeply pessimistic.[3]

Most introductions in the various commentaries cover the wide range of interpretations available. Duane Garrett summarizes many of these under five headings:

1. A Pessimistic Skeptic?
2. The Preacher of Joy?
3. A Thinker Caught in the Tensions of Life?
4. An Apologetic Work?
5. The Original Existentialist?

The question marks indicate his rejection of those views. It's not that he thinks they're totally wrong (he acknowledges some truth in each of them); rather, he considers each inadequate as a complete explanation. He then adds two further headings:

1. Reflections for the Wise
2. Reflections on Creation and the Fall

These headings contain additional helpful comments—but don't actually provide an overall purpose.[4]

This is not the place to discuss whether Garrett's headings cover all the possibilities. I doubt anyone could achieve that feat. Nor is this the place to solve what scholars have argued about for centuries. My purpose is to highlight that there are some difficulties interpreting this book—and thus I recognize that not everyone will agree with what I write below. Indeed, with many of the issues surrounding the interpretation of this book, it's difficult to identify a majority view—and so it's fairly easy to find someone who disagrees. Ecclesiastes does contain significant tensions. Yet I think those tensions are deliberate.

At one level, Qohelet wishes to affirm the wisdom of a book like Proverbs. Generally, following such wisdom will result in a successful life. But such wisdom only gets you so far. It doesn't answer all of life's conundrums. In particular, it fails to resolve two issues. First, following such wisdom doesn't always result in success. There are significant blips on the radar. The wise don't always win. The righteous don't always succeed. In this, Qohelet aligns himself with the book of Job (this element is also present in Psalms and Proverbs[5]). And second, those who do succeed on the basis of godly wisdom must still confront death. And death undermines all that they've done in life. It removes any sense of permanence or purpose or meaning. And so Qohelet faces this tension in affirming both the value of wisdom and its insufficiency.

I find Stephan de Jong's proposed structure for Ecclesiastes helpful—and I think it also highlights this tension. He argues that Qohelet alternates between what he calls observation and instruction complexes. In the *observation complexes*, Qohelet primarily reports his observations of and reflections on human life; his conclusions are fairly bleak. Then, in the *instruction complexes*, Qohelet provides advice and admonitions on how to live within the context of his observations; here the tone is more positive. De Jong's outline of the book is as follows:

1:1	Introduction
1:2	Motto
1:3–4:16	Observation Complex
4:17–5:8	Instruction Complex
5:9–6:9	Observation Complex
6:10–7:22	Instruction Complex
7:23–29	Observation Complex
8:1–8	Instruction Complex
8:9–9:12	Observation Complex
9:13–12:7	Instruction Complex
12:8	Motto
12:9–14	Epilogue[6]

Ecclesiastes delineates Qohelet's search for purpose in life.[7] It describes the reality of life in our current world (theologically, I would add *fallen* world). We humans don't control life. We don't determine our own destiny. Everything doesn't always work out the way we expect. Life is transient. Life is not predictable. Even more, we're not even sure what life's about. We're very busy with a wide range of activities. The activities look like they're getting somewhere. But we're not really sure where we should be headed—or even if we should be headed anywhere. And, on top of that, life is often tough.

By way of warning, in this chapter, I don't have the space to deal with all the details of the passages we'll examine. Instead, I'll paint with broad brushstrokes. What I'm aiming for is an overall impression of what Qohelet contributes to our understanding of work—and any possible implications that has for a concept of retirement.

THE NEGATIVE

Let's begin with the negative passages—the material that's in the observation complexes. Qohelet sets the scene right at the beginning.

> What does man gain from all his labor
>> at which he toils under the sun? (Ecclesiastes 1:3)

Does he mean each person as an individual or humanity as a whole? I suspect it makes no real difference. After all, this question comes on the heels of his opening exclamation, in which Qohelet tells us the conclusion to his observations up front:

> Utterly meaningless!
>> Everything is meaningless. (Ecclesiastes 1:2)

That's fairly comprehensive. It incorporates both humanity in general and any individual who may contemplate the issues.

These two verses also introduce us to two key terms in this book. As the NIV translates them, they are *meaningless* and *under the sun*. Both terms require some explanation because they influence how we interpret the book. (Or is it that how we interpret the book influences how we translate these terms?)

The phrase *under the sun* occurs twenty-nine times in Ecclesiastes—and nowhere else in the Old Testament.[8] It reflects the perspective from which Qohelet views human life—that it's lived on this earth and is confined to what happens on this earth. It's what he can observe. It may sometimes have an additional nuance such as the generally cyclical, repetitive and unchanging nature of life on this earth; the fact that we live in a fallen world and God's good creation is marred; or the sometimes troubled and oppressive nature of life. But I think those elements are found in the specific contexts rather than the phrase itself.

It does leave open the possibility that other factors "beyond the sun" may have relevance for our life on earth. For example, it's likely that "the expression 'under heaven' carries the additional nuance of the divine government of the world in which human beings live."[9] After all, Qohelet refers to God on several occasions. Yet such matters are beyond direct human observation and thus not available to Qohelet. His conclusions are based on his observations of life *under the sun.*

The Hebrew word *hebel,* here translated "meaningless," occurs thirty-eight times in the book. The basic meaning of the word is "breath" or "vapor."[10] If you try putting either of those words into verse 2, you will realize why translators opt for something else. But what is the something else for which they should opt? Craig Bartholomew reports:

> Traditionally translated as "vanity," in recent decades an astonishing variety of translations of *hebel* have been proposed, such as "meaningless," "useless" (GNB), "absurd," "futility," "bubble," "trace," "transience," and "breath."[11]

It can also have the sense of being weightless or insubstantial.[12] So there's quite an array from which to choose—and a range of scholars who argue for each of them.

Given the regularity with which the word is used in Ecclesiastes, the choice of meaning is important. It impacts our basic understanding of Qohelet's message. Yet I think Barry Webb (following Eugene Peterson) makes an important point:

> It is a mistake to try to nail this word down, as though one "right" meaning could be found for it in Ecclesiastes. "Various meanings glance off [its] surface . . . as the context shifts." It is like the whole category of things it refers to: rootless, unstable, subject to continuous change. But in Qohelet's hands it will become a powerful weapon. For what this motto tells us in no uncertain terms is that Qohelet is a debunker. He will not tolerate pretension, or allow anything to appear more solid or satisfying than it really is.[13]

I suspect no one English word will adequately fit all contexts in Ecclesiastes. *Under the sun*, human life appears temporary, insubstantial, and insignificant. In that context, it seems meaningless. But I don't believe Qohelet affirms that life is meaningless; rather, his main point is that access to meaning is not open to us from our current perspective.

From this opening, one could easily get the impression that work's a total waste of time—that there is absolutely no value to it whatsoever. I think that would be to overstate Qohelet's case. After all, work is necessary for survival. It supplies the calories we burn up each day. It keeps the cycle of life ticking over. But is there anything else to work? Does it somehow add to the cycle—does it cause the cycle to progress or turn the cycle into a spiral that's heading somewhere? It's at that point that there seems to be no *gain* or *profit*. I think Qohelet provides several supporting reasons for this conclusion.

Death Takes the Profit out of Work

First, the reality of death removes any potential for ultimate profit. For what happens when you come to the end of life? After all that work you've put in over all those years, what do you have to show for it?

> Naked a man comes from his mother's womb,
>   and as he comes, so he departs.
> He takes nothing from his labor
>   that he can carry in his hand.

> This too is a grievous evil:

> As a man comes, so he departs,
>   and what does he gain,
>   since he toils for the wind?
> All his days he eats in darkness,
>   with great frustration, affliction and anger.
>   (Ecclesiastes 5:15–17)

At that point, you have nothing. You may have a big bank account, but it will give you no benefit whatsoever.

The Australian motto of life is something like: The one with the most toys wins. We value people by their net financial worth. Of course, we don't do this officially—that would contradict our egalitarian philosophy—but that's how we establish our unofficial pecking order. We work to accumulate as much stuff as possible. It gives us a sense of achievement and self-importance. Qohelet asks the obvious question: what about when you die? You think you've gained some profit from all of your work. You think you can calculate your net financial worth. What's its value when you die? Not, what's its dollar value, but how does it benefit you at that point?

Well, you say, it may not mean anything to me at that point, but at least it can benefit my descendants. Qohelet deals with that too.

> So I hated life, because the work that is done under the sun was griev-ous to me. All of it is meaningless, a chasing after the wind. I hated all the things I had toiled for under the sun, because I must leave them to the one who comes after me. And who knows whether he will be a wise man or a fool? Yet he will have control over all the work into which I have poured my effort and skill under the sun. This too is meaningless. (Ecclesiastes 2:17–19)

Hopefully, you've had some say in whether or not the one who comes after you is a fool by the way you've brought them up and trained them in wisdom! Then again, perhaps you were too busy working and accumulating stuff to notice. But surely, you say, it counts for something that you've given the next generation an eas-ier life. That may not provide you any direct benefit, but won't it provide some benefit for them? But, Qohelet might answer, won't they just follow your example and work to accumulate more stuff and turn out just as much a fool as you? Won't they face the same issue as you in the long run? At the point of their death, how will this benefit them?

But perhaps they could break the pattern and retire early. They still won't get any benefit at the point of death, but perhaps they can gain something during life itself. Qohelet doesn't deal with that directly. He says some things about pleasure that are relevant, and we'll come to some of those shortly. In the meantime, I'd simply ask: Is accumulating pleasures really any different from accumulating stuff? Doesn't death still achieve the same result—that it removes any gain?

Time Removes Any Gain

Second, even before death, so much of our work seems to make no real progress. Rather, we have the frustration of going round in circles or doing the same thing over and over again. At one time, it's right to work in one way; and, at another time, it's right to work in exactly the opposite way. That's part of what that well-known time-poem in Ecclesiastes 3 is saying:

> There is a time for everything,
>   and a season for every activity under heaven:
>   a time to be born and a time to die,
>   a time to plant and a time to uproot,
>   a time to kill and a time to heal,
>   a time to tear down and a time to build. . . .

And so it goes on. Not every pairing has to do with work, but quite a few do.

We take Qohelet's words about farming here for granted— perhaps because it's such a regular cycle (or perhaps because so few of us city slickers have personal experience of farming!). At the right time of the year, the farmer plants the seed. Then, when the crops have grown, it's time to harvest and reap the fruit of the earlier work. And, after that, the now dead plants are turned back into the ground so the process can start all over again. Where's the gain in the work? What progress is made? Sure, it provides the farmer's food and sustains the farmer's life. What's the profit of that? It simply enables the farmer to plant the next crop—and perhaps adds a couple of centimeters to the waistline. It achieves no lasting result.

Well, what about buildings—since Qohelet says there is "a time to tear down and a time to build"? They seem more permanent.

You draw up the plans. You bring the materials together. Perhaps you call on your neighbors to help. You take care to construct everything properly. And so you build your house for your household. Over the years, you make the necessary repairs. So does the next generation. But eventually the house wears out (or, in modern terms, goes out of style) and it's time to pull it down and start from scratch (unless it's Heritage Listed). Nothing lasts forever. It's all fleeting. As Qohelet puts it:

> All man's efforts are for his mouth,
>> yet his appetite is never satisfied. (6:7)

Work Produces Nothing Ultimate

Third, everyone who works has to go through the same cycle again and again. It feels like we're running in circles. And there's so much of the circle we don't control. We don't determine the time to plant or the time to harvest. We just learn what's appropriate and fit our schedules to that. Much of our work has that pattern. It's as if we're dancing to a tune, but we didn't write the melody and we're not even sure we understand the rhythm. How do we know if our work has any significance? And here's where we run into that word *meaningless* again.

> So I hated life, because the work that is done under the sun was grievous to me. All of it is meaningless, a chasing after the wind. (Ecclesiastes 2:17)

Or a few verses earlier:

> I denied myself nothing my eyes desired;
>> I refused my heart no pleasure.
> My heart took delight in all my work,
>> and this was the reward for all my labor.
> Yet when I surveyed all that my hands had done
>> and what I had toiled to achieve,
> everything was meaningless, a chasing after the wind;
>> nothing was gained under the sun. (Ecclesiastes 2:10–11)

In what sense is our work *meaningless*? Is our work fleeting? Is it futile? Incomprehensible? Can we find no meaning in the work we do (and the pleasure we enjoy!)?

I don't think Qohelet argues that our work is meaningless. Rather, I think his main point is that we can't work out its meaning—that we don't (and can't) know the significance of our work (at least, not in any ultimate sense). It's clearer in 8:16–17.

> When I applied my mind to know wisdom and to observe man's labor on earth—his eyes not seeing sleep day or night—then I saw all that God has done. No one can comprehend what goes on under the sun. Despite all his efforts to search it out, man cannot discover its meaning. Even if a wise man claims he knows, he cannot really comprehend it.

Our work may very well have some ultimate meaning. It's just that we don't know what it is.

Qohelet does note some other negative things about work—such as the case of the person who works from envy (4:4) and the workaholic who has no relatives (4:7–8)—but I think those three reasons form the basis for what appears a rather depressing attitude toward work.

THE POSITIVE

It's certainly enough to raise the question: Why work at all? If work is such a "meaningless" activity according to Qohelet, why not give your life over to something else? It too may be just as "meaningless," but at least it could be more fun!

Qohelet does mention the usual mundane reason for work in passing—that if you don't work you won't eat (4:5)—but his main thrust follows a different direction. Qohelet actually encourages us to find satisfaction and pleasure in our work.

> Then I realized that it is good and proper for a man to eat and drink, and to find satisfaction in his toilsome labor under the sun during

the few days of life God has given him—for this is his lot. Moreover, when God gives any man wealth and possessions, and enables him to enjoy them, to accept his lot and be happy in his work—this is a gift of God. He seldom reflects on the days of his life, because God keeps him occupied with gladness of heart. (Ecclesiastes 5:18–20)

You can find similar expressions in 2:24–26; 3:12–13, 22; 8:15; and 9:9–10. That final reference concludes by exhorting:

Whatever your hand finds to do, do it with all your might, for in the grave, where you are going, there is neither working nor planning nor knowledge nor wisdom.

In other words, put your best effort into your work.

Four facets are worth highlighting about Qohelet's theology of work. First, Qohelet believes work is one of God's gifts. Second, he expects us to experience satisfaction in work. Third, he thinks work should be a source of pleasure. And fourth, he adds that we are to enjoy the fruit of our work (here expressed in terms of food and drink). It's not simply that work provides the resources to pursue other pleasurable activities (though an element of that is also present), but that work itself should involve a level of pleasure or contentment or happiness.

Now, we could follow each of those themes through with great benefit—and I'm very tempted to do so—but on this occasion I'll keep our main purpose in focus. The point is that Qohelet doesn't simply promote a negative, pessimistic attitude toward work. He doesn't say it's a necessary evil that we should avoid if at all possible. To simply take his negative statements and use them to justify a concept of retirement would be to ignore their context in two ways. First, in essence, Qohelet is not negative about work itself; rather he affirms that work (as well as a whole host of other things, including pleasure) doesn't bring any ultimate profit. In itself, it doesn't provide the meaning for our existence. Second, Qohelet, consistent with the Jewish tradition based on Genesis 1–3, does view work as one of God's good gifts. We are to exercise this gift with thankfulness.

THE BALANCE

And so Qohelet does not advise us to abandon work. Why would we wish to despise God's gift? On the other hand, neither does he advise us to abandon God's other gifts—the enjoyment of God's good creation and the fruit of our work. Rather, he urges us to keep both in proper perspective. He advocates what we today would call balance. Notice his juxtaposition of the two extremes in 4:5–6.

> The fool folds his hands
>> and ruins himself.
> Better one handful with tranquility
>> than two handfuls with toil
>> and chasing after the wind.

Laziness (the folding of the hands) leads to disaster—to the consumption of one's own body.[14] But merely pursuing toil (filling both hands with labor) is also not the way to go. As he has already indicated, that brings no ultimate profit. Rather, we should aim to balance labor and rest—to emulate neither the sluggard nor the workaholic—to work and find satisfaction in that and also to enjoy the results of our work.

Within a Jewish context, Qohelet is advocating observance of the Sabbath and Jewish festivals (as well as daily rest). These were times set aside by God for his people to rest and celebrate. Would it be legitimate to extend that concept to retirement? If we should aim for a weekly balance of work and rest, could we perhaps also aim for a lifetime balance of work and rest—work for the first sixty years and rest for the last ten, plus whatever bonus years God may grant (Psalm 90:10)?

Again, I want to highlight that we can only draw inferences. Qohelet does not specifically address this issue. I think a good case can be made to argue that Qohelet would oppose such a conclusion. As already noted, he considers work to be one of God's gifts to us. Because it's given by God, we're responsible not to ignore it. Rather, we're to use it with thankfulness. And because it's a *good* gift, he points out that we should find a certain level of contentment and pleasure in our work. He knows work has its frustrations and involves toil and sweat and sometimes drudgery, but he still affirms these positive aspects of our labor.

Does Qohelet show a preference for pleasure? That's not an easy question to answer. Certainly, he doesn't encourage the rejection of pleasure—he doesn't idealize ascetic tendencies. Legitimate pleasures also fall within the category of God's good gifts and should be enjoyed with gratitude. The point is, though pleasures are real, they too are also transitory. As with work, they don't get behind the mystery of life. They don't provide the knowledge that enables us "to fathom what God has done from beginning to end (3:11)."

Qohelet does outline the futility of work that's designed simply to accumulate more stuff (2:17–21; 4:7–8). He claims there's no point in having possessions if you don't enjoy them (6:1–3). That certainly could imply that he thinks pleasure is preferable to work. Yet that's not a step Qohelet himself takes. On the one hand, that's not the comparison that interests him—his focus is whether either work or pleasure avoids the conclusion of *hebel*. On the other hand, he thinks you can also find pleasure in work—so he might then ask us whether it's appropriate to forego the pleasure of work for the sake of leisure.

To look at this question of whether pleasure should be preferred to work from a different perspective, some scholars suggest Ecclesiastes is directed toward leisured young men. Whybray, for example, writes:

> Qoheleth's teaching was evidently addressed primarily to the leisured young men who sought his advice on how they should live their lives, and also on the deeper problems of life: in particular, "Is it all worth while?"[15]

Though it's certainly worth pondering who the likely original intended readers were, this is not the place to delve into that question in detail. It's not difficult to see why scholars make this suggestion. If it is correct, I find it interesting that Qohelet doesn't encourage them into a life of idle leisure. Rather, among other things, his advice includes finding pleasure in work. Yet, I recognize that conclusion is based on speculation about the intended audience—and so I wouldn't place much weight on that argument.

In the long run, perhaps Qohelet would answer this question of retirement by pointing to his overall conclusion.

> Now all has been heard;
>> here is the conclusion of the matter:
> Fear God and keep his commandments,
>> for this is the whole duty of man. (Ecclesiastes 12:13)

It boils down to this: If God tells us to work, we should work; if God tells us to retire, we should retire. We don't understand all God's ways. Nor do we understand all God's purposes in the tasks he gives us to do. Since we're finite creatures, we should expect that. Qohelet may also add that it's part of the burden of living *under the sun*. Still, our duty is to conform to what God has told us—even if we don't understand the purpose. That's what's involved in trusting God.

BRINGING BALANCE TO QOHELET

One final matter is worth mentioning. It seems to me that Ecclesiastes has a strongly individualistic tone.[16] The first person singular pronoun is prominent throughout the narrative. Qohelet embarks on a personal quest to find some profit in his work—to discover some meaning and purpose in life. He focuses on his own actions and observations. He doesn't completely ignore the wisdom of other people. And he does acknowledge that companionship provides advantages in at least some aspects of life (4:9–12; 9:9; on the other hand, 5:11 notes there may also be disadvantages!). Yet the overall tone is individualistic. Even the advice he gives seems directed to individuals.

And so it seems to me that his discussion of work lacks the concept of the common good. His criticism of accumulating possessions focuses on the individualistic perspective: what benefit is there for me? I can't take it with me when I die. I may leave it to a fool who may squander it. I don't get any lasting profit from it. There's no sense that my legacy may benefit other people.

And so, in considering whether we should prioritize pleasure over work (that if we can accumulate sufficient resources we should take the opportunity to retire and pursue pleasure), I think we should consider this additional aspect. Duane Garrett puts it well (although I should point out that his comments are not directed to the topic of retirement).

> Until work becomes a blessing to everyone, God's people are called to struggle for the benefit of all workers. We are indeed meant to eat, drink and find enjoyment in all the toil we are blessed with. But we do this while striving—as also we pray—that God's kingdom come.[17]

SUMMARY

Thus I admit that some statements in Ecclesiastes appear, on the surface, to provide a very negative assessment of work—and would thus support the conclusion that we should avoid work if at all possible, including via retirement. Yet, I think an understanding of the overall message of the document points in the opposite direction. Neither work nor pleasure will provide us purpose and meaning in life. Yet, we are to receive both as God's gifts to us and seek to be obedient to him in how we use those gifts.

9

RETIRING LEVITES?

So far this book has examined the concepts of work and rest only in general terms. We have seen that the Bible provides a broad theology of work that is introduced in the Garden of Eden. Work is one of God's good gifts to humans and continues to be so throughout the biblical narrative—even, as I've argued, into the new creation. As we've seen so far, the idea of leisure that is associated with modern retirement—complete freedom from responsibilities, and a chance to indulge one's own pursuits rather than continue to contribute to the communal good—does not fit well with the biblical invitation to exercise God's good gift of work. Nor does it correspond to the biblical invitation to enter God's rest. But it's possible that the Bible gives the elderly exemptions because of the frailties that usually accompany the aging process. The next few chapters will examine various biblical laws and practices that may be thought to support the modern concept of retirement.

The biblical passage that most readily springs to mind is Numbers 8:23–26. The NIV puts it this way:

> The LORD said to Moses, "This applies to the Levites: Men twenty-five years old or more shall come to take part in the work at the Tent of Meeting, but at the age of fifty, they must retire from their regular service and work no longer. They may assist their brothers in performing their duties at the Tent of Meeting, but they themselves must not do the work. This, then, is how you are to assign the responsibilities of the Levites."

There it is in black and white. The Levities are to retire, not at age sixty-five, but at age fifty. Talk about your public service perks!

IN WHAT SENSE DO THEY "RETIRE"?

But it's not that simple. Did you really think we'd reach a definitive conclusion that easily? Look at how the KJV translates verses 25 and 26:

> And from the age of fifty years they shall cease waiting upon the service thereof, and shall serve no more: But shall minister with their brethren in the tabernacle of the congregation, to keep the charge, and shall do no service. Thus shalt thou do unto the Levites touching their charge.

Rather inconsiderately, the translators omitted the word *retire*. Well, it's not really inconsiderately. This translation was made in 1611. They had no concept of retirement in seventeenth-century England (remember that history section back in chapter 1?). The practice was not yet invented. Thus, it's not surprising that the translators of the KJV fail to use *retirement* language. What would people have understood by it? Imagine the preacher on Sunday morning:

> Brothers and sisters, we come to a difficult part of the text this morning. The translators here have indulged in a bit of prophecy. This is meaningless to you and I. We'll keep working till the day we die. But that won't always be the case. A time's coming when people will stop working. They'll work until a fixed age. And then, because people will revere their elders so much, they'll tell them to stop. They'll still be alive, but they won't have to work anymore. I'd tell you it's like having a permanent holiday—but you don't really have their concept of holidays either!

For us, the word *retire* evokes all sorts of cultural images. We picture Mr. Levite enjoying a Mediterranean cruise with his wife or relishing regular fishing expeditions to the Dead Sea with his mates. Or maybe he's the stay-at-home type—the guy who's content perpetually snacking while watching the sports channel on his big-screen TV.

We must resist reading our culture into Numbers 8. They had no entertainment industry. Nor was there a leisure sector of the economy. They didn't dream about things not yet invented. They didn't know they were missing out on anything. They simply got on with life as they knew it. People worked. People ate. People slept. People related to each other. And people died.

So, what's going on in Numbers 8? Israel is camped at Mount Sinai. They've been there since Exodus 19. God has recently and dramatically delivered them from slavery in Egypt. God is now giving them his instructions for what it means to be his people—for what it means to have God dwell in their midst. His law covers all aspects of life. Much of the material in Numbers 3–8 relates to the Levites. God set apart this tribe to serve in and around the sanctuary—the tent they called the tabernacle. For this service, they're divided into two groups: the priests come from Aaron's family and the rest function as their assistants. This chapter focuses on the latter group.

There are two Hebrew verbs in verse 25, both of them quite common. The first means to "turn back" or "return"—in this case "to turn back from cultic service" (the noun could also mean "army service"). The second verb means "to serve" or "to work" or "to toil." The context identifies this as "the work at the Tent of Meeting." The previous passage (8:5–22), describing the consecration of the Levites, also refers to this work (verses 15, 19, and 22). Verse 11 refers to it more generally as "the work of Yahweh." But this passage does not specify what that work was.

For that, we need to look back at Numbers 1–4. There we read that the work of the Levites includes erecting and dismantling the tabernacle (1:50–51), maintaining or taking care of the tent and its furnishings (3:8, 25–26, 31, 36–37), being responsible for carrying the tent and its furnishings when the tabernacle moved (4:15, 24–28, 31–33), and providing a protective barrier between the tabernacle and the nation—guard duty (1:53). All this was to be done under the supervision of the priests. Essentially, the Levites were chosen by God for the purpose of serving as the priests' assistants (3:6–9). Yet they also performed their duties for the sake of the community (3:7; 8:9–11) and in place of the firstborn (3:11–51). In effect, they acted as a "buffer zone" between God and the people so that the latter could "come into God's presence with safety."[1]

It was this work that the Levites were to cease on attaining the age of fifty (8:25). However, the law tells us they were permitted to "assist their brothers" beyond that age. We'll return to what's involved in this assistance later.

WHY STOP?

But first, what's the rationale for this commandment? Why are the Levites commanded to cease this work at age fifty? At this point, I must admit that the text doesn't tell us. Thus, what I and others say about this is speculation. It is not wrong to speculate, and various commentators may produce good reasons to support their speculations. But, in the long run, we need to remember that it remains speculation—and to remember that we have a tendency to read our culture into the text.

Much of the speculation surrounds the lower age limit for Levitical service because this varies across several passages and people naturally wish to find reasons for the variations. In Numbers 8:24, Levitical service begins at age twenty-five. In Numbers 4:3—which apparently records a command that comes slightly later than Numbers 8:24 (see Numbers 7:1 and 1:1)—the lower limit is age thirty. Jewish scholars have proposed a five-year apprenticeship to explain the difference. Later in Israel's history, David reduced the lower limit to age twenty (1 Chronicles 23:24–27). This new minimum age was retained both in Hezekiah's reign (2 Chronicles 31:17) and in the post-exilic period (Ezra 3:8). No upper age limit for Levites is mentioned in these last three references.

Gordon Wenham, among others, suggests it was a question of supply and demand.[2] The priority of maintaining right relationship with Yahweh meant it was important to have a sufficient number of Levites on hand to complete the work associated with the tabernacle. The priority of providing the community's food under subsistence conditions meant having idle Levites would have been a waste of important resources. According to Wenham, they varied the minimum age (and perhaps removed the permission to voluntarily help beyond age fifty) according to their religious personnel needs at the time. It's a bit like us today—either keeping young people in education or moving older people out of the workforce—in an effort to minimize the unemployment figures.

Timothy Ashley suggests a required level of maturity may be involved—and that the intervening Nadab and Abihu incident (Leviticus 10) may have resulted in raising the lower age limit to avoid having immature people performing this "dangerous role."[3] This makes sense about the lower age limit (the aspect which Ashley reviews in some detail), but fails to explain the upper limit. Why ask those with the highest levels of maturity to cease working? Then again, I guess that's also what happens with retirement today—we ask those with the most experience to stop contributing.

B. Maarsingh proposes that retirement is required for the Levites because it's "time for the younger brothers to take over."[4] Similarly, Anastasia Boniface-Malle highlights the difficulties faced by younger generations when older people cling to leadership positions.[5] Those sentiments resonate strongly in a youth-focused culture like Australia, but I'm not convinced they would have similar traction in cultures where the elderly are more valued (like ancient Israel). While such cultures certainly would desire to prevent idleness among their youth, they wouldn't achieve that at the expense of the elderly. Nor, I suspect, would their youth be as well-trained in impatience and self-fulfillment as those in modern Western cultures.

Iain Duguid suggests it's related to physical strength—that "the Levites' task was a work that demanded the very peak of their powers."[6] That fails to explain raising the lower age limit—are not men aged twenty-five to thirty *more* at their physical peak than they are once they pass thirty? At the other end, this theory does relate well with the modern concept of retirement, where the physical decline of our bodies (whether it's our strength, reflexes, or mental agility) often provides the rationale for ceasing work. And this too makes sense. Caring for people involves relieving them from burdens they can no longer bear. God's instructions relieve aged Levites from heavy lifting and carrying and allow them, if they desire, to continue with the lighter duties of guarding. But why set an age limit? Not everyone declines physically at the same rate. Why not allow more flexibility? True, blanket rules are often easier to enforce (for example, consider the modern difficulties involved with licensing aged motorists), but would they have realized that in ancient Israel?

HOW DID THEIR ROLE CHANGE?

This seems a good point to add an interesting complication. Over time, the Levites' role changed. Many of the tasks outlined in Numbers 1–4 relate particularly to the wilderness journeys. Once they dwelt in Canaan, circumstances changed. The Israelites dispersed to the land allotted to them. The tribes no longer camped in formation around the tabernacle with the Levites' tents forming a buffer zone between Yahweh and the people. The tabernacle itself was not moved on a regular basis—and thus did not require dismantling, carrying and reassembling very often. Indeed the historical narrative rarely refers to the tabernacle itself after this point. After the conquest of Canaan, we have a passing reference to the Ark of the Covenant in Judges 20:27. At the opening of 1 Samuel, it appears the Ark is housed in a permanent building at Shiloh.

The narrative provides little additional insight into the Levites' role during this period. We do meet two Levites at the end of Judges: the young, upwardly mobile Levite who first becomes the personal priest for the dishonest Micah and then the priest for the migrating tribe of Dan; and the jilted Levite whose pursuit of his concubine leads eventually to civil war against the tribe of Benjamin. But there are no indications of them fulfilling the roles assigned them in Numbers.

Eventually, David establishes Jerusalem as the permanent location for the Ark of the Covenant. Apparently, he provides a new tent for it (2 Samuel 6:17; 1 Chronicles 15:1; 16:1). In this context, the Levites' role changes. The details are itemized in 1 Chronicles 23:28–31 (and the following chapters). It included things like caring for the courtyards, acting as gatekeepers, purifying or cleansing the sacred things, baking the bread, and thanking and praising Yahweh. At some point, the Levites also picked up a teaching role in relation to the Law (2 Chronicles 17:7–9).[7] The heavy manual labor described in Numbers seems to be absent. As noted above, the upper age limit for Levites is also absent in this period. Was it simply assumed to remain at fifty? Was it removed because it was no longer necessary?

Constructing a history of the Levites is not an easy task. Scholars have proposed a broad range of possibilities for how that history unfolded.[8] The term *Levite/s* occurs over 280 times in the NIV—a large number of references, although they are concentrated in Numbers, Deuteronomy, Chronicles, and Ezra/Nehemiah (strangely, very few occurrences appear in Leviticus). Despite this, large gaps remain in our knowledge of them. As mentioned above, we know little of their activities between the times of Joshua and David. On those rare occasions when the Ark is mentioned, we see little evidence of them performing the duties outlined in Numbers.

WHY STOP?—AGAIN

But I must come back to the matter at hand—the command that the Levites cease work at age fifty. The digression above has highlighted how their work pattern changed over time—and particularly that the more strenuous aspects of their work ceased. But why should they stop work at all? So far, we've touched on three possible rationales:

- To balance the number of Levites with the required work (the supply and demand reason).
- To make room for the next generation.
- To ensure those on active duty have sufficient physical capabilities.

Each is speculative, because the text doesn't give us a reason. You can make a reasonable argument in relation to each—though the third rationale perhaps became less relevant in Israel's later history. In the twenty-five commentaries I looked at on this subject, the first and third options were the most popular. That, of course, doesn't make them right—Bible interpretation isn't determined by the ballot box. But it does indicate that those options each make sense to several scholars.

Interestingly, they're all rationales associated with our modern concept of retirement. First, we think it's important to balance employment supply and demand and thus to reduce unemployment. Retirement allows us to exclude a large segment of the population from the unemployment figures. Second, we emphasize youth and encourage the next generation to step up to the mark—and often do this at the expense of older generations. Third, we recognize that the aging process makes it unwise to retain older people in a whole range of occupations that require strength, vitality, mental agility, quick reflexes, and the like. Again, this doesn't mean that any of these rationales are correct. The way ancient Hebrews approached this issue may have been vastly different from our current approach. It does mean, however, that we should seriously ask whether we're just reading our situation into the text rather than dealing with the text on its own terms.

Those three rationales are not an exhaustive list. For example, it's possible that the age limit had to do with physical appearance. Perhaps ancient Israelites had a preference for unwrinkled faces and God accommodated that preference so they weren't confronted by wrinkled faces when they entered the sanctuary. That seems highly unlikely—and I guess that's why I've found no scholars suggesting it—but technically it's a possibility. Perhaps more credible is the suggestion that wrinkled faces symbolized uncleanness and thus were excluded from service. Several of the Old Testament laws relate uncleanness with either a lack of wholeness or death.[9] Wrinkles indicate the aging process, a move away from what's often considered wholeness (perhaps a modern perception?), and the inevitable approach of death. Maybe that's the rationale. After all, various bodily imperfections prevented those from Aaron's line serving as priests (Leviticus 21:16–23).

Overall, our exploration of the possible rationales behind this command has not been particularly helpful because no one possibility commands the field. Thus, we are left with the bare command as it appears in the text.

STOP WHAT?

Let's consider the issue from a slightly different angle. What happened when a Levite turned fifty? Scholars disagree about how to interpret the command. Samuel ben Meir argues that their ceasing work only applied to the work of dismantling, hauling, and reassembling the tabernacle (the work described in Numbers 4 as being done by those aged thirty to fifty). He claims that aged Levites still had full responsibility for the work of guarding.[10] The ESV translators also take this view.

At the other end of the spectrum, Dennis Olson claims that aged Levites could do no further work at the tabernacle. He interprets *brothers* in 8:26 as a reference to *priests* (since the priests and Levites belonged to the same tribe), rather than to *Levites*. Thus, he claims verse 26 applies to their activities while they're aged twenty-five to fifty: they are assistants to the priests, but must not engage in the priestly work itself. This reading is consistent with chapter 4—the upper age for Levitical service is fixed at fifty and once they reach that age they must cease from all cultic service.[11]

However, most commentators interpret *brothers* as other Levites who are still eligible for full Levitical service. But they disagree about the level of assistance these aged Levites could provide. The possibilities include the following:

- They could still do everything except the heavy work of carrying and erecting the tabernacle (this tends to assume the rationale relates to declining physical strength).[12]
- They could only assist others, that is, they couldn't take sole responsibility for an activity.[13]
- They could only assist in times of shortage (such as the annual festivals).[14]
- They remain at the tabernacle in only a supervisory, advisory, and teaching capacity.[15]

Again, the text doesn't provide specifics. For our purposes that doesn't matter too much, since all of the proposed possibilities constitute ongoing work at some level. Perhaps some allowance is being made for their age, but they are not retiring as we understand the term.

What about those who didn't take up the "assistance" option? For whatever reason, they may have decided they no longer wished to continue in Levitical service. What happened to them? Most likely, they would have returned to the Levitical cities. Because they were chosen for service at the sanctuary, the Levites received no allotment of tribal territory in the distribution of land amongst the tribes. Instead, God was their inheritance (Deuteronomy 10:8–9; 18:2). Further, God provides for them from Israel's tithes (Numbers 18:21–32; Deuteronomy 14:22–29). Israel was also instructed to remember them during the festivals (Deuteronomy 16:9–15). In addition, God gave them use of forty-eight towns, along with their surrounding pasturelands, scattered throughout Israel. These included the six cities of refuge (Numbers 35:1–8; Joshua 21). This describes the situation once the Israelites entered the land.

It seems to me this implies several things that aren't explicitly stated in the biblical narrative. First, at any particular time after the Israelites entered Canaan, not all of the Levites were present serving at the central sanctuary. Some remained in the Levitical towns. (This implies an overall excess of Levites and tends to undermine the "supply and demand" rationale.) Second, there was likely some system of organizing which Levites were serving in Jerusalem at any given time: perhaps a rotational roster or a permanent workforce determined by lot and supplemented by others at peak times. Third, Levites could move in and out of Jerusalem—and thus in and out of the Levitical towns (Leviticus 25:32–34). Fourth, in the Levitical towns, there was some expectation that Levites would do "normal" work. The text strongly suggests this work was pasturing animals rather than farming crops (Numbers 35:1–5).

God had some purpose in scattering the Levites among the tribes. A common suggestion is that they reminded the people of the need for faithfulness in response to their calling to be God's holy people.[16] It also seems likely they had some Levitical work in their local communities—the suggestions include collecting tithes, teaching the laws, providing legal services (including being judges), involvement in local sacrifices (before the establishment of the central sanctuary in Jerusalem), and ensuring the correct slaughter of animals.

All this implies a far more complex situation than is suggested by a first reading of Numbers 8:23–26. I think it also implies that ceasing the work of the sanctuary at age fifty did not result in acquiring a life of recreation and relaxation—nor in simply putting their feet up. Rather, it meant moving to other spheres of work. That is, while they may have "retired" from their official Levitical position, they didn't retire from the workforce.

THE QUMRAN COMMUNITY

The following is something of an appendix to this chapter. It's not directly related to Numbers 8 or to the Levites—but it may help to shed light on the rationale for the command we've been examining in this chapter. This material comes from a later period of Israel's history (closer to New Testament times) and a particular community within Israel (the Qumran community). I include this mainly for illustrative purposes. This Jewish community also instituted upper age limits for several of their positions. And at one point they do provide a rationale for their decision—one that is a significant variation on one of the rationales suggested above.

Because this material is not usually on the average Christian's bookshelf, I have quoted several paragraphs in full, highlighting the relevant parts (bold type). The quotes are taken from Geza Vermes, *The Complete Dead Sea Scrolls in English*.[17] The most relevant section of the Damascus Document states:

> Ten shall be elected from the congregation for a definite time, four from the tribe of Levi and Aaron, and six from Israel. (They shall be) learned in the Book of Meditation and in the constitutions of the Covenant, **and aged between twenty-five and sixty years. No man over the age of sixty shall hold office as Judge of the Congrega-**

**tion, for "because man sinned his days have been shortened, and
in the heat of His anger against the inhabitants of the earth God
ordained that their understanding should depart even before their
days are completed."** (Jubilees, xxiii, II; p. 176)

Here the rationale for limiting the age of judges explicitly relates to
the aging process—but to the loss of mental ability rather than physical strength. The text fails to indicate what happens on reaching
age sixty other than that men can no longer hold the office of Judge.

This community rule quotes from the pseudepigraphical Jewish
book of Jubilees (another source that may not be on the average
Christian's bookshelf). This book, which was likely written about
a century before Jesus lived, claims to record the complete history
from the time of creation to the time of the exodus. It claims to be
a revelation from God to Moses and is organized according to fifty-
year periods (jubilees). The context in Jubilees is a discussion of
the decline of human longevity after the flood. The writer refers to
Abraham in 23:8–10 and notes that he failed to reach four jubilees
(that is, two hundred years of age). Jubilees 23:11–12 then states:

> And all of the generations which will arise henceforth and until the
> day of the great judgment will grow old quickly before they com-
> plete two jubilees, **and their knowledge will forsake them because
> of their old age**. And all of their knowledge will be removed. And in
> those days if a man will live a jubilee and a half, they will say about
> him, "He prolonged his life, but the majority of his days were suffer-
> ing and anxiety and affliction."[18]

Returning to the Damascus Document, two other offices are
given upper and lower age limits. The two upper age limits are different. Neither provides any rationale for the ages chosen.

> They shall all be enrolled by name: first the Priests, second the Le-
> vites, third the Israelites, and fourth the proselytes. And they shall be
> inscribed by name, one after the other: the Priests first, the Levites
> second, the Israelites third, and the proselytes fourth. And thus shall
> they sit and thus be questioned on all matters. **And the Priest who
> is appointed {to head}** (4Q267, fr. 9 v, II) the Congregation shall be

from thirty to sixty years old, learned in the Book of Meditation and in all the judgements of the Law so as to pronounce them correctly.

The Guardian of all the camps shall be from thirty to fifty years old, one who has mastered all the secrets of men and the languages of all their clans. (181)

A later section provides details of a man's progression through the various stages of life. No "retiring age" is given, but the community clearly recognizes that the assigned duties may require adjustment to make allowances for the elderly.

And this is the Rule for all the hosts of the congregation, for every man born in Israel.

From [his] youth they shall instruct him in the Book of Meditation and shall teach him, according to his age, the precepts of the Covenant. He [shall be edu]cated in their statutes for ten years. . . .

At the age of twenty years [he shall be] enrolled, that he may enter upon his allotted duties in the midst of his family [and] be joined to the holy congregation. He shall not [approach] a woman to know her by lying with her before he is fully twenty years old, when he shall know [good] and evil. And thereafter, he shall be accepted when he calls to witness the judgements of the Law, and shall be [allowed] to assist at the hearing of judgements.

At the age of twenty-five years he may take his place among the foundations (i.e. the officials) of the holy congregation to work in the service of the congregation.

At the age of thirty years he may approach to participate in lawsuits and judgements, and may take his place among the chiefs of the Thousands of Israel, the chiefs of the Hundreds, Fifties, and Tens, the Judges and the officers of their tribes, in all their families, [under the authority] of the sons of [Aar]on the Priests. And every head of family in the congregation who is chosen to hold office, [to go] and come before the congregation, shall strengthen his loins that he may perform his tasks among his brethren in accordance with his understanding and the perfection of his way. According to whether this is great or little, so shall one man be honoured more than another.

When a man is advanced in years, he shall be given a duty in the [ser]vice of the congregation in proportion to his strength. (198)

It seems to me that this affirms the expectation that people continue to contribute to the communal well-being throughout their life, while also recognizing that the aging process often reduces one's capacity to do so fully.

SUMMARY

In this chapter, I've explored the meaning of the passage in Numbers 8 where the Levites are instructed to cease their service at age fifty. I've particularly concentrated on any possible implications this instruction may have to support a concept of retirement.

We began by considering some of the possible rationales for this instruction. That, however, proved disappointing. While we may propose several possible rationales—and provide good reasons to support them—none of them is completely persuasive. Thus, we can't be confident in assigning any particular reason to this instruction for them to cease their service.

We then examined what happened when a Levite turned fifty. For those taking the option of continuing as assistants, they clearly remained workers even if their job description was altered. For those who did not choose that option, the most likely result was a return to work associated with residence in the Levitical towns. In neither case was the outcome what we understand by a retired lifestyle.

Finally, we looked at material from the Qumran community—material that arises from a later time period. There is evidence that this community made allowances for the declining abilities that accompany aging, but not that they advocated a system of retirement. Rather, the norm was that everyone contributed to the community's needs according to their abilities.

10

VOWS AND VALUING PEOPLE

The next passage we'll examine makes no reference to work or to ceasing work. Instead, it may give us another glimpse into the biblical view of aging—hence its possible relevance for a theology of retirement. This passage from the Old Testament law provides regulations about the amounts to be paid in order to redeem people who were dedicated or vowed to God. The values vary depending on the person's age. Leviticus 27:1–8 sets out the details.

> The LORD said to Moses, "Speak to the Israelites and say to them: 'If anyone makes a special vow to dedicate persons to the LORD by giving equivalent values, set the value of a male between the ages of twenty and sixty at fifty shekels of silver, according to the sanctuary shekel; and if it is a female, set her value at thirty shekels. If it is a person between the ages of five and twenty, set the value of a male at twenty shekels and of a female at ten shekels. If it is a person between one month and five years, set the value of a male at five shekels of silver and that of a female at three shekels of silver. If it is a person sixty years old or more, set the value of a male at fifteen shekels and of a female at ten shekels. If anyone making the vow is too poor to pay the specified amount, he is to present the person to the priest, who will set the value for him according to what the man making the vow can afford.'"

So, what's the possible relevance of this passage to retirement? The required value declines significantly once a person turns sixty—down to 30 percent for a man and 33.3 percent for a woman compared with the twenty to sixty age bracket. Why this big drop in value? Could it somehow be connected to some idea akin to retiring at age sixty? That, it seems to me, would depend on the rationale behind these values. And, as far as I can tell, once again the text doesn't specify what that is. That means we're left to weigh up the speculative suggestions that may be proposed.

Now, I found this a difficult passage. On the surface, it looks fairly straightforward. But once you start to dig a little, you run into all sorts of unknowns and additional questions. This brief summary appears to rely on lots of assumed knowledge—things known to the ancient Israelites which aren't recorded in any surviving documents. Before we get to the actual issue of retirement, it will be helpful to discuss some of these other matters in an effort to gain a better understanding of what these particular vows were about. That should then help us better assess whether they have any implications for a concept of retirement.

Thus, the plan for this chapter is to consider first why someone would take the step of vowing a person—either themselves or someone else—to God. Then we'll think about why there is the provision of an option to buy back a vowed person. That's the background material. Hopefully, that will provide some foundation for understanding the basis on which the values are calculated. And, if we can understand that, it should help us work out whether the significantly reduced values for those over sixty imply something like retirement for these older people.

WHY VOW PEOPLE TO GOD?

So, the first matter: what's happening here? Why would people make vows that involved dedicating people to God? And who, other than themselves, could they so dedicate? The text is quite general in how it describes this potential event. The NIV does describe it as a *special* vow. But the only thing in the context that indicates anything *special* is the fact that humans are being dedicated, rather than animals or property (Leviticus 27:9–33). Nothing else distinguishes any particular circumstances surrounding this dedication as being somehow *special*.[1]

The biblical narrative itself records few examples of humans being dedicated to God. I've identified only three occasions. On the first occasion, the Israelites dedicate their yet-to-be-defeated enemies to God, indicating they will totally destroy them (Numbers 21:1–3). The second occasion is when Jephthah vows to sacrifice as a burnt offering whatever first comes out the door of his house on the condition that God gives him military victory (Judges 11:30–31). And then Hannah dedicates her son Samuel before he is conceived, indicating that he will serve God for his whole life (1 Samuel 1:11).

In all, it's a mixed bunch. Interestingly, none of these people vow themselves. What they have in common is the desire that God act for them in some specified way. On the surface, the vow looks like an inducement to enlist God's favor.

That sentiment can be readily understood. Throughout history and across cultures, humans have appealed to their various gods for assistance. It's not unusual for such appeals to be accompanied by inducements: promises of some reciprocating service done for the god if the requested assistance is granted. Such vows are especially common in situations of duress. It has been quipped that there are no atheists in foxholes. Whether that is a theologically correct way to deal with the God of the Bible is another matter—he is not one to succumb to bribes or to allow himself to be the subject of manipulation. That, of course, doesn't stop people from trying. For example, J. D. Douglas notes that in the post-exilic period, Nazirite vows were often undertaken to gain favors from God.[2]

Of course, we're likely to remind ourselves that calamitous situations are not the only times such vows are made to God. People may make these vows purely from thankfulness or a desire to serve God or a wish to please God. While not denying the existence of that sentiment among ancient Israelites, Tony Cartledge argues that's a modern use of the word *vows*. He demonstrates that the use of this particular Hebrew word in the Old Testament relates to a person making a conditional promise to God: that if God responds favorably to the person's prayer, then the person will fulfill whatever is vowed. Other terminology is used for those other occasions.[3]

The Nazirite vow (Numbers 6:1–21) was one of separation in which a people consecrated themselves to God for a specific period. Regrettably, though the text is clear about actions forbidden to Nazirites during the period of their vow (consuming grape products, cutting hair, touching dead bodies), it supplies few details of any positive requirements: for example, did they have to serve at the sanctuary? The text assumes any such obligations were known already by the ancient Israelites. On the basis of the regulations in Numbers 6, it's questionable whether these Nazirite vows are the type envisaged by Leviticus 27. First, the Nazirite vow was made for a limited period, whereas the vows in Leviticus 27 appear open-ended (it's possible this is an unwarranted assumption, since the relative values indicated are more understandable if they are in lieu of a fixed period of service). Second, if the Nazirite vow is interrupted, the person must restart the vowed period. It does not appear that any substitute can be made in the way that Leviticus 27 describes.

On the other hand, we have God's instructions to the parents of the unborn Samson that he is to be a Nazirite for life (Judges 13). And though the term "Nazirite" is not used in 1 Samuel,[4] many consider Hannah to have also vowed that the unborn Samuel be such for life. These examples seem to fall within the category of vows described in Leviticus 27.

All this is to indicate two things: the reasons for dedicating people were varied and there are many gaps in our knowledge of the nature of these vows.

WHY VALUE THE PEOPLE VOWED?

An obvious question that arises is: why does Leviticus 27 place values on these vowed persons? If someone is dedicated to God's service, shouldn't that simply involve service—whether that be for a fixed period or for life? Why should there be an opt-out clause? Was that intended as part of the original contract?

On the one hand, the way the NIV translates verse 2 implies this indeed was the intention of the person making the vow. And within the cultural context envisaged by the biblical text, that makes sense. Israel's law prohibited human sacrifice—so the vowed person couldn't be burnt on the altar. The law also prohibited cultic prostitution—so the Jewish sanctuary was distinct from many other temples in their world. And Israel's law provided the Levites to assist the priests in their work—so, in principle, there was no work for a vowed person to perform at the sanctuary.

In effect, the vowed person was converted to cash (or the equivalent value in kind) and the money given to the priests and Levites.[5] It seems to me that the vow of a person becomes a form of legal fiction: it would be much simpler just to vow the particular amount of cash in the first place.[6]

On the other hand, there is another strand of interpretation that thinks the original vow actually involved giving the person wholly to God's service the way Hannah dedicated Samuel. This passage then provides an opportunity for the person making the vow to change their mind. Perhaps they were under duress and made their vow rashly without fully understanding the consequences. Perhaps their personal circumstances have changed and they have great need for the vowed person. God, in his kindness, provides an option for them to redeem their vow.[7]

But to discuss that fully is to move away from our main topic— and you may be wondering if we'll ever get to retirement. The point is, either way, there was the option of substituting cash for the person's ongoing service to God.

WHAT'S THE BASIS OF THE VALUATION?

One further question arises before we get to retirement: How did they arrive at these particular cash values? This is where we encounter further uncertainty. I have a mathematical bias and so like seeing things in tables. In Leviticus 27, a person's shekel value is:

	MALES	FEMALES
< 5 years	5[8]	3
5 years–20 years	20	10
20 years–60 years	50	30
> 60 years	15	10

The values are set for each category. They are determined by age and gender alone. There is no further distinction to reflect individual attributes—whether in terms of health, strength, attractiveness, social class, or whatever. Within the categories specified (which we moderns may object to as sexist or ageist), everyone is treated equally. The only exception is for those who can't afford the set value (verse 8).

The most common proposal for explaining these values relates them to the person's potential production, that is, the amount of economic output they're likely to contribute in terms of manual labor. Because of our modern tendency to equate monetary value with a person's perceived worth, many commentators also note that these values were not related to a person's inherent worth.[9] The differences in values have been explained as follows.

- Young children (one month to five years) had low values because they added very little to household income. Further, the high infant mortality rates left a large question mark over their future potential.

- Children and young adults (five to twenty years) had survived the initial threats to life and now made a significant contribution to household labor.

- Adults (twenty to sixty years) were in the prime of life and at the height of their production levels. They could undertake heavy labor. The census in Numbers 1 also considers men eligible for the army at age twenty.

- Older adults (over sixty years) were past their prime. They experienced declining strength and energy levels. They could no longer work at peak capacity. Thus, their value was reduced.

As to the lower value for women, Carol Meyers argues that in gender-balanced communities (and not denying the patriarchal nature of ancient Israel society), women contributed around 40 percent of the labor involved in providing subsistence (in a context where the production element was shared between men and women). She then demonstrates that the figures in Leviticus 27:1–8 generally are consistent with this ratio (the exception is the five to twenty years age bracket, which she suggests could be more equally balanced because the major portion of a woman's childbearing responsibilities fell within that period). This lends support to the theory that economic production capabilities provide the rationale for this range of values.[10] It is worth noting that this relative valuation is different from that applied when a bull known to gore kills a slave (Exodus 21:28–32). In that case, the male or female slave is valued equally at 30 shekels.

There are a couple of minor variations on this theme among the various modern-day interpretations of the passage. Mark Rooker mentions the possibility that the amount represents "the relative worth of the value of the person's services in the tabernacle"— which is a helpful way of more directly relating the values to the vow's presumed purpose.[11] Gordon Wenham suggests it's the price that would be received in the slave market—an amount also related to the value of their potential work.[12] These are important variations and some people rightly claim there are important distinctions between them—but they share the underlying foundation of potential economic output.

Now, on the basis of this commonly proposed rationale, it doesn't look like there's much support for a concept of retirement. The values may decline sharply following age sixty, but they don't reduce to zero. Indeed, for women, they only reduce to the same value as the five to twenty age bracket—and no one wants to suggest those people aren't working. And that also conforms to my overall understanding that the biblical narrative expects humans to work according to their capacity. Older people may have had reduced capacity for work, but they still contributed to the household's production.

But, for me, this proposed rationale (economic productivity) fails to convince. Consider several examples. The production capacity of one-month-old children is nil (at least, in terms of economic production!), yet they receive a value. The production capacity of an eighteen-year-old is far greater than that of a six-year-old, yet they are valued the same. The production capacity (and experience) of a twenty-two-year-old would not be much greater than that of an eighteen-year-old and yet the former is assessed at two and a half times the value of the latter (three times for females). And statistically, twenty-year-olds have many more years of work ahead of them than fifty-year-olds, yet they both have the same value. To me, this explanation of the system just doesn't add up.

Some commentators have attempted to solve some of the issues involved. Perhaps the vow was intended as an annual payment and would vary as the person grew older.[13] Yet given that the average wage is estimated at a shekel a month, this would then appear excessive for the twenty to sixty age bracket. Perhaps, like the Nazirite vow, the dedication of the person was for a fixed period only—perhaps five years. But there's no hint of this in the text (and there are comparable hints when it comes to redeeming dedicated family land—27:16–21), and it still doesn't explain the variations in value (the cost for a twenty-two-year-old compared to that for an eighteen-year-old). For me, these suggestions could be read into the text and they do improve the proposed economic rationale, but they don't solve all my issues.

Are there any other possibilities? Could the values be related more generally to the person's "value to the community"? The differences between males and females could be explained on the basis of patriarchal prejudices. The differences between the age groups could be explained as follows:

- Infants basically exist. They belong to the community, but they don't understand it. Nor do they know their role in it. Their enculturation is just beginning.

- Children and young adults (five to twenty age group) cooperate in the process of enculturation. They learn their place in the community and increasingly take that place by accepting their communal responsibilities.

- Adults (twenty to sixty age group) are fully participating members of the community.

- Older people (sixty and above age group).

This is where this theory breaks down. It may work in our society where older people are moved to the side. They've had their time in the spotlight—now it's time for the next generation to take center stage. But in ancient Israel, they highly valued older people. In particular, the elders exercised a central role in the community. So, on this theory, I'd expect a higher value for this age group.

Maybe this rationale could be rescued by partially incorporating a production element—although I get the feeling I'm clutching at straws. I could argue that "value to the community" includes full participation in economic production and that those over sixty have "retired" from that element, but not from their other community responsibilities. This explains the lower value for this age group and opens up the possibility of a theory of retirement. But there is no evidence to support the assumption they no longer participate in economic production (this means the theory is not refuted; just that it's not proven—which perhaps still leaves it in better condition than the other theories discussed). More to the point for our inquiry, however: it would be a change in job description rather than what we consider retirement.

I should confess that I do struggle to think of value in non-economic terms (a long time ago, I worked as an auditor) and so I find it difficult to think outside that particular box. So it's quite possible there are other rationales that haven't entered my head.

TO WHAT WERE THEY VOWED?

Before concluding this chapter, I think it's important to step back and look at the bigger picture. It's too easy to get lost in the details as we try to work out the rationale behind these values and the circumstances in which they operate. By focusing on the values, we run the risk of overlooking something basic.

This passage is about people dedicated to God's service. Now, it's hard for us to think about that without importing some concept of a division between the sacred and the secular. But that was foreign to Israel's law. The law makes it very clear that every aspect of life is lived under God's jurisdiction. Sure, they had what we'd label "religious" aspects of that law—regulations regarding priests and sacrifices and the tabernacle and its holy furniture. But "religious" is not a label you find in the law itself. God doesn't separate his statutes into moral, civil, and religious categories. God gives them the whole lot as part of the one package. And God is equally offended no matter what aspect (in terms of how we would categorize things) of his will they ignore.

We're tempted to import later thinking into this transaction. We may think the person being dedicated to God's service is pursuing a higher calling, taking a cushy clergy job, moving into the realm of the sacred, or getting an inside track to God. I don't think ancient Israel thought in those terms. Yes, this was work done in relation to God's sanctuary. And yes, this work was extremely important in the nation's life if the holy God was to continue dwelling in their midst. But it didn't somehow make the person who was vowed closer to God or more valuable to God. These people still had to offer sin offerings like everyone else.

Certainly, sacrifice was involved in dedicating a person to God's service. There was one less pair of hands to work on the family farm. In subsistence conditions, every person counted. And there will be some reason why that sacrifice was made (as discussed above). But, when you boil it down, from the perspective of the person involved, they were simply swapping one job for another.

And that remains true for those over sixty. Yes, the monetary value for their redemption may have been lower. Perhaps that was because of their reduced capacity to provide labor for the sanctuary. But it was still expected that they would supply labor. They weren't dedicated in a vow so they could retire—unless you take the cynical approach that this was one way for households to rid themselves of old people who could no longer pull their weight on the farm (and yes, given human nature, some probably did try that!). Their service involved work.

SUMMARY

Can we reach any conclusions about this passage? There are quite a few unknowns here. The most important, for our purposes, is the basis on which these values were calculated. The significant issue is: Is there anything in this passage to support the notion that those over sixty "retired"? As noted above, I find all the proposed theories unsatisfying. To me, none of them fully explains the data we have. So, I have to admit that someone may propose a different theory that alters my basic understanding of this passage. Yet, on the basis of the current proposals, it appears to me there's nothing in this passage to support a notion of retirement for those over sixty. Rather, I think the text strongly suggests older people continued to work once they reached that age.

As a final (random) note: the next sequential chapter in the Bible—Numbers 1—records a census of those eligible to serve in the army. This census was confined to men who had reached the age of twenty. No maximum age is specified—that is, there seems to have been no provision for "retirement" from military service.

11

PUTTING WIDOWS
ON THE LIST

We turn next to a New Testament passage—not because we've finished with the Old Testament, but because this is a passage that indicates a possible change of status at a set age. The age in question is sixty and the group in view is widows. Paul's instructions appear in 1 Timothy 5:3–16. Although his directions concerning those over sixty form only a segment of this passage, it's helpful to see those directions in their broader context—for, as we shall see, some of the other things mentioned influence how we interpret what Paul says about those over sixty.

> Give proper recognition to those widows who are really in need. But if a widow has children or grandchildren, these should learn first of all to put their religion into practice by caring for their own family and so repaying their parents and grandparents, for this is pleasing to God. The widow who is really in need and left all alone puts her hope in God and continues night and day to pray and to ask God for help. But the widow who lives for pleasure is dead even while she lives. Give the people these instructions, too, so that no one may be open to blame. If anyone does not provide for his relatives, and especially for his immediate family, he has denied the faith and is worse than an unbeliever.
>
> No widow may be put on the list of widows unless she is over sixty, has been faithful to her husband, and is well known for her good deeds, such as bringing up children, showing hospitality, washing the feet of the saints, helping those in trouble and devoting herself to all kinds of good deeds.
>
> As for younger widows, do not put them on such a list. For when their sensual desires overcome their dedication to Christ, they want

to marry. Thus they bring judgment on themselves, because they have broken their first pledge. Besides, they get into the habit of being idle and going about from house to house. And not only do they become idlers, but also gossips and busybodies, saying things they ought not to. So I counsel younger widows to marry, to have children, to manage their homes and to give the enemy no opportunity for slander. Some have in fact already turned away to follow Satan.

If any woman who is a believer has widows in her family, she should help them and not let the church be burdened with them, so that the church can help those widows who are really in need.

Within the Old Testament law, God instructed Israel to care for the disadvantaged. That included providing for widows (for example, Deuteronomy 24:17–22). After Jesus returned to his Father, the early church expressed this same concern in a Jewish context, taking steps to ensure widows' daily needs were met (Acts 6:1–6). Now, a few decades later and in a Greco-Roman context, Paul wants Timothy to display a similar concern within the church at Ephesus. Unlike in Israel, this practice was distinct from the cultural norms of Ephesus. Yet given Paul's Jewish heritage and his lengthy stay in the city when he first established the church there (Acts 19:9–10), it's unlikely that he now introduces a totally new concept to them.

Widows were a vulnerable class in the ancient world. The exact extent of their vulnerability is unclear. Most likely, it varied in different locations and in different circumstances. On the one hand, Robert Karris paints a bleak picture:

> The widow in Greco-Roman tradition was trapped in a patriarchal system. Once her protector and "breadwinner" died, she was cast adrift. There was no welfare system, no social security to come to her rescue."[1]

On the other hand, Bruce Winter lists several ways in which the Greco-Roman society did provide for widows. First, the law defined how a widow's dowry was used upon her husband's death. If she had children, she could remain in her deceased husband's household and be maintained by the new master (possibly her son). Or she could return with her dowry to her father's house. Second, any children a widow had were morally obliged to care for her. In Athens, this was also a legal obligation. Third, widows were expected to remarry. At one period, Augustus made this compulsory for widows under fifty. Fourth, in some places, food was distributed to the poor, including widows.[2] Unfortunately, as Winter himself notes, we're unsure of the extent to which these provisions were enforced. Human nature has a tendency to exploit loopholes, especially when the other party is in a vulnerable position. Further, provisions that applied for citizens and those with means didn't always apply across the board.[3] And so we have the situation that confronts us in 1 Timothy 5 where it seems the church at Ephesus had an excess of widows looking for assistance.

On the surface, Paul's instructions seem straightforward. But I should warn you that surface appearances may be deceptive. Luke Johnson notes that this passage "is so specific and complex that its untangling is a notorious problem for the history of earliest Christianity."[4] He's not unique in voicing that sentiment. For our purposes, we won't need to untangle all the difficulties; but we will need to work our way through some of them.

NARROWING IT DOWN TO THE WIDOWS IN "REAL" NEED

To commence that process, ponder the broad canvas. Within 1 Timothy 5, the particular widows we're considering (those over age sixty) are a subcategory of a much bigger class. I think it's helpful to identify the distinctions Paul makes—some explicit, some implicit. Paul's concern is to provide for all widows, but how they're provided for depends on how they're categorized.

First, notice that Paul only deals with the situation of Christian widows. The church may very well have helped non-Christian widows as well—after all, they did develop a reputation of caring for the empire's orphans—but I don't think non-Christian widows are mentioned in this passage.

The first distinction Paul draws within the category of Christian widows is between widows with family members still alive and those without. For widows with families, they should receive their support from those families. The church should not need to contribute to their upkeep. Paul focuses here on children and grandchildren (though I don't think he would exclude other family options—like a widow returning to her father's house). These relatives should take the initiative and provide for their mother or grandmother. For Paul, that's a straightforward application of the Fifth Word about honoring parents. It's a debt they owe—not simply because God commands it of his people, but also because their culture valued the "repayment" of the investment their parents made in them (also implied by verse 8) and it's inappropriate for Christian standards to be inferior to those of the surrounding pagan society. We'll come back to the Fifth Word in the next chapter.

As noted in chapter 3, by New Testament times, the organization of households in the Roman Empire was far more varied than in ancient Israel. Yet, whatever those variations, it's unlikely that widows who were absorbed into family households would remain idle. Households still constituted the basic production unit. It was a communal effort with each person playing their part. Every member of the household was responsible to contribute productively to the household's common good.

Paul then distinguishes between different groups of Christian widows without families to support them. Three options were open to them: they could remarry; they could support themselves; or they could receive support from the church. In passing, it's worth noting the first two of these three options were also available to those widows with families to support them. But to resolve the issue in Ephesus—which widows should receive church support—Paul doesn't need to explore those avenues in relation to them. It's sufficient that they have families to care for them such that the church need not be burdened.

It's possible Paul briefly touches on the option of widows supporting themselves in verse 6. Donald Guthrie tentatively suggests the word translated "lives for pleasure" may refer to widows prostituting themselves—whether generally or to one client—in order to survive.[5] If so, Paul clearly rejects that option. Luke Johnson believes the word refers to pleasures in general (Lea and Griffin go as far as identifying it as "luxurious, voluptuous indulgence"[6]) and notes that a widow with sufficient resources to indulge herself in that manner hardly needs the church to provide her basic necessities.[7] But whatever Paul's precise meaning here (clearly negative), there were legitimate ways women could support themselves. The New Testament presents several examples of women (whether they were widows or not is unclear) who ran their own households (for example, Lydia and Nympha).[8] While Paul doesn't address the possibility of widows working in this passage, I'm sure he wouldn't object to widows earning their own keep.[9]

Paul here does deal with the other two options. His approach is simple: if they're under sixty, they should marry again; if they're over sixty, they may be put on the "widows' list" if they meet the other qualifications.

But I did warn you that things are not always as simple as they appear. It seems to me that Paul omits two important groups: those under sixty who can't find another husband; and those over sixty who don't meet the qualifications (the qualifications he identifies in verses 9–10). Does the church ignore those widows? Are they left destitute? I suspect not—and I'm not alone in that suspicion[10]—but the passage doesn't say. What we have here is a letter written to a pastoral colleague in a specific situation. It addresses the main issue that Paul wished to resolve in Ephesus. But it's not parliamentary legislation designed to prevent all loopholes. Paul provides general principles and expects Timothy (and the church) to fill in the details where necessary. I don't think there's anything in the passage that forbids supporting widows who don't make the list—but such support would need to conform to the general tone of Paul's overall strategy.

Some scholars take a different approach. Margaret Davies, for example, suggests Paul identifies two groups of widows the church should help: those who are really in need (5:3–8); and those who qualify for enrollment on the list regardless of their need (5:9–15).[11] This provides satisfactory answers to the questions raised above: the church does support other widows in need. It also raises two issues relevant to our task. First, it provides the potential for a second "leisured" group—one based on marital status rather than age. While such a group doesn't strictly fit our concept of retirement, widows in this category would be an example of people with the capacity to work who are no longer required to work—and that state would be achieved through material support from the church. Second, if widows in need can receive church support without being enrolled on the list, what's the point of the list? Does it perhaps give extra benefits? Does it provide additional status? Does it have some other significance? We'll deal with this second issue first.

ENROLLING WIDOWS ON THE LIST

In verse 9, Paul refers to a "list of widows." He then details the qualifications to be met for a widow to be *put on* this list: While scholars have raised interesting discussions about the precise meaning of some of Paul's expressions (for example, what it means that she be a "one man woman," the NIV's "faithful to her husband," and whether the foot-washing was literal), for our purposes the requirement that she be over sixty is the most relevant. Those other qualifications were certainly important. They demonstrated growing Christian maturity and ministry. But in relation to retirement, the age factor is the one that most naturally grabs our attention.

Why pick on sixty? Several possible reasons have been suggested by scholars.

1. It was the figure at which the culture recognized a person had reached old age.[12]

2. At this age the widows would be infirm (on the basis that their age sixty was perhaps the equivalent of eighty years of age today) and no longer able to support themselves.[13]

3. It was extremely unlikely a woman would remarry after this age (an issue that's prominent in excluding younger widows from the list).[14]

4. Church men supporting women under this age may have given the appearance of immorality—the idea that the widows were "kept women."

5. It ensured that those included were mature, experienced, and reliable (and unlikely to fall into the traps identified in verse 13).[15]

They all make good sense at some level.

Within the broader context of this passage, the third reason above finds some support. One of the reasons Paul gives for not putting younger widows on the list is that they're likely to succumb to a desire to marry again. In itself, there's nothing wrong with that desire. Paul himself counsels these younger widows to marry (verse 14). Yet verses 11 and 12 strongly imply there's some inconsistency if a widow already enrolled on the list subsequently remarries—a problem that's not present if she remarries before being enrolled. The exact nature of the problem is unclear—and therefore disputed.

The most common suggestion, and the one that makes most sense to me, is that enrollment on the list involved an understanding (perhaps even a pledge) that the widow made a commitment to remain in the single state, usually understood to be for the purpose of serving the church (something that will be discussed further below).[16] It should be noted that this argument would lose much of its force if enrolled widows were not expected to involve themselves in ministry.

Other scholars suggest that Paul restricts the list to widows over sixty years old because younger widows might be tempted to abandon Christian principles by marrying unbelieving husbands.[17] I'm not convinced by this argument. It introduces the concept of an unbelieving husband into the text. While this is a feasible explanation, nothing in the context directly suggests it. Instead, the issue with younger widows in verse 11 is that they wish to marry after being enrolled—not the identity of their new husband. Further, this interpretation fails to explain why it's a problem to put them on the list. If they made no commitment on enrollment, why would it have been an issue to remove them if they no longer qualified?

And that leads to my next question: Why do widows need to qualify in the first place? Isn't the church a grace-oriented group of believers? Surely the fact that a widow is destitute is sufficient qualification for supporting her. That seems to be good enough for the church in Acts 6. Why these extra hoops to jump through? What if a widow had converted at age fifty-five and thus had no real opportunity to build up this lengthy résumé of Christian service? To me, all these extra qualifications imply that there's more to this list than simply providing for destitute widows.

THE LIFESTYLE OF WIDOWS ON THE LIST

To tease this out, ponder another question: What happens to these women after sixty? Certainly widows may qualify for the list. And since the passage deals with widows *who are really in need* (5:3) and wants those with surviving children to have their children *repay* their mother (5:4), the strong implication is that widows on the list receive material support (whether money or provisions) from the church. If we put it in modern terms, we might say they got a "church pension."

Living It Up on the Pension?

But does Paul envision that this material support will enable them to enjoy leisure and idleness? Such a conclusion runs counter to my impression of the entire passage. As is clear from this passage, Paul wants people to be productive. He tells Timothy that the families of widows should be productive in caring for them (5:4, 8). The widows who qualify for the list have certainly been productive in the past—good deeds, raising children, hospitality, assisting others (5:9–10). The younger widows are to remarry and be productive—both in bearing children and managing homes—so that they don't become idle (5:13–14). It seems the contrast between leisure and industriousness is strong throughout the passage. Idleness is a bad habit that, if not a sin in itself, leads to various sinful problems, such as *gossiping* and being *busybodies*. It's far better for Christians to occupy themselves in productive pursuits that contribute good for others.

But could I be misreading Paul? Certainly he talks about the past deeds that qualify widows for the list. Up to the age of sixty, they're required to be busy with all manner of good works as itemized in verse 10. But isn't that the whole point of retirement? Isn't retirement when you don't have to do that stuff anymore? Paul doesn't specify they must keep doing these things once they've made the list. Isn't retirement a reward for the hard yards you've completed in the past—that you can now stop doing that kind of work? In the past you spent your time focusing on the work God wanted you to do; now you can do as you please. In the past these widows showed hospitality; now they can ignore the needs of others.

Somehow I just can't imagine Paul buying into that philosophy of life. God saved these women that they might experience saved lives—lives to be lived in God's service and for his glory. Is it reasonable to think that, having made significant progress in both godliness and Christian service—highly desirable elements of their actual salvation—Paul now gives them a holiday from the good life to indulge in self-centeredness?

I've approached this slightly out of left field because I want to highlight a point that I think is easily overlooked: namely, this underlying theme that Christians should lead productive lives (remembering that a "productive life" or "work" is much broader than paid employment). This theme is not that uncommon in Paul's writings (for example, see 2 Thessalonians 3:6–14). Now, I admit it's not the only underlying theme in this passage. Paul does want the church to care for widows in need. He's also concerned that church finances not be burdened unnecessarily—and so he excludes certain groups of widows from help.[18] He's concerned for the church's reputation in the wider community and that Christians reject activities or situations that would bring dishonor to the gospel.[19] And it may well be that Paul's overall concern for false teaching in this letter also lies behind this passage.[20] But, in addition to these issues, he also seems concerned to combat idleness.

What Exactly Is the List?

Thus, I think it seems more likely that the widows placed on this list continue to serve God—even that the material support they receive allows them to more fully devote themselves to the work of ministry. At this point, I need to indicate (again!) that scholars disagree as to just what this "list" was—even if there was a "certified list." The main options they propose are:

1. The church was merely given general instructions and people were encouraged (as individuals or households) to make their own contributions directly to those whom they believed met the qualifications.

2. Same as 1, except the church maintained a register of qualified widows.

3. Same as 2, except people contributed to a common fund maintained by the church out of which widows were supported.[21]

4. Same as 3, with the addition that those on the list, being now freed from the burden of laboring for their material needs, were to avail themselves of the resultant opportunity to give themselves more fully to functions of church ministry.[22]

5. Same as 4, with the addition that there was an official position of widow, similar to elders and deacons.[23]

I think we need to be careful of reading our situations and our structures back into the early church. For example, others have noted that the early church focused more on function than position. Rather than set up a roster of necessary positions for people to fill, they simply got on with the work of ministry according to how God gifted them. Thus, option 5 most likely belongs to a much later era, when the church exhibited a more formal structure.[24] At the other end of the scale, the example of Acts 6 suggests it's unlikely they had a completely ad hoc approach. In that instance, people contributed to a common fund from which distributions were made as required. So I think it is doubtful that options 1 and 2 were adopted. Yet having said that, the greater communal culture of the early church[25] may mean that the difference between options 2 and 3 was not as great as we would view them today.

What Expectations Accompany Enrollment?

The more significant issue for our purposes is whether the church expected any work from these widows on the list. It must be admitted that some factors can be used to argue against this possibility. Perhaps some women over sixty were too infirm for most ministry activities and so were now involved in prayer alone. Yet infirmity isn't a feature of Paul's argument in this passage—importantly, it's not one of the qualifications for those enrolled on the list. Further, he does advise those under sixty to marry and manage a household. It seems unlikely that he intends us to presume that these women suddenly become infirm upon turning sixty.

Based on Paul's description of their activities, it may be argued that these widows haved ceased work. The aorist tenses used in verses 9 and 10 indicate that, from the perspective of their enrollment on the list, these were past activities for these candidates. Yet when examining qualifications for a position, it's normal to check a person's past record. And nothing indicates they should no longer pursue these activities. These widows would no longer have the financial resources to continue extensive ministries of hospitality and service. Yet, if they serve officially on the church's behalf, surely the church would also supply any needed resources for such service.

Based on these factors, it's possible these widows did no work. But by now it's probably clear that I don't find those factors persuasive.

Instead, I think other factors suggest an expectation of ongoing ministry. As noted already, the general tone of the passage upholds productivity rather than idleness. Second, the qualifications for the list appear too strict if the sole purpose is to support those in financial need.[26] Third, Paul's comments about the younger widows going house to house *may* also suggest those enrolled on the list were authorized and expected to exercise a ministry of visitation.[27] Fourth, the fact that the following passage (5:17–18) speaks of payments to elders in relation to their ministry *may* suggest a link in Paul's mind—that he saw both groups being financially supported by the church in their work of ministry. Fifth, when the full-fledged office of widow developed later in the history of the church, the appointment was for the purpose of ministry. It seems more likely that this formalized existing practice that developed over time than that it was an innovation.

Then, there are additional arguments that are dependent on particular interpretations of other disputed aspects of the passage. For those who argue that Paul identifies two groups of widows in this passage, the main distinction is that those enrolled on the list are expected to minister as a result of their support. And for those who argue these women made a vow of celibacy, the point of that vow was that they might devote themselves more fully to serving the church. None of these arguments are conclusive—after all, it remains an area of significant debate among scholars. For myself, I find the arguments in favor of the widows' ongoing ministry more persuasive.

What was the nature of the ministry expected of them? Hanson thinks it was intercessory prayer and assistance in entertaining the church's guests.[28] Kelly adds to that the various matters listed in verse 10 and pastoral visitation.[29] Karris further adds the devoted life which in itself provides an example and challenge to the community of total dedication to God.[30] They all have some relationship to the passage. At a later time, "registered widows gave themselves to prayer, nursed the sick, cared for the orphans, visited Christians in prison, evangelized pagan women, and taught female converts in preparation for their baptism."[31] But perhaps to phrase the question as I have is to focus more on position than function. These women have a demonstrated track record of ministry. That's one major aspect of the qualifications Paul establishes. Surely the point is that each widow will continue, as the ongoing expression of her Christian maturity, to exercise her ministry in accordance with the gifts given her by God. And perhaps that's why no official duties are specified.

So, in this passage, I don't think enrollment on the list at age sixty signifies a transition to leisured retirement. Rather, I think it refers to a specific group of widows who had dedicated themselves to the work of the church's ministry. But I realize there are other possible interpretations. Perhaps those enrolled on the list were too infirm to work. That certainly happens in old age—both then and today. It can also happen for reasons other than the aging process. And it is right that such people not be expected to work. But that is not comparable to the concept of leisured retirement simply because a particular age has been attained. Or again perhaps those enrolled on the list were still physically able, but are no longer required, to work. I think that's the least likely interpretation of the passage—but I don't think I can rule it out conclusively.

SUPPORTED WIDOWS NOT ON THE LIST

We must now return to the other issue raised earlier: does this passage envisage a second group of supported widows who aren't enrolled on the list—and, if so, do these widows provide an example of people with the capacity to work who are no longer required to do so?

As I indicated earlier, I think it's unlikely that church support was limited to destitute widows over the age of sixty who could demonstrate a lifetime of Christian service. Qualifications like that were not required in Acts 6. And it's contrary to the fundamental nature of the church—where Jesus indicated his followers would be known by their love for one another. Part of the essence of true religion is to look after widows (James 1:27). Whether we reach this conclusion by emphasizing the two separate paragraphs of this passage (5:3–8 and 5:9–15) or by importing a Christian ethos into the passage doesn't matter for our purposes. The result will be the same.

Can this group be used to justify a concept of retirement? I think not. The support of these widows is of a different nature than those on the list. For those on the list, there's a mutual commitment for the remainder of their lives. For this other group, support is based on their needs. Those needs may continue for the rest of their lives—but they may not. To put it in today's terms, it's more like unemployment benefits than retirement. While they remain in the state of destitute widow, the church will support them. But that state may change. They may remarry (something Paul encourages here). They may find employment. They may have children who mature and care for them. The concept that they can now draw a widow's pension so they can spend the rest of their life at the club was foreign to their thinking. Well, given verse 6, maybe it wasn't foreign to their thinking. Paul certainly thinks it should be foreign to a Christian's thinking.

A PATRIARCHAL BACKLASH?

Before concluding this chapter, I should mention yet another interpretation of this passage. Jouette Bassler argues that the socio-historical situation underlying these instructions was the mushrooming numbers of widows in the church. She contends that early Christianity was strongly egalitarian, and this was highly attractive for women who were dissatisfied with the strictures on their lives within patriarchal society. The Christian order of widows offered them opportunities to exercise new-found freedoms and ministries. Bassler suggests the term translated *widow* could be understood as meaning "woman living without a husband" and could thus include divorced women and those who had never married (celibacy was the defining element of the group). This resulted in an influx of younger "widows" (some of whom were wealthy) ministering from house to house, challenging the male eldership and asserting their authority to teach. Some of these women defected to the heretics because the lifestyle they advocated resonated with the freedoms that attracted these women. In this passage, Bassler argues, Paul responds by reasserting patriarchal traditions for the sake of restoring both order within the church and the church's reputation in the community. It's not written to establish a new order; rather, its aim is to severely curtail an existing practice.[32]

This approach solves some of the difficulties in this passage. But as Bassler herself notes, some unanswered questions remain.[33] Be that as it may, what are the implications of this interpretation for our thoughts on retirement? In relation to the older women still enrolled in the order, this doesn't alter the conclusions reached above. They remain involved in ministry. In relation to the younger women now excluded from the order, their idleness remains a problem. Paul's insistence that they lead productive lives is still valuable for our discussion of retirement. While the work he allots to these younger women—marrying and starting households of their own—may seem to betray a patriarchal bias, it's still the case that he holds both groups of women accountable to the same standard. No one, young or old, is to be idle.

Thus I don't think this particular interpretation has anything new to contribute to our particular concerns.

SUMMARY

For us, being absent from the actual situation in Ephesus, not knowing all the details, and only hearing one side of the "conversation," 1 Timothy 5:3–16 is a complex passage—perhaps made even more complex by the sorts of questions scholars have brought to it over the years (and I know I have ignored many of those questions). But I felt it important to provide sufficient information to understand enough of the background to this passage so that we can be fairly confident we know the significance of the age sixty and what transpired for these widows on reaching that age.

I'm reasonably confident it had nothing to do with what we imagine by retirement. Indeed, if I'm correct in how I understand this passage, it actually presents a strong challenge to our concept of retirement. Rather than seeing sixty as an age to sit back and put up one's feet, Paul sees it as the age for these widows to more fully give themselves to mission work on the church's behalf.[34]

12

Caring for Aged Parents

We return to the Old Testament and the fifth commandment[1]—
the one about honoring parents. Now, if your background is similar
to mine, you're probably asking: What's this got to do with retirement? When I learned about this command in Sunday school and
Christian Endeavour, teachers focused on me (as a child) obeying
my parents. That was good and proper. They sought to apply the
biblical text to my particular context.

As I matured into the youth group, the focus shifted. It's not
that the obedience aspect was absent. It was certainly still there.
From our leaders' perspective, it was probably still 95 percent of
what they wished to communicate. But, in our trajectory toward
maturity and independence, we asked questions like: When should
we obey God rather than our parents? At what age do we no longer
have to obey? What if our parents are not very honorable? (I hasten
to add that, for me personally, that was not an issue: my parents
were very honorable!) Do we still have to honor them when we set
up our own homes? And if so, what does that look like?

As an adult, my understanding of this commandment didn't
change much. We taught our children the requirement to obey us.
I did the same as I taught various children in Sunday school and
adolescents in youth group. Certainly, *honor* remained a lifelong
obligation. I didn't question that. But neither did I particularly
focus on it. I simply assumed this command was addressed primarily to non-adults. And, on that basis, it would have no relevance
whatsoever to retirement.

Imagine my surprise when I recently discovered that most
scholars think this commandment was primarily addressed to
adults in relation to their aging parents. That's a big paradigm shift.
Perhaps, then, it could be saying: "Relieve your parents of the need
to work in their old age. Let them sit out their last days in comfort

and ease. Encourage them to get out, have a good time and spend your inheritance!"

Again, we face the danger of reading our culture into the text— or, at least, of allowing our culture to dictate what questions we ask of the text. I tend to look for independence. That's part of my culture and how I'm trained. I ask about the age when it's okay for me to no longer obey my parents. I want to know when I can do my own thing and make my own way in life. I live in an individualistic society. I look for my rights and privileges rather than my responsibilities. I search for my own advantage rather than serving others for the common good. The Israelite culture had a more communal focus. They asked about the well-being of the household and the wider community first. Individual self-fulfillment was not a major priority.

THE TWO FORMS

With that lengthy introduction, let's turn to the text. The first time the Decalogue occurs within the narrative, Israel is camped at Mount Sinai. Yahweh speaks to the newly released slaves, explaining the covenant relationship between them (Exodus 19–20). The Fifth Word states:

> Honor your father and your mother, so that you may live long in the land the LORD your God is giving you. (20:12)

Then, forty years later, on the Plains of Moab, Moses stands before the next Israelite generation and reminds them of Yahweh's covenantal words.

> Honor your father and your mother, as the LORD your God has commanded you, so that you may live long and that it may go well with you in the land the Lord your God is giving you. (Deuteronomy 5:16)

On both occasions the narrative stresses the covenant context.

If we compare the two accounts of the Fifth Word, the Deuteronomy version contains two additions. First, as with the previous Sabbath Word, Moses reminds them that this is what God commanded. Some scholars propose imaginative rationales for this addition. For example, Telford Work suggests:

> Affirmative commandments require more reinforcement and struc-
> ture than negative ones, especially in times of personal and social
> change. As the absence of manna in the land will be a temptation to
> overwork, so this generation's success in entering the land after the
> last generation's failure will be a temptation to arrogance.[2]

Eugene Merrill claims there was "some infraction of the statute in the interim."[3] Raymond Brown proposes that "this command had a special significance for the nation as it went into the promised land."[4]

These proposals fail to convince. For example, idolatry was a significant problem for Israel in their wilderness journeys (and remained so after their settlement in Canaan); yet, Moses provides no similar addition when reminding Israel of that Word. More likely, Moses simply reinforces the narrative context: these Words are not new revelation from God; yet they retain the same authority as when first given.

The second addition extends the promise to include the experience of ongoing goodness in the land. While this is not linked explicitly to this Word in Exodus, the overall context indicates that adherence to all of God's words will result in overall blessing (Exodus 19:3–6; 20:24; 23:25–26). Further, it is implicit in the shortened form of the promise, since longevity in adverse circumstances would provide little incentive for obedience.

Thus, I think neither addition adds material substance to the actual requirement—especially in relation to its relevance to any concept of retirement.

WHO IS ADDRESSED?

To whom is this Word addressed? Clearly, if it targets non-adults alone, it's of no relevance to our current enquiry. To answer this question, we need first to look at the overall context. To whom is the Decalogue as a whole addressed?

At first glance, the answer appears straightforward. In both Exodus 19 and Deuteronomy 5, it's quite clear that these Words are spoken to all Israel. But the Words themselves use the second person masculine *singular* forms (what we translate as the word "you"). To explain this, I need to inject some *grammar* (sorry if, as with *history*, you also have a negative reaction to that word!). I'll keep it brief. In English, we do three things differently from Hebrew (actually, there's lots more than three, but only three are relevant here).

- We tend to keep our various parts of speech (especially verbs and pronouns) separate. To write "I know" or "she knows" or "they know" in English, I have to use two separate words. In Hebrew, the pronoun is part of the verb. To write "I know" requires only one word. And in the Decalogue, each of the verbs indicates a second person masculine singular subject.
- We, in our second person pronouns, don't distinguish between singular and plural. If I write "you know," I could be talking to one of you or lots of you. In Hebrew, the verbal form clearly distinguishes between singular and plural.
- Similarly, we also don't distinguish between feminine and masculine in our second person pronouns. If I write "you know," "you" could be either feminine or masculine. In Hebrew, the verbal form clearly makes that distinction.

The point is that the form of these words is both singular and masculine. And so we need to ask: Is that significant? Now, it could be like our third person singular pronouns in English. In days before our current emphasis on gender-neutral language, the pronoun "he" was often used inclusively to refer to both male and female. It was not appropriate to use "it," because the reference was to people, not things; nor was it appropriate to use "they," because the reference was singular, not plural. The convention was to use the masculine pronoun. That use of the masculine pronoun is no longer acceptable for us today. It may be like that with the Decalogue. The crowd included both males and females. In biblical Hebrew, the normal way to address both men and women at the same time was to use the masculine forms. Normally, the masculine *plural* forms would be expected, but the singular form here may "underscore the importance of each individual member of the Covenant between God and Israel."[5]

But not everyone agrees with that interpretation. In the twelfth century, the Jewish scholar Maimonides suggested that God addressed these words directly to Moses (and thus the masculine singular language), who then was responsible to relay them to Israel. Since that fails to fit the Deuteronomy 5 context, few have followed that option.[6] I think it's an unlikely explanation.

Far more popular is the view that these words are addressed to the Israelite adult men or male adult household heads. In addition to the grammatical features already mentioned, scholars highlight four other aspects to support this view.[7]

1. In preparation for receiving the law, the "men" are instructed not to approach a woman for three days (the NIV obscures this by translating generically: "Abstain from sexual relations"—Exodus 19:15). There is no corresponding instruction to the women.[8]

2. In the Second Word, the phrase "the sin of the fathers" hints that the household head's actions are primarily in view—that he is warned not to lead his household into idolatry.

3. In the Fourth Word, the instructions about the Sabbath are addressed to the male and then extended to include all people and animals in terms of their relationship to the male household head.

4. In the Tenth Word, the instruction forbids coveting one's neighbor's wife, but not one's neighbor's husband.

This, so it is argued, reflects the patriarchal nature of their society. The male heads of households are addressed because their cultural understanding of their responsibilities included both instructing household members concerning God's words and exercising judicial functions within the household. This doesn't exclude other community members from adherence to God's instructions; rather, it simply means they receive those instructions through the structures of their community. A woman, for example, couldn't claim she was free to steal because she wasn't addressed directly by the Decalogue.[9]

For our purposes, it's unnecessary to choose—both of these common interpretations affirm that every Israelite was included in the covenant and thus required to observe God's instructions. As Ben Witherington points out: "Even a Jewish child who had not yet personally embraced the call to be a 'son of the commandments' was still expected to obey the Mosaic Law."[10]

The next issue is whether something in the Fifth Word itself justifies a narrower audience for this particular instruction. For example, the Seventh Word concerning adultery is aimed at adults rather than children.

At this point, Robert Martin-Achard provides assistance. He identifies three common interpretive approaches to this Fifth Word. The first, the "socio-phenomenological approach," emphasizes the obedience of non-adults. The second, the "more theological approach," stresses "the pedagogical role of parents"—that is, that parents are responsible to train their children concerning their covenant obligations. While this argues that the Fifth Word is directed toward adults, the envisaged outcome benefits their children. The third interpretive approach focuses on the responsibility of adult children to care for their aging parents, especially when their productive capabilities fail.[11]

I think it's important to note that those three approaches are not mutually exclusive. It's quite feasible that the Fifth Word intends to include all three aspects—and perhaps more. For our current purposes, it's only necessary to show the third is included.

As I've read various commentaries explaining the Fifth Word, I've discovered a wide diversity of reasons that scholars use to argue that this instruction expects care of aged parents. Many of them, I find unconvincing. For example, Walter Harrelson links the Fourth and Fifth Words—the instructions about honoring parents and observing the Sabbath. He claims that, as humans require weekly rest from their toil, so they also need a "sabbath" rest when their productive years finish. To me, that seems a rather tenuous connection

between the two Words and one that imports our cultural under-
standings and practices. A straightforward reading of the two Words
reveals no direct verbal or contextual links.[12]

Now, I could go through all of those reasons—both the good
and the not so good. Instead, I want to concentrate on two things
that have convinced me this instruction includes care of aged parents—and that this was probably its primary focus. That's not to say
the other two aspects Martin-Achard identifies are irrelevant. The
first, the obedience of non-adult children, was a cultural given—
something considered a normal part of life (see Proverbs for how
that works out). Assnat Bartor notes: "The requirement of obedience is taken for granted by a patriarchal society, and someone
who disobeys the head of the family is seen as someone who rebels
against society's foundations."[13] Other parts of the law encouraged
the second aspect—parents' responsibility to train the next generation in covenantal fidelity (see Deuteronomy 6:1–9). These are
certainly important aspects for promoting *shalom*. But so is this
third aspect.

To return to the two things that convince me that this instruction includes the requirement for adult children to honor their aged
parents by caring for them: the first is simply understanding the
Israelites' culture. As explained in chapter 3, their household extended beyond our nuclear family. Male children remained under
their father's authority until his death. They worked alongside their
parents each day. They stayed in their parents' home or, if that
became too crowded, they constructed another building nearby.
It was the same for female children, except that they transferred
to their father-in-law's household when they married. Maturity
brought increased responsibility within households that were characterized by interdependence, rather than independence. Together
they shared the tasks necessary for survival, producing everything
they required. The very structure of their households required that
this commandment apply to children for as long as their parents
remained alive.[14]

The second reason I think this instruction includes care for
aged parents is based on examining how the New Testament treats
the Fifth Word. (Incidentally, these New Testament passages indi-

cate that this Fifth Word has ongoing significance for God's people in the church.) The New Testament contains instructions for children to obey their parents based on this Word (Ephesians 6:1–3; Colossians 3:20). In that same context, fathers are instructed to train and instruct their children in the Lord (Ephesians 6:4). Those two aspects were emphasized in the church tradition of my pre-adult years.

But the New Testament also refers to the third aspect. In one of the less well-known incidents from Jesus' life, Jesus clearly applies the Fifth Word to the situation of adult children relating to their parents. Mark 7:9–13 tells us (Matthew 15:1–9 records the same incident):

> And he said to [the Pharisees and scribes]: "You have a fine way of setting aside the commands of God in order to observe your own traditions! For Moses said, 'Honor your father and your mother,' and, 'Anyone who curses his father or mother must be put to death.' But you say that if a man says to his father or mother: 'Whatever help you might otherwise have received from me is Corban' (that is, a gift devoted to God), then you no longer let him do anything for his father or mother. Thus you nullify the word of God by your tradition that you have handed down. And you do many things like that."

Now, that's not an easy passage for us to understand. We don't know exactly what was involved in the tradition of Corban—especially how it worked that the adult child still seems to have use of this property but it's denied to his parents. We don't know why the property has already passed from the parents to their child—perhaps it reflects an urban, rather than rural, setting. But what is important for our purposes is crystal clear: Jesus thinks the Fifth Word includes caring for aged parents. I'd suggest the passage shows that the Jewish leaders of his time also thought in those terms. Why else would they take such elaborate steps to find a "legal" way to circumvent the commandment's intentions?

And so, I've had the paradigm shift. It's not that the things I was taught in my childhood are now excluded from my understanding of this Word. Rather, this other dimension is now added to it—or added to it more strongly—so that I see this as the prime focus.

THE MORE SPECIFIC COMMANDS

Other laws in the Old Testament that explain how children relate to parents also support the argument that the Fifth Word includes adult children within its intentions. They can also help us think through further how we (or, at least, I) import our culture into our understanding of the text.

As we read other parts of the Pentateuch, we come across other legislative items that instruct people how to relate to parents.

- Exodus 21:15 prohibits attacking parents. The penalty imposed for breaking this law is death.

- Exodus 21:17 and Leviticus 20:9 prohibit cursing parents. Again, the breach of this law incurs the penalty of death.

- Deuteronomy 21:18–21 legislates the procedure for dealing with stubborn and rebellious sons. Yet again, the death penalty is imposed for those declared guilty.

- Deuteronomy 27:16 indicates that anyone[15] who dishonors their parents is cursed.

The biblical narrative contains no examples of these laws being enforced—and, thus, no clues to their interpretation in particular life situations.[16] (Note that in the book of Proverbs, there are comparable warnings against robbing, mocking or cursing parents: Proverbs 19:26; 20:20; 28:24; 30:11, 17.)

Have you ever contemplated what those instructions may have meant for your typical four-year-old Israelite boy? For some reason, he can't get his own way. Rage boils up inside him. He throws a tantrum—lashing out with his arms and fists. His mother, being the closest object (and perhaps also wishing to prevent him harming himself), bears the brunt of this tantrum. She is struck by him. Is he to be executed? To us, that seems a bit excessive (but then, lots of things in the law seem a bit excessive to us—so perhaps we aren't good judges of that). Or perhaps children back then never threw tantrums. Maybe these unfortunate episodes are inventions of modern Western culture.

The point I'm making is that I don't think these regulations were directed at young children. I think it's far more likely they're directed at adults—remembering that adulthood for them began around the age of thirteen. I think this perspective is clearest in relation to the stubborn and rebellious son described in Deuteronomy 21. This isn't a spur-of-the-moment thing. It's not the occasional expression of moody sullenness. It's a settled attitude and disposition of character that's clearly demonstrable. It takes time to develop and manifest these characteristics. He is further described as a profligate and drunkard in verse 20; that is, he pursues a lazy and self-indulgent lifestyle and wastes both the household's and community's precious resources. He's not suitable to be entrusted with the family's inheritance. He threatens the very stability and good order of the village. This is not a young child.

HOW ARE AGED PARENTS HONORED?

Returning now to our main purpose: given that the Fifth Word includes the requirement to care for aged parents, how was that to be done? Were they encouraged to retire with dignity—to sit out their remaining days lounging in shaded deck-chairs on the household roof or gossiping with fellow retirees at the village gate? Those sorts of images simply ignore the reality and harshness of life in ancient Israel.

It's worth highlighting several factors. First, conditions were tough in Israel's rural communities.[17] Work was physically exacting and took its toll on human bodies. They faced many dangers that could result in reduced work capacity or early death. Minor scrapes and cuts could result in serious infection. The steep hillsides that often constituted the workplace environment contributed to accidents. Poor harvests would result in undernourishment. And childbirth was a very risky business; yet birthing many new workers was important for long-term survival. To add to these occupational hazards, invading armies and raiding desert tribes resulted in stolen crops and war casualties.

These all contributed to low life expectancies. That in turn impacted the definition of old age in ancient Israel. Our culture may think old age begins at seventy (it tends to be a shifting target); they thought it began much earlier.[18] Yet, like us, their physical condition on reaching old age varied from person to person. Attaining the status of old age didn't automatically leave one incapable of work. If there was no apparent reason for them to stop work, it seems to me they were unlikely to do so.

Second, the subsistence level of their existence required everyone to contribute whatever they could to the household's survival, including the elderly. It's unlikely that the idea of the elderly ceasing their work for their offspring's survival would have entered their heads. Far less would the elderly dream of using household resources to support a lifestyle of idleness. That would have run counter to the communal nature of their existence and the priority given to household necessities.

Third, if the decline of their bodies did prevent their continued involvement in regular work (such as farming), they could be assigned less strenuous tasks within the household. Taking care of infants so that they survived to become workers was an important task that could free able-bodied adults for the more demanding tasks. Supervising the training of younger children was another essential assignment. Food preparation, mending clothes, and minor household repairs could still be managed. Older men could lead religious functions within the household and perform judicial functions for the community. Thus, the nature of their work may have changed during their later years, but they would have continued to contribute to the household economy.[19]

One other important contribution of the aged was their own person as a cherished "commodity." Jon Berquist describes it well.

> These men and women would have formed a valuable resource for the village, because their great accumulation of knowledge could offer a community significant advantages. Such respected elders operated as a community's institutional memory, having lived through many more life situations than the younger members and thus could share insights and analogies to teach the next generation about the world and to help the village make important decisions.[20]

All this, of course, is not to say that no elderly people became completely incapacitated for work. As noted in the introduction, that's not the subject of this investigation. People who can't work, whatever the reason, are not in the same category as those who embrace the modern concept of retirement. The former stems from necessity, the latter from personal choice.

When older people could no longer work, their children had the responsibility to care for them.[21] Such care included not only providing materially for them, but also personally serving them as required.[22] Gerald Blidstein helpfully sums up the human rationales for valuing this Fifth Word.

> Jewish reflection upon filial responsibility focused on these dimensions of significance: (a) parents are creators, and the recognition of human creators forms a continuum with the recognition of God the creator; (b) the ethical value of gratitude is first encountered in filial thankfulness towards those who gave one being and sustenance; (c) the structures of authority essential to human life are dependent upon the model of filial piety; (d) filial piety is a "natural" component of the humanity of man and his culture.[23]

The closing verses of Ruth (4:14–15) also point to this expectation of caring for aged parents:

> The women said to Naomi: "Praise be to the LORD, who this day has not left you without a kinsman-redeemer. May he become famous throughout Israel! He will renew your life and sustain you in your old age. For your daughter-in-law, who loves you and who is better to you than seven sons, has given him birth."

Jan de Waard and Eugene Albert Nida explain the sense of the phrase the NIV translates "sustain you in your old age."

> Give you security in your old age may also be rendered as "will support you in your old age," "will take care of you in your old age," "will see that you have enough when you are old," or "will take care of you when you are old."[24]

Some other ancient cultures discarded the nonproductive older population, expelling them from their villages. They thought of them as liabilities—people who no longer contributed to the production of the community's resources. Especially when those resources became scarce because of drought or war or pestilence, the older people were forced into the wilderness areas to fend for themselves. Not so in Israel. They were to care for the disadvantaged: the orphan, the widow, the landless foreigner—and even the elderly who could no longer care for themselves.[25]

After reading the above discussion about the meaning of the Fifth Word, one could still suggest that ancient Israel lacked retirement for purely practical reasons—and that these reasons no longer apply to most of us today. Very few of us live in a subsistence economy. Our adult children often don't need our help to sustain their own families (except, perhaps, to provide child-minding services while both parents engage in paid employment). In fact, we usually encourage them to become independent as soon as possible! Unlike the ancient Israelites, many of us may be able to afford to retire voluntarily before we become physically unable to work. Should we permit this option if people have the means?

The answer to that particular question is beyond the scope of this book. Our present task is to determine whether anything in the Scriptures may be used to support the modern concept of retirement. If we fail to find any support for the idea that humans are excused from exercising the God-given privilege of work, there remains the further question of whether we are permitted to structure our economic systems in a way that includes some concept of retirement.

WHAT ABOUT NAOMI?

Having mentioned the book of Ruth, an obvious question to ask is: What about Naomi? After they arrive in Bethlehem, Ruth asks Naomi for permission to glean in the fields (2:2). Naomi grants that permission but doesn't join Ruth in the work. Why not? The text isn't interested in disclosing this information, nor does it draw attention to it. The focus is on Ruth's astounding loyalty to her mother-in-law. She leaves her homeland to accompany Naomi to

Israel (1:16–19). She then provides for her mother-in-law through the work of gleaning (2:2–23). She exemplifies adherence to the Fifth Word, even though she's a foreigner.

It took me a while to track down a commentary that touches on the issue of Naomi's nonwork. That's not really surprising, since the narrative has other concerns. It's only in the context of a study like the present one that anyone is likely to raise the issue. Even then, it's not a passage that quickly springs to mind. It's only because of that reference to old age in Ruth 4:15 that it entered my thoughts.

So is Naomi perhaps retired? First, we should note she's a relatively old woman in that culture. The narrator supplies few time references, yet we are left some clues. By chapter 2, Naomi had two sons who had both grown to maturity and got married. They also both died. It's likely they died soon after their marriages, since they were childless. Ruth 1:4 refers to "ten years"—likely this refers to the sons' total time in Moab, not the length of their marriages. After that, Naomi returns to Bethlehem. So she is at least at the "grandmother" stage of life.[26]

Second, she has recently journeyed home from Moab. This isn't a couple of hours down the freeway in air-conditioned comfort. Given her relatively destitute state, it's unlikely she even had an animal to ride. So it was a lengthy hike through fairly rugged terrain over at least several days with no plush hotels along the route. That she could make such a journey indicates she's still capable of physical labor. But it may be she's still recovering from the trip.

Third, the years and her life's circumstances have taken a heavy toll on Naomi. She gives voice to this in Ruth 1:20–21,

> "Don't call me Naomi," she told them. "Call me Mara, because the Almighty has made my life very bitter. I went away full, but the LORD has brought me back empty. Why call me Naomi? The LORD has afflicted me; the Almighty has brought misfortune upon me."

Now, I don't think we're in a position to psychoanalyze Naomi. That's certainly not the narrator's intention. But it's worth noting there are other factors that may contribute to Naomi not working at this particular time. For example, Frederic Bush asks: "Is it advanced age that keeps her from gleaning with Ruth in the fields, or has she pursued her suffering into the withdrawal of despair?"[27] And Katharine Sakenfeld suggests: "Naomi's response is as brief as possible; she seems still caught up in her grief and bitterness, unable to take any step or assist with any plan for her own survival."[28]

Fourth, there are many gaps in our knowledge. For example, where do these women stay? Did the place need repairs? Was there other work involved in setting up their life in the town? Did Naomi need to concentrate on reestablishing her position in the community? Did she have other responsibilities? Just because she was not gleaning with Ruth doesn't mean she was idle.

It's possible Naomi was in some sense "retired" or resting while her younger daughter-in-law worked for both of them. But, at best, it's an argument from silence, and there are other possible explanations that don't require that she has ceased work.

HAVING CHILDREN TO
PROVIDE FOR OLD AGE

One further matter should be considered. Several scholars indicate that one of the purposes for having children in the ancient world—and for having lots of them—was that in the event you yourself survived to old age, you increased the odds that at least one of them would still be around to provide for you. Victor Matthews, writing about the ancient Near East in general, notes:

> Since the ancient world did not have government programs that attempted to provide for the needs of the aged and the infirm, it fell upon the extended family to take up these duties. One of the chief purposes, therefore, of having children, aside from insuring that there would be an orderly inheritance pattern, was to create care givers for their aging parents. Failure either to conceive children or to raise them to adulthood because of disease, famine or war would have forced the head of the household either to obtain another wife or concubine or to impregnate a slave.[29]

Likewise, S. M. Baugh writes of Greek culture:

> Sons in particular represented the only form of social security available to the Greek couple, for children were expected and in some cases required by law to support their parents in their old age.[30]

And Daniel Block notes that similar concerns existed in ancient Israel—even suggesting that the eldest sons' double portion of the inheritance may have included the responsibility to care for aging parents.[31]

While it's easy for us to interpret this attitude to aged parents in line with our modern concepts of retirement, I don't think it undermines what we've already noted. Like us, people in the ancient world recognized their bodies declined with age. They made adjustments to accommodate these realities of life. They realized they might even reach the point where they could achieve little effective work. As they say, this isn't rocket science. But here's where our individualistic mind-set intrudes. I suspect we tend to think in terms of self-sufficiency—that the aging process brings us to the point where we're forced to acknowledge we're no longer self-sufficient (though personal superannuation savings are even pushing that point further back). They, on the other hand, always knew they weren't self-sufficient. All household members contributed to the group's survival. How they did this varied depending on their stage of life. But to retire from any form of contribution would be totally foreign to them.

SUMMARY

Much more could be said about honoring parents. I'm convinced that God's Fifth Word includes the responsibility for adult children to care for their aged parents, especially those no longer able to care or provide for themselves. Ancient Israelite society acknowledged the aging process. The human body deteriorates and older people have less ability to contribute effective labor to the household economy. At one level, the Fifth Word is similar to God's instructions for the people to care for those who are vulnerable: widows, orphans, and landless foreigners. At another level, the relationship with parents is much closer and involves the interplay of family bonds over a lifetime. This is part of how everyone in the community can enjoy *shalom* together. As they receive God's blessings, so they are to share and enjoy them with the wider community.

Thus a solid argument might perhaps be made that the parents' command included the concept of ceasing productive labor. Yet there is no command for them to stop work or for the adult children to facilitate a cessation of work. Honoring parents requires intervention at the point of their inabilities—not preventing them from continuing to exercise their God-given abilities for the benefit of the household and community.

Again, I think our view of work is skewed. Instead of fully receiving work as one of God's good gifts, we tend to have a love-hate relationship with it. Most people experience both joy and frustration in their work. As mentioned earlier, that's a result of humanity's rebellion against God. As the years of work mount up, most people also experience a growing tiredness or lethargy or accumulated weariness in their work. As we grow older, we tend to view work less as a gift and more as a burden. I think the structure of our culture and the hype about retirement push us strongly in that direction. Perhaps the aging process also contributes, but it doesn't have to be that way. I've met plenty of people still enthusiastic about work well beyond the official retirement age. And I think the overall theology of work presented by the biblical material would question why we would want to cease exercising the privilege.

If we come to the Fifth Word with our culture's perspective—that leisured retirement is the great goal of life—then it's natural we would think caring for aged parents involves ensuring that they have that experience of leisure. But if we come with the view that work is the privilege of serving others for the common good, why would we encourage the aged to forsake that privilege just because they reach a certain age?

But these are modern ponderings. In ancient rural Israel, it wasn't really an option. Their subsistence existence required "all hands on deck." By New Testament times, advances in technology and a greater variety of occupations perhaps gave some the potential to accumulate the wealth needed to "retire." But for the vast majority, having sufficient resources to sustain life remained a constant challenge—made even more difficult by the vast array of Roman and local taxes. Far from dreams of "retirement," many found themselves increasingly in debt with the end result that they were sold into slavery.

13

THE ELDERS AT THE GATE

There's another group in ancient Israel that may have enjoyed a somewhat leisured existence: "the elders at the gate." I don't remember them receiving a prominent place in my childhood Sunday school lessons. They probably got a mention every now and then—but, let's face it, they don't play a conspicuous role in the biblical narrative. That, of course, doesn't stop us forming mental pictures about them.

By my late teenage years, I'd acquired a somewhat romantic image of these guys—though where I got it from I have no idea. These were "retired" gentlemen. They were community leaders who, among other things, formed the local judiciary. They sat around in the public square near the town gate and waited for people to approach them with various legal matters. They gave due consideration to these matters brought before them and rendered legal verdicts. But that consumed just a small portion of their time. Mostly, they pursued their own interests. When no disputants presented themselves, they were free to lounge around, sipping cappuccinos and idly discussing politics.

I even had a culturally sensitive mental image of these elders. After all, I thought, they didn't have fancy courthouses to impress. They didn't wear ornamental clothes to intimidate their legal opponents. They didn't have lawyers to muddy the waters. And they didn't have set court schedules where you had to book a time slot months in advance. They didn't even have full calendars!

These were relatively small local communities where people were usually related to each other. Everyone in the village had a personal relationship with the elders. The aim was to uphold justice and maintain harmony. And when no one approached the elders with a matter requiring decision, they were free to spend their time as they liked. In short, I thought they were semi-retired. Little did I know how much my image was still shaped by my own culture and my perceptions of modern judicial systems!

In thinking through any possible implications that this group of elders may have in relation to retirement, I will focus on three questions. First, who were the elders at the gate? Second, what functions did they perform? Third, what did they do with their time? We could skip straight to the third question but, because of our general ignorance about this group, I think it's helpful to consider it in the broader context raised by the first two questions.

WHO WERE THE ELDERS AT THE GATE?

The Hebrew term translated "elder" has a range of nuances. Sometimes it simply refers to those who are advanced in years— the elderly (for example, Leviticus 19:32). It's descriptive of an age category. However, on other occasions, it designates an official group. The Old Testament identifies several different groups of elders.

Some of these groups seem to operate at a national level. Several descriptive phrases are used, including "elders of the tribes," "elders of Israel," and "elders of the land." It's not clear whether these designate the same basic group or several different levels of leadership. Nor is it clear how much their functions overlapped with those of other officials (for example, judges) who were appointed after the establishment of the monarchy. This group isn't my focus in this chapter, and so for our purposes we can ignore those issues.[1]

Sometimes the Hebrew term may refer to the leadership of a smaller group within Israel. For example, in 2 Kings 19:2 the word is associated with "priests." The NIV translates the phrase as "the leading priests," implying that these older priests exercise a leadership role within the group. But the ESV translates the phrase as "the senior priests," thus leaving some ambiguity as to whether it's descriptive of age or function. This use also isn't my focus in this chapter.

The group I do wish to focus on here is more clearly defined. They are elders who exercise leadership of local communities—the village, town, or city. Sometimes the text identifies them as "the elders at the gate" because that was the location of public business. At other times, the text simply calls them "elders," and the context makes clear that local leadership is intended. They were people appointed by the community to exercise important leadership roles both within and on behalf of the community.

That much is clear. What's not clear to us is how they were appointed. I suspect it had little resemblance to our modern elections for local government. But just as we know the process for electing leaders today, so everyone back then knew how their system operated. Because they knew that, they saw no reason to record it—and thus our current ignorance. It may even be that there was no official "appointment"; simply a tacit recognition that these people demonstrated significant influence within the community.

I should mention that some commentators think all adult men qualified as elders on the basis that the Hebrew term for "elder" derives from the Hebrew word for "beard."[2] But it's more usual to view them as a sub-group of these "bearded" males. Frederic Bush, for example, distinguishes two significant subgroups: the first group, the legal assembly, consisted of all men who occupied their own property; and the second group, the elders, consisted of those within the legal assembly who were appointed to this particular office.[3]

Can we say anything further about the elders? The term itself implies younger people were excluded. The patriarchal societal structure of ancient Israel suggests this group was likely limited to male heads of households (to reiterate what was noted in the last paragraph). And the official nature of the position probably demanded a high level of community respect. The functions of the position would require knowledge of community customs and traditions and an ability to mediate between disputing parties— abilities that come with experience over a number of years. We might also expect that the job description would emphasize wisdom—a characteristic the Bible often associates with older generations (while also recognizing that age in itself does not guarantee wisdom). Clearly, that still leaves many unanswered questions, but it should prove sufficient for our current purposes.

WHAT WERE THE RESPONSIBILITIES OF THE ELDERS?

Part of the reason for our unanswered questions is our tendency to focus on aspects in which the Bible shows no interest—like the subject of retirement! In relation to these elders, the Bible focuses more on their functions than their appointment. From this I infer that, at least in this instance, God allows his people to decide how the appointments are made. As long as the candidates are suitably qualified for the task, it doesn't matter how they're selected. That's not always the case. In the case of the priests and Levites, God is very specific as to who is appointed—but not with the elders.

Even when we turn to the elders' functions, we find that many of them arise more from tradition than from specific statutes legislated by God. As we today would categorize them, the main areas of responsibility were hearing criminal proceedings, adjudicating disputes, notarizing business transactions, and representing the community in intercommunity matters. They may also have performed some cultic duties and given general oversight to the community. John Wilch notes:

> The elders were responsible for the theological integrity of the community which was based on the LORD's covenant and their fidelity to it. They also worked for reconciliation of social rifts and for social and economic solidarity.[4]

On five occasions, the biblical law speaks of the involvement of the elders. First, "cities of refuge" were established for the protection of those who accidentally killed a person. The elders of the dead person's village were responsible to determine whether it truly was accidental—and, if not, to ensure justice was done (Deuteronomy 19:1–13). The elders of the city of refuge were also responsible to hear the killer's case when he first arrived at the gate of their city (Joshua 20:4). In terms of modern classifications, this would fit neatly into our concept of criminal law.

Second, the law recognized that some murders would remain unsolved (and the discovery of new forensic tests to solve these cold cases was not anticipated any century soon!). The elders of the town nearest the location of the body were responsible to declare their ignorance of the identity of the killer and to make atonement for the wrongful death on behalf of the people (Deuteronomy 21:1–9). This cultic duty is foreign to our modern practices.

Third, we mentioned the law regarding the rebellious son in the last chapter. In this case, the parents were to present the charges against such a son before the elders at the gate of their town. The actions of this son would impact the household's economic viability and would also likely influence the prosperity of the wider community. Thus the matter was handled at the public level (Deuteronomy 21:18–21). Maybe this could be viewed as a form of embezzlement or theft—but more likely we'd struggle to categorize it within our criminal law. Rather, we'd consider it a more private matter (unless public damage was proven)—perhaps a situation to be solved by counseling.

Fourth, the law dealing with a groom's accusation that he found his bride not to be a virgin also involved the elders at the gate. They were to hear the accusation, examine evidence brought by the parents, and make their adjudication (Deuteronomy 22:13–21). This whole concept is foreign to expectations within modern Western culture. We live the other side of the sexual revolution. It also reflects a different emphasis on the place of marriage within the community. As Daniel Block writes,

> In a kinship-based society, healthy marriages are fundamental to the health of the community, linking families that have negotiated the marital agreement in the first place. Because the divorce sought by this man and the rumors he has spread have the potential to divide the community, elders representing the extended family units must intervene.[5]

Fifth, the refusal of a man to marry his dead brother's wife and produce a son for his dead brother was to be taken, by the widow, to the elders at the town gate. Their role was to persuade her brother-in-law to fulfill his family duty and, if that proved unsuccessful, to witness his identification as being "unsandaled" (Deuteronomy 25:5–10). This too is completely foreign within our modern Western context. Its purpose was to maintain the family line.

Outside its law books, the Bible contains several hints to other functions performed by the elders. The town gate (where the elders conducted their business) was to be a place of justice. Unfortunately, this was not always the case. In his day, Amos complains that, because of bribery, the elders "turn away the needy in the gate." God strongly objects to this. And so Amos encourages them instead to "establish justice in the gate" (5:11–15, ESV; the NIV uses the word *courts*—a word that brings some unhelpful modern connotations). Likewise, Zechariah later exhorts his audience to "render in your gates judgments that are true and make for peace" (8:14–17, ESV; again the NIV translates this as "courts"). I think there's also a sense of this "elder" function in the way Absalom conducts his conspiracy against David at the town gate (2 Samuel 15:1–4). At that traditional location, he intercepts those coming to the king for justice and promises to provide more equitable solutions.

There are also hints of the elders' involvement as witnesses to legal or business transactions. On the death of his wife Sarah, Abraham bargains at the city gate for the purchase of a burial plot (Genesis 23:3–20). This, of course, was before Israel's existence as a nation. Admittedly, the passage makes no reference to elders. Yet "the gate of the city" is mentioned twice (verses 10 and 18). This was the traditional place for conducting property transactions. The crucial factor is the necessity for witnesses. In the book of Ruth, Boaz redeems all the property of Elimelech, Kilion, and Mahlon at Bethlehem's town gate. He gathers ten elders for the occasion. Their specific function is to act as witnesses (Ruth 4:1–12).

In modern terms, one could describe the elders' role as the provision of a complete legal service covering many of the tasks performed by judges and lawyers today. But there was more to it than that. They functioned as community leaders who both protected and promoted the community's welfare. At the local level, they were both government and judiciary. They worked (or were supposed to work) to advance the community's *shalom*—both its prosperity and its harmony.

Now, I confess that I've gone into more detail here than was strictly necessary for our current purposes. Why? Because I think we tend to approach this whole subject with our modern categories and impose them on how we view these elders and their roles. I know I tend to do that.

For example, I tend to view "the system" as somewhat distant. I don't personally know any politicians and judges. I know they perform important functions and, generally, I'm grateful they do those things (though I am occasionally known to voice the odd complaint about how politicians run the country). I realize that their work ensures a stable environment for my own life—an environment that provides a high level of predictability for my own plans and decisions. But there's still a sense in which it's very remote from my day-to-day activities.

Of course, there will be times when I encounter difficulties. A purchase may fail to meet my expectations. A dispute may arise with someone in my community (or beyond). I may fall victim to some criminal activity. At those times, I expect the "system" to come to my aid. I can take my adversary to court and have my individual rights upheld. But I still won't have a personal relationship with the judge. Indeed, the judge will have no interest in my personal life except as it pertains to the circumstances of the legal matter before the court.

That wasn't the case in an ancient Israelite town. In their small communities, they all knew one another. They all certainly knew the elders personally. They worked together for the survival and prosperity of their town. When disputes arose, it was important they be resolved in a just manner. Certainly, unjust decisions were unacceptable. But justice wasn't the ultimate goal. That was community well-being and harmony. Today, I may take some company to court in relation to the faulty goods they sold me, with the full intention of never doing business with them again no matter what the outcome of the judicial process. I hope to receive justice from the court, but the relationship (as impersonal as it was) will remain broken. The elders' function in ancient Israel was to achieve justice in a way that promoted good relationships in the community.

My individualistic mind-set shapes my interpretation. For me, justice is about protecting my individual rights—perhaps even using "the system" for my individual benefit. I've even been known to complain about contributing my fair share to the community via the taxation system. For the Israelites, justice includes promoting community harmony and well-being. That would, of course, have benefits for each individual—but not at the expense of other individuals (except to the extent that their wrongdoing requires redress). The Israelites functioned with a communal, rather than an adversarial, mind-set. At least, that was the ideal—though the sharp rebukes of Israel's later prophets demonstrate they increasingly failed to maintain that ideal.

HOW DID THE ELDERS SPEND THEIR TIME?

Now with all that background we come to the central question for our current purposes: What did the elders do all day? Did they, for example, have a backlog of cases that they slowly worked through while people waited in a queue? Or, as in my teenage romantic image, were cases fairly rare? Did they just sit around at the gates on the off-chance that other people would come along? Or were some seasons busier than others?

At one level, of course, we could argue that their role as elders was still a job, no matter how few cases they dealt with each week. Sure, it didn't involve the back-breaking manual labor of farming. But it required knowledge and wisdom acquired through years of life experience. And it included the stress of dealing with strained relationships on a regular basis. It was an important task that contributed significantly to the community's overall well-being. We might imagine that it would be like someone today transitioning from the hands-on work of a blue-collar job into a management position.

But I think that would still be an inaccurate perception of the elders' position. Look at the example of Boaz in Ruth 4. He has two interrelated legal matters: the buying (redemption) of Elimelech's land[6] and the production of an heir for that land through Elimelech's daughter-in-law Ruth. In reality, these matters are between Boaz and the unnamed kinsman-redeemer who has a legal right to redeem the land and marry Ruth. It's not a lawsuit as such—but because it involves property Boaz wants the elders to witness the transaction. The narrator introduces the scene:

Meanwhile Boaz went up to the town gate and sat there. When the kinsman-redeemer he had mentioned came along, Boaz said, "Come over here, my friend, and sit down." So he went over and sat down. Boaz took ten of the elders of the town and said, "Sit here," and they did so.

What image comes to mind? Boaz has a legal matter and so he heads off to court (the town gate). He arrives early (before the elders arrive) and sits down to wait. While he waits, the other party in this case (the kinsman-redeemer) just happens to walk by. Boaz thinks this must be divine providence—with both parties present, he should be able to finalize the matter in one session. He calls the guy over and asks him to wait for the elders to take their place at their judicial bench. I don't think that visualizes the real scenario.

What image should come to mind? Boaz has a legal matter and so he heads off to court (the town gate). He deliberately arrives early because he wants to catch people on their way to work. He knows everyone must pass through the town gate as they head to their fields for their day's work. The first one he catches is the kinsman-redeemer. He then stops ten elders on their way to work in their fields. Other people also stop (see verse 11). They sense a legal case in the wind and their curiosity takes over. After all, it's a relatively small kinship-based community, and what goes on here will likely impact them all. No point waiting to read about it in tomorrow's newspaper!

For these community elder statesmen, their function as elders is not a transition into a new profession. Nor is it some sort of halfway cutting back in preparation for full retirement. Rather, it's an extra responsibility incorporated into their already full days—and there's no indication that it comes with a public service salary.

Thus it seems to me that the role of these elders in the gates has no connection with any notion of retirement. Unlike today, when the aged are expected to yield leadership positions to up-and-coming younger workers, this particular responsibility was reserved for those with the most life experience.

ELDERS IN THE NEW TESTAMENT

At this point, it seems appropriate to mention references to "elders" in the New Testament. Clearly, there are some differences. These New Testament elders are responsible for churches, not towns. These elders operate in a variety of cultural situations across the Roman Empire, not just in Israel. These elders are not part of the official legal system. However, there also remain similarities. It's likely that the position and role of church elders originated from the structure of Jewish synagogues, which had connections with the earlier elders at the city gate. And the function of church elders included maintaining the overall order, discipline, and harmony of the local church. The qualifications required of potential candidates for eldership in the church (1 Timothy 3:1–7; Titus 1:5–9) overlap with those noted above.

Again, the Bible doesn't answer all the questions we have about church elders. In New Testament times, it's likely this role was usually voluntary—that is, unpaid. As with the elders at the gate, it was a task people undertook in addition to their regular occupations. In this regard, it's like most voluntary organizations today in which those in leadership exercise their roles both in an honorary capacity and in their spare time.

There are, however, indications in the New Testament that at least some elders received financial remuneration. First Timothy 5:17–18 instructs:

> The elders who direct the affairs of the church well are worthy of double honor, especially those whose work is preaching and teaching. For the Scripture says, "Do not muzzle the ox while it is treading out the grain," and "The worker deserves his wages."

Several questions arise concerning the interpretation of this text. For example, is there a connection between these elders and the widows in the preceding verses (for example, is this simply the male equivalent of that group?)? What's the relationship between the elders in this passage and the overseers in 1 Timothy 3:1–7? Does Paul here distinguish between different groups of elders (for example, elders generally, those who serve well and those who preach and teach)?

Did all elders receive remuneration or only a subgroup? What's the nature of the remuneration (for example, is it more like a salary or an honorarium?)? William Mounce, in his commentary on the Pastoral Epistles, provides a useful discussion of most of these issues.[7]

While that discussion is interesting, for our purposes I think it's unnecessary to explore it at present. Whoever these elders are, the context and the supporting quotes clearly indicate that any payment being made in this instance is not a pension to support those too frail to continue working, or those looking for a life of leisure. It's payment for labor—and the Greek verb used implies a measure of hard work involving difficulties and troubles. We can envisage that the elders of the early churches had numerous responsibilities (which they often carried out in societies that were hostile to their Christian community).

SUMMARY

There are two main reasons why I think the existence of elders at the gate (and also church elders in the New Testament) does not provide justification for the concept of retirement.

First, this was an additional responsibility undertaken. People didn't "retire" into these positions. Rather, because of their recognized abilities and overall standing in the community, in addition to their normal work, they were entrusted with this extra task. They served the community in this way in order to maintain its overall well-being.

Second, this was a task. It was not idleness or leisure or retirement. It involved work. The work may have been significantly different from what was classed as normal labor, but it was still work (and, in the case of church elders, may have attracted some form of remuneration). Indeed, the task could be quite taxing—especially where significant disputes occurred. Overall, it was important toil performed for the good of the community.

All of this suggests that the biblical ideal for the aged was much more active, engaged, and responsible to the community than the modern practice of retirement encourages us to be.

14

BITS AND PIECES

As I noted at the outset, one of the dangers with looking for "proof-texts" is that we may fail to be comprehensive. In the previous chapters, I've dealt with several passages that may be thought to support the concept of retirement. I've indicated why I think those passages fail to do so. Instead, we've seen that the biblical view of aging assumes that the elderly are valuable members of the community, precisely because they continue to work as part of the family and to take on responsibilities within the community. We've also seen that the Mosaic Law and Israelite culture in general had a practical approach to aging that still upheld the God-ordained value of work. Based on the passages we've surveyed, we can see a picture emerging: the aged continue to work to serve their communities and to promote *shalom*. The community in turn supports and honors its aged members when they are no longer able to work. The modern practice of retirement doesn't seem to be consistent with this biblical picture.

But I haven't scoured the Bible with the proverbial fine-tooth comb to ensure I've found all the possible potential passages. Besides the obvious possibility of laziness, one reason I haven't done that is because of the amazing ingenuity (and perhaps duplicity) of the human mind. After years of listening to sermons and discussions among Christians, I've reached the conclusion that if we ignore the context and apply our creative imaginative abilities, then we can enlist any text in the service of our pet theories. There are probably passages some people think are relevant that I've failed to include in the detailed discussion so far.

Some of those passages are in this chapter. I've included them here for the sake of completeness. There are two main reasons why they didn't get their own chapter. Some don't add any further justification for the concept of retirement beyond what is suggested by the earlier passages. Others don't appear to be prime contenders on which to base a serious case for retirement.

JESUS AND THE AGE OF FIFTY YEARS OLD

One such text is John 8:57. It's certainly not one that automatically came to my mind when I started writing on retirement. Even after thinking about this subject for several years, I hadn't come across a reference to this text. The context is a discussion between Jesus and the Jews. Their conversation goes back and forth, with various accusations being thrown around. Toward the end, Jesus says: "Your father Abraham rejoiced at the thought of seeing my day; he saw it and was glad." To this, the Jews respond: "You are not yet fifty years old and you have seen Abraham!" My wife was listening to a sermon on this passage and the preacher commented in passing that the Jews picked this figure because it was the age of entering inactivity.

Personally, I thought they picked that figure for two reasons: first, it was clear to everyone that Jesus was not yet fifty; and second, fifty is fairly minuscule when compared with the two thousand years that had floated by since Abraham's death. They interpreted Jesus' words as a claim to have rubbed shoulders with Abraham and found a witty way of pointing out the obvious ridiculousness of his claim. The figure of fifty isn't particularly significant—sixty or seventy or one hundred would have done just as well. I doubt I even bothered checking it out when I preached on this passage; it seems such a minor point in a lengthy and detailed dialogue.

But now that my attention was drawn to it, I thought I should check it out in the commentaries. I discovered an interesting array of suggestions. After stating that it's unlikely to be a reference to Jesus' actual age, Leon Morris notes:

> More probably fifty is thought of as a good age, possibly as the completion of a man's working life and the entrance on to old age. It is the age at which the Levites completed their service (Num. 4:3). Or it may be meant to contrast one short life-time with the centuries that had elapsed since Abraham's day.[1]

George Beasley-Murray similarly writes, "It simply indicates the common view of the end of a man's working life."[2]

Perhaps one of these was the preacher's source—but, unfortunately, the only support either provides for this claim is the "retirement age" for Levites (which we've covered in chapter 9). While that may be consistent with the broader claim they make, it's insufficient to prove it as general practice.

Part of this discussion goes back to one of the early Christians—a church father by the name of Irenaeus. He uses this text to claim that Jesus was nearly fifty at the time—and that meant he was close to the final stage of human life. I think it's worth quoting him at some length to get a feel for his argument.

> Now, such language is fittingly applied to one who has already passed the age of forty, without having as yet reached his fiftieth year, yet is not far from this latter period. But to one who is only thirty years old it would unquestionably be said, "Thou art not yet forty years old." For those who wished to convict Him of falsehood would certainly not extend the number of His years far beyond the age which they saw He had attained; but they mentioned a period near His real age, whether they had truly ascertained this out of the entry in the public register, or simply made a conjecture from what they observed that He was above forty years old, and that He certainly was not one of only thirty years of age.[3]

It's important to understand why Irenaeus argues this way and why he thinks it's significant that Jesus was older than the generally accepted tradition.

> For He came to save all through means of Himself—all, I say, who through Him are born again to God—infants, and children, and boys, and youths, and old men. He therefore passed through every age, becoming an infant for infants, thus sanctifying infants; a child for children, thus sanctifying those who are of this age, being at the same time made to them an example of piety, righteousness, and submission; a youth for youths, becoming an example to youths, and thus sanctifying them for the Lord. So likewise He was an old man for old men, that He might be a perfect Master for all, not merely as respects the setting forth of the truth, but also as regards

age, sanctifying at the same time the aged also, and becoming an example to them likewise.[4]

For Irenaeus, it's important that Jesus pass through every stage of life if he is effectively to save people of all ages. How Irenaeus interpreted this text was driven by the theological point he wished to establish. Thus, for him, Jesus must enter old age, not because this is a period of inactivity that follows an active life, but because it's the final recognized stage of life. For Irenaeus, old age (as opposed to youth and middle age) begins around fifty. The issue of whether or not that involves ceasing work isn't part of his picture. Further, for Irenaeus, it's also the age at which one becomes a full "Master" or teacher—again, not a position of inactivity.

Very few agree with the chronology of Jesus' life presented by Irenaeus. Rather, most follow the traditional chronology that Jesus suffered death in his mid-thirties after a three-year ministry. Thus most modern interpreters (rightly, in my opinion) reject Irenaeus's proposal that Jesus had to pass through every stage of life in order to save people from every stage of life. Yet it seems, for some at least, that the link Irenaeus made between the Jews' reference to the age of fifty and the onset of old age persists.

To be fair, usually that link is not based solely on Irenaeus. Craig Keener provides an extensive list of possible reasons why the Pharisees may have selected this age in their remark to Jesus.

> When Jesus' adversaries note that Jesus is not yet fifty, this observation does not suggest that he looked nearly fifty. Fifty may be a round number for a period very short compared with how long before Abraham had lived, or a way of saying, "You are not yet an old man," so how could you have been around for two thousand years? Perhaps most importantly, in addition to emphasizing the chronological impossibility, it provides Jewish leaders a way to put Jesus in his place. Many in the Greek world considered fifty an ideal age for ruling; many Jewish offices also required a person to be at least fifty years of age, though there were exceptions. Thus, when one assumed a prominent position around the age of thirty, this apparent breach of seniority would arouse envy. . . . His opponents think that Jesus is too young to have seen Abraham, but they are probably also annoyed by his claims to authority despite his relative youth![5]

He provides supporting references, many from ancient times, for each point.

Certainly, Keener presents a plausible scenario. He may well be right. However, for our purposes, we don't need to decide why they picked the age of fifty. For none of the possible reasons Keener mentions suggests they were talking about a form of retirement or inactivity. To the ancients, fifty may well have been a significant milestone—but it doesn't correspond to what we associate with turning sixty. That's reading our culture back into their context. For them, based on Keener's additional reason, this milestone meant they were finally eligible to be leaders.

In itself, the text has nothing to do with work. It may reflect a tradition that fifty was a significant milestone in a person's life—but it doesn't define the nature of that milestone. It's possible that Marshall and Beasley-Murray are right when they claim that this milestone began a period of inactivity, but I have found no evidence to support their claim. Thus I think there is nothing here to alter my earlier conclusions about either the significance or the experience of old age in the ancient world.

THE ELDERLY IN THE STREETS

Another biblical text that may appear to suggest some form of vision for retirement occurs within Zechariah's image of Jerusalem's future. He ministered in the renewed Jerusalem after the exile—except that at his time, Jerusalem still didn't really look renewed. Some Israelites had returned to the land, but far from all of them. The group that did return found life difficult. Jerusalem and its surrounds were underpopulated. Many struggled to survive. It didn't live up to the expectations aroused by prophets such as Isaiah, Jeremiah, and Ezekiel. In that situation, Zechariah speaks of a future when:

> Once again men and women of ripe old age will sit in the streets of Jerusalem, each with cane in hand because of his age. The city streets will be filled with boys and girls playing there. (8:4–5)

The overall message is clear: Jerusalem will prosper and enjoy peaceful times. Here, the elderly and the young represent the two extremes of human existence. The technical term for this literary device is a merism—using the two extremes to represent the whole. It's a way of saying that Jerusalem (and presumably its surrounds) will be well populated and include the whole range of ages. The elderly and the young also represent two vulnerable groups in a community. The fact that they're in the streets (or open spaces) indicates a measure of peace and security. These two groups aren't threatened—either externally by invading armies, or internally by crime and corruption. Further, the elderly and the young also represent two of the physically weaker groups in a community. The fact that they appear to be "idle" suggests a measure of prosperity and perhaps leisure.

Zechariah pictures better times ahead. He does so with images that contrast with those used to describe the destruction of Jerusalem by the Babylonians. Then, because of widespread death and devastation, there was weeping (for example, see Lamentations 2:10–12); in the future, because the situation will be completely reversed, there will be rejoicing. It also contrasts with the returned exiles' current subsistence struggle for survival. In effect, God promises to give his people *shalom*—peace and prosperity, abundance and protection. They'll live to a ripe old age and enjoy the harmony of a secure community.

Is this a picture of retirement? Perhaps. I confess that my mind automatically moves in that direction when I read this passage—my default position because of my cultural upbringing. And I'm not alone in that. One commentary puts it this way:

> This passage shows men and women not at work. In an agrarian society, such a situation could only represent, whether in a city or on a farm, the existence of a healthy and stable economy whereby the senior citizens are relieved of the necessity of contributing substantially to subsistence tasks. . . . Older people will be released from the demands of productive labor and will have the leisure to gather in a public place. . . .
>
> Their leisure to sit in social gatherings in public places indicates that the normal constraints of the Palestinian economy which required

at least some contributive labor both from the very old and the very young have been removed.[6]

That's certainly a coherent, culturally sensitive interpretation. It may well be correct.

But there are other possibilities. First, what's the status of these old people? They represent one end of the spectrum of human life, and Zechariah's image deliberately pushes them toward the extreme of that end: they use canes because of their advanced age. They suffer at least some of the disabilities associated with age. Perhaps (I admit this is conjecture—but because of its brevity so are most things written about this passage) these people are now incapable of working in the fields or of putting in a full day's work. Maybe, with their canes, it even takes them too long to walk to the fields. This may be a case of forced inactivity rather than voluntary "retirement."

Second, what's the age of these children? We're not told. Are they nine- and ten-year-olds letting off steam after a day cooped up in classes? Or are they two- and three-year-olds taking their caregivers to Playgroup? Perhaps these old people are actually working—doing the work of caring for children still too young to start their farming careers. That would release those capable of greater physical exertion (such as young mothers) to work in the fields.

Third, what's the timing of this picture? For example, one older commentator presents this as an image of day's end:

> The image here presented is one of great force and beauty. The city rises before us as the glow of sunset begins to steal over Olivet, and the lengthening shadows begin to warn the laborer home. The streets are not silent or deserted, as they have hitherto been, but there sits the old man gazing on the scenes of peaceful beauty before him, while the aged companion of his earlier years sits by his side, to enjoy with him the freshening breeze that comes cool and sweet from the distant sea, while before them and around them are the merry shout, the joyous glee, and glad gambols of happy childhood, whose ringing echoes mingle sweetly with the tinkle of the bells and the lowing and bleating of the flocks that come softly from the hills as they hie them homeward to the nightly fold. There is an exquisite beauty in this picture that would strike a Jewish mind with peculiar force, to which the promise of old age and posterity was one of the richest that could be made.[7]

I don't envisage Zechariah's scene as picturing the end of the day, but can I definitively exclude that as a possibility? Alternatively, is there anything in the passage that would exclude someone suggesting that Zechariah here presents a scene from a typical future Sabbath or future feast day?

The main point I wish to make about this passage is that Zechariah provides an image that portrays an idyllic future. He doesn't intend it to be interpreted in isolation from Israel's past. The future he pictures contrasts with earlier images of destruction and insecurity and scarcity—images associated with the exile. The future he pictures reaffirms God's earlier promises to Israel—especially promises of peace and security in the land. Unfortunately, the image of an idyllic lifestyle that we already have fixed in our minds influences how we interpret Zechariah's words. If our image highlights idleness and leisure, that's what we'll likely see in Zechariah 8:4–5. But if our image values both work and enjoying the fruits of God's creation, it's equally possible to see that in the passage.

Let me put it another way. If you think the Bible's overall trajectory heads toward *inactive* rest in God's eternal kingdom, then that's most likely what you'll see in this passage. After all, this passage looks eschatological. If the eschatological goal is the cessation of human work, then it's not hard to interpret this as an idyllic picture of that goal—as long as you don't ask what the rest of the population is doing. If, on the other hand, you think the Bible's overall trajectory heads toward *active* rest (an ongoing enjoyment of God's good creation that includes human work) in God's eternal kingdom, then it's also not hard to interpret this as an idyllic picture of that goal—a picture of security and harmony.

SUMMARY

Let me remind you what we've covered in terms of texts that may be thought to support some concept of retirement.

- The concept of God's rest and what it means for us to enter that rest.

- The whole range of Sabbatical legislation.
- The requirement that the Levites "retire" from active service at age fifty.
- The reduced values placed on redeeming people over the age of sixty.
- Paul's instructions to Timothy not to enroll widows on the church list before they turn sixty.
- The command for children to honor their parents by caring for them in their old age.
- The concept of elders at the gate.
- The negative comments about work in Ecclesiastes.
- The Jews' comment about Jesus not having reached age fifty.
- Zechariah's image of the future that pictures old people sitting peacefully in the streets of Jerusalem.

In each case, I've argued there is insufficient evidence to justify a concept of retirement from the biblical text. That is, I don't think these passages provide a reason to overturn the Bible's presumption in favor of human work. Not only was retirement not available in the cultures in which the Bible was written, but God's people were taught to value the work of the elderly and to appreciate their ongoing contribution to the community. Thus, if we adopt our society's concept of retirement, then I think we fail to fulfill the task God entrusts to us. In doing so, it appears to me that we adopt a cultural value that's contrary to God's word.

15

HINTS IN THE OTHER DIRECTION

Having surveyed a range of biblical texts that could perhaps be used to support a concept of retirement, it's worth approaching the issue from the other direction. Are there texts that could be used to argue against retirement? Does the Bible have anything direct to say about the elderly continuing to work?

As noted at the outset, I believe the Bible's theology of work is such that the onus of proof falls on those who wish to justify retirement. Thus I think our main focus should remain on restoring our appreciation for the goodness of God's gift of work (within the context of the goodness of all his gifts in creation). Still, other biblical material may support that conclusion.

THOSE WHO DON'T RETIRE

One fairly obvious area to note is the variety of biblical characters who "die in the saddle" having reached an advanced age. Moses is the first such leader who comes to mind. According to Deuteronomy 34:7, he died when he was one hundred and twenty. He continues in his role as Israel's leader and prophet until the time God removes him from their presence (in fairness, it should also be noted that he didn't commence this role until age eighty). The text indicates that "his eyes were not weak, nor his strength gone"—in other words, that his abilities weren't diminished by the usual deteriorations associated with old age. Moses' successor Joshua has a similar story—he dies at the age of one hundred and ten (Joshua 24:29). He also continues in his role as Israel's leader until the time of his death. Like Moses, toward the close of his life, he delivers a stirring challenge for Israel to remain faithful to God after his departure. Later in Israel's history, the judge Gideon is said to have "died at a good old age" (Judges 8:32)—yet not only is that a vague expression, it's also unclear whether he continued to exercise any leadership role in the nation after his defeat of the Midianites. Perhaps he simply lived off the spoils of war.

Samuel facilitates Israel's transition to rule by kings. At one level, Samuel "retires" after Saul's appointment as king (1 Samuel 12); yet the text makes plain that he continues to exercise a prophetic ministry within Israel until the time of his death, although we're not told how old he was at that time.

Of King David it's also said he "died at a good old age, having enjoyed long life, wealth and honor." We're not told David's age at his accession to the throne but, given the length of his reign, it's unlikely he was under sixty at his death. He continued his work as king until he died—even if the latter part of his reign proved somewhat ineffective.

Later on, the books of Kings record the reigns of the various monarchs of Judah and Israel. While we're always told the length of their reigns, their ages at death make it into the text less often (though Chronicles enables us to calculate the ages of the kings of Judah). We may note two main things: first, all of these kings remain in office until death (except those taken off into exile); and second, some have co-regencies toward the end of their reign—for example, Azariah, because of his leprosy (2 Kings 15:5). Further, the priest Jehoiada, who orchestrated Joash becoming king, continued in an active role and died at age one hundred and thirty (2 Chronicles 24:16).

At first glance, that's an impressive list—but it must be quickly admitted that it has significant limitations. It's a very select group. They're all leaders. Some of them may have begun life as common farmers, but they left the rigors of that lifestyle behind when they assumed leadership. This cuts both ways. On the one hand, their leadership position often brought privileges that resulted in longer lives (although being king during periods of war could also reduce one's longevity!). The point is that, on average, these people lived longer than the ordinary Israelite and thus are more likely to provide possible examples of those who "retire." On the other hand, this isn't your average Israelite running the family farm. There may be reasons why leaders don't "retire" that don't apply to ordinary Israelites. On the positive side, perhaps they're so invaluable as leaders that others encourage them to continue their work as long as possible. On the more negative side, perhaps the reason for their working so late in life was less godly. Perhaps people in power don't like relinquishing their sense of control. Maybe too many problems arise for the new leader if the old leader is still floating around behind the scenes (if they're sufficiently humble to even remain behind the scenes). Perhaps leadership in the Bible is simply a different category of "work" altogether—something that's more of a role rather than "real work."

Thus, while these leaders provide solid examples of those who continued to work during their senior years, it's also relatively easy to build a case that this list of examples should not be taken as the general norm.

AN OPPORTUNITY MISSED

A second possibility relies on an argument from silence—a place in the text where the writer failed to take advantage of a good opportunity to refer to exceptions to the expectation that people work. Because it is an argument from silence, it can't constitute proof. At best, it provides only corroborating evidence.

Some Christians in the Thessalonian church apparently chose not to work (1 Thessalonians 4:11–12; 5:14; 2 Thessalonians 3:6–15). The interpretation I heard during my youth linked this action (or should that be inaction?) to expectations regarding Jesus' imminent return. After all, their misunderstanding on this subject is a major concern in Paul's correspondence with this church. These nonworkers reasoned, so the argument went, along these lines:

If Jesus is coming back this week (or this month, or this year), why bother working? That's a waste of time and effort. Instead, why not rather waste time sitting around waiting?

Okay, they probably didn't ask that last question—but perhaps they should have! Paul responded by telling them to get back to work—in line, I believe, with the Bible's presumption that humans are expected to work. He doesn't want them sponging off their fellow Christians. Not only is that unloving, it's also a terrible witness to the wider community.

More recently, I've learned of other proposed backgrounds to Paul's instructions. Ben Witherington, for example, argues that the ethical issue (their failure to work) was completely separate from the theological issue (the timing of Jesus' return and its implications). He proposes that the primary problem involves the entanglement of these young Christians in patron/client relationships. Paul's solution remains the same (it's difficult to sidestep his quite explicit instructions), but the rationale now includes additional features connected with the potential compromises associated with patron/client relationships.[1]

They are two very different proposed backgrounds—and they aren't the only possibilities. The choice of background will significantly impact our overall interpretation of the passage. Yet whatever the background, it's difficult to avoid concluding that Paul wants everyone to work. He gives clear instructions to that end. He commends his own example (working to support his gospel ministry among them) as worth imitating. He doesn't appear to admit any exceptions—other than that he did have the right to be financially supported in his mission work (a right he didn't exercise while preaching the gospel to them).

Consider some of the potential exceptions he doesn't highlight. These are the things he could have said but didn't.

- "The contemplative life is the Greek ideal. If you can achieve that without sponging off others, then that's a good goal to have." (As an aside, it's worth considering whether Paul would think something the world values could ever automatically qualify as a Christian goal. Didn't he write something about being transformed by God's word rather than allowing the world to squeeze us into its mold?)

- "Leisure and idleness are our future existence in God's kingdom—that's the goal we've set our eyes on that directs our current lives." (I don't think Paul thinks that is the goal, but those who wish to argue for retirement may think so.) "If you can accumulate enough possessions and reach that state ahead of time, then go for it. Just make sure you're not achieving that goal by an improper dependence on others."

- "Everyone should work as normal until you reach the generally accepted age for stopping. When you reach that age, you can follow the norms of our culture (even if it means putting aside the norms of God's kingdom!)."

He doesn't write anything that hints at any of those options. He doesn't even write anything about the comparative values of work and rest. There is, for example, no suggestion about pushing for a five-day work week.

Now, to be fair, Paul is not here writing a complete theology of work and rest. For example, he makes no reference to the rest we need because of our human finiteness, but I don't think he expects these Christians to forego sleep. And there are all sorts of other reasons why Paul may not have included the "potential exceptions" suggested above. This is the inherent weakness in arguments from silence: they argue from what's not in the text rather than what is in it. Maybe Paul wrote in a hurry and only emphasized the basics. Perhaps he simply focused on the problem at hand and didn't think about exceptions. Maybe the exceptions were generally well known and so he didn't have to spell them out (after all, he doesn't say anything about those unable to work because of disability). But it's hard to escape the overall impression that Paul expected everyone to involve themselves with work.[2]

THE SILENCE OF THE SABBATH

A third possibility relies on another argument from silence. We examined the Sabbatical legislation earlier. This legislation includes the instructions to stop work every seventh day, to let the land be fallow every seventh year, and to celebrate the Jubilee after seven cycles of seven years. Each of those instructions limits work in some way. They thus show that work is not the be-all-and-end-all of life. Work in itself isn't the purpose of life.

Earlier, I disagreed with a link that Walter Harrelson draws between the Fourth and Fifth Words—as humans require weekly rest from their toil, so they also need a "sabbath" rest when their productive years finish.[3] This illustrates that we intuitively feel retirement should somehow be connected with this Sabbatical legislation. And so, to us, it perhaps seems unusual that we don't have any command to that effect. We can imagine how it might fit into the law. "Once you reach your personal Jubilee, you can have a permanent Sabbath." Or "Work for the first six decades of your life, but in your seventh decade you must take a sabbatical—and you don't need to return to work after that." There's nothing remotely like that in Israel's legal code.

A SHORT RETIREMENT

Consider a fourth possibility. It seems to me that the guy in the Bible who comes closest to our concept of retirement is the rich fool in Jesus' parable (Luke 12:13–21). Maybe it should be renamed the Parable of the Superannuated Retiree! This guy gets his superannuation scheme solidly in place—in the form of big barns filled with grain and other goods. Then he decides to sit back for a few years—to "take life easy; eat, drink and be merry." To be fair, he doesn't ignore the possibility that he may need to return to work because his retirement savings may run out before he dies—but that's not part of his immediate future.

The parallel isn't perfect. And, of course, he's never even heard of retirement—although he may be aware of the Greek preference for leisure. In addition, he's just a fictional character. But overall, he looks pretty close to the great Australian dream of retirement.

His retirement doesn't last long. It's not that there's a global financial crisis and his retirement fund is wiped out. Rather, he himself is wiped out—God demands his life before he can settle his feet into his footstool and turn on the TV.

Now, it would be nice to conclude that this is God's assessment of our concept of retirement. But that would abuse the parable. Jesus doesn't indicate that death is God's judgment on the man's apparent "retirement." Nor does Jesus indicate it's a judgment on his self-indulgent attitude. Indeed, there's no mention that his death is any sort of punishment. It's simply that his time's up—as determined by God.

Yet I believe the parable still speaks to issues surrounding retirement—especially as it's practiced in Australian culture. Jesus identifies his purpose in telling this story. "Watch out! Be on your guard against all kinds of greed; a man's life does not consist in the abundance of his possessions" (Luke 12:15). I like John Nolland's description of greed: "Greed is the desire to have more, to get one's hands on whatever one can, to acquire without reference to one's own specific needs or the situation of others."[4] It's a self-centered attitude that seeks to acquire and accumulate for one's own benefit. It tends to measure success in life by the extent of one's possessions. This becomes a measure of self-worth. Jesus warns of the dangers of that attitude and tells this parable to drive home his point.

God identifies the rich man as a *fool*. In what sense is this true? From most people's perspective, this man demonstrates wisdom. He's wise enough to run a successful farm, to become rich, and to provide for the future. From our modern perspective, he's even wise enough to be in the position to retire. From a purely pragmatic point of view, those things aren't in question. Nor, I think, does Jesus question those things in themselves.

This man is a fool because he lives his life only at that level—the level determined by greed that values a life on the basis of possessions. Interestingly, at the point when God addresses him, this rich fool has actually stopped accumulating. Maybe he could claim he's now satisfied—that he's finally conquered greed because he no longer chases the extra dollar. Yet his underlying value system hasn't changed. He simply swaps the accumulation of leisure experiences for the accumulation of possessions. He still focuses on self. And he assumes that his "self" is something he controls.

The man's a fool because he believes he determines how to value life. That is, he follows the choice the original human pair made in the garden. He hasn't considered God and God's assessment of what's important in life or the purposes God may have for his life. He assumes it's okay for him to accumulate resources solely for his private use and personal pleasure and that this is a worthwhile task. He feels responsible only to make his own way in life. He works for himself and not for the common good. He fails to consider that God may have blessed him (perhaps he thinks his abundance results solely from his own wise planning and hard work) so he in turn can bless others. He feels no responsibility to others—and thus no responsibility toward God.

Jesus concludes with this warning: "This is how it will be with anyone who stores up things for himself but is not rich toward God." The man impressed himself with his success in life. And, in terms of his measure, he did in fact succeed. But he's got the wrong measure. He chases a faulty goal. The real goal is to be rich toward God. In the verses that follow, Jesus explains that more fully to his disciples. It involves seeking God's kingdom and caring for the poor.

Doesn't our current version of retirement pursue the same values as the rich fool? We seek to accumulate sufficient capital in our superannuation funds (with the additional top-up from the government pension—our neighbors' taxes) to demonstrate that we can make our own way in life. We thus fulfill our responsibility to ourselves. Have we no ongoing responsibility to God? Are we entitled to stop seeking God's kingdom and caring for the poor? Why should I be entitled to "take life easy, eat, drink, and be merry" while I retain the ability to benefit others by working for God's kingdom and the common good? Sure, my government gives me that right—but does God?

I think that particular idea of a government-given entitlement runs deep in the Australian psyche. Something that began as a generous privilege quickly morphed into a definite expectation and then solidified into an inalienable right. Some years ago, I remember hearing people assert their perceived right to the government old-age pension in these terms:

> I've worked hard throughout my life. I've paid my taxes all these years. I've earned my retirement. I've paid my dues to society. Now, it's time for me to relax and enjoy myself. Now, it's time for society to look after me. Now, it's time for me to get some return on all those taxes I've paid over the years (as if they'd never driven on roads or taken advantage of the public health and education systems!).

I don't hear that explanation so often these days—maybe I now move in different circles; maybe it's a function of the shift in focus to compulsory superannuation.

It seems to me that while this attitude acknowledges some notion of responsibility to others ("paid my dues to society"), it's inadequate from a Christian perspective. In seeking to live for God's purposes, should we not desire to be involved in the task God originally set humanity—as well as any other tasks God has added since that time? And as part of that task, should we not care for God's creatures—especially our fellow human creatures? How can we retire from that task while some of our fellow humans have insufficient resources to adequately rejoice in the goodness of God's creation?

ANOTHER OPPORTUNITY MISSED

A few chapters after the parable of the rich fool, we're told of another fictitious rich man (Luke 16:19–31). The text doesn't say he was idle, but it does tell us he lived in luxury. This rich man is also condemned. He's not condemned for enjoying the good gifts of God's creation. Rather, it's that he enjoyed them excessively while poor Lazarus experienced scarcity right under his nose. He too failed to work for the common good. He too assumed his own good fortune—perhaps even a fortune accumulated through sheer hard work—was for his personal use only.

This continues a theme from the prophets, which is not surprising since Abraham reminds the tormented dead rich man that his still-living brothers have Moses and the prophets to warn them (Luke 16:29). They too condemn the rich who enjoy their luxury and even idleness in the face of the poverty of their fellow-countrymen. Consider how the Old Testament prophet Amos described his targets:

You lie on beds inlaid with ivory
　　and lounge on your couches.
You dine on choice lambs
　　and fattened calves.
You strum away on your harps like David
　　and improvise on musical instruments.
You drink wine by the bowlful
　　and use the finest lotions,
　　but you do not grieve over the ruin of Joseph.
Therefore you will be among the first to go into exile;
　　your feasting and lounging will end. (Amos 6:4–7)

Alec Motyer comments that this passage "reveals scenes of ag-
gravated self-indulgence: extravagant laziness (4a), improvident
gluttony (4b), specious frivolity (5), artificial—even sacrilegious—
stimulation (6a), and excessive personal vanity (6b)."[5]

Now, on the surface at least, Amos isn't attacking idleness and
self-indulgence in itself. For example, I don't think he condemns
David for playing the harp. The problem was these people—the
upper echelons of Israelite society at that time—maintained their
lifestyle at the expense of the general population. Amos makes that
clear in the preceding chapters. For example, he has some choice
words for the wealthy women of Israel in 4:1:

Hear this word, you cows of Bashan on Mount Samaria,
　　you women who oppress the poor and crush the needy
　　and say to your husbands, "Bring us some drinks!"

These people had power. Instead of following the law's exhortation
to use political power to serve the community (for example, Deuteronomy 17:14–20), they used it to serve their own ends. Through their
power, they protected their own position and accumulated more
wealth. Through their power, they oppressed the general populace
and exploited them to maintain their own self-indulgent lifestyle.

Now Jesus doesn't go that far with the rich man in his parable.
There's no hint that the rich man caused Lazarus's poverty. There's
no hint that he took steps to oppress Lazarus. He simply enjoyed his
own lifestyle—and probably mouthed words of thanks to God for
his generous provision. He failed to relieve Lazarus's condition, even

though it was in his power to do so. He felt no responsibility toward Lazarus—or, if he did, he apparently had no trouble suppressing it.

Again, it strikes me that our vision of retirement has features in common with the rich man. It encourages us to shift our focus away from the common good and toward self. Sure, we may still give to charitable causes—we may even do so generously. But does that entitle us to stop working for the common good if we still have the ability to do so?

THE NATURE OF THE CHRISTIAN LIFE

Sixth, it seems to me that the whole nature of the Christian life is to serve others. When his disciples got into a discussion about greatness in God's kingdom, Jesus instructed them:

> "You know that those who are regarded as rulers of the Gentiles lord it over them, and their high officials exercise authority over them. Not so with you. Instead, whoever wants to become great among you must be your servant, and whoever wants to be first must be slave of all. For even the Son of Man did not come to be served, but to serve, and to give his life as a ransom for many." (Mark 10:42–45)

Jesus expects his disciples to be different from the culture around them. Our aim is not to demonstrate our superiority to others, whether in terms of accumulating power or wealth or popularity or leisure experiences or anything else of which we like to boast. We're not climbing the pecking order—however our culture defines that order. Rather, we're to seek to serve others. Another way to put it is that we're to work for the common good—not just of our own culture but of humanity as a whole.

The New Testament reiterates this message in a variety of ways. Perhaps it's so common that we overlook it. Consider the following examples.

> "A new command I give you: Love one another. As I have loved you, so you must love one another. By this all men will know that you are my disciples, if you love one another." (John 13:34–35)

Let no debt remain outstanding, except the continuing debt to love one another, for he who loves his fellowman has fulfilled the law. (Romans 13:8)

There are different kinds of gifts, but the same Spirit. There are different kinds of service, but the same Lord. There are different kinds of working, but the same God works all of them in all men. Now to each one the manifestation of the Spirit is given for the common good. (1 Corinthians 12:4–7)

Let us not become weary in doing good, for at the proper time we will reap a harvest if we do not give up. Therefore, as we have opportunity, let us do good to all people, especially to those who belong to the family of believers. (Galatians 6:9–10)

Remind the people to be subject to rulers and authorities, to be obedient, to be ready to do whatever is good, to slander no one, to be peaceable and considerate, and to show true humility toward all men. (Titus 3:1–2)

Each one should use whatever gift he has received to serve others, faithfully administering God's grace in its various forms. (1 Peter 4:10)

In context, some of those verses refer primarily to serving and loving other Christians; some of them refer to Christians and non-Christians alike. The point is that such love and service remain an ongoing responsibility for Christians. Just as there is no retirement from the Christian life (at least, not one that ends well for the one who chooses to abandon the faith), so there is no retirement from the task delegated to us as Christians. The two are part of the one package. While we retain the capability, we're responsible to God for the continued exercise of the abilities he's entrusted to us.

In concluding his letter to the church at Corinth, Paul writes:

Therefore, my dear brothers, stand firm. Let nothing move you. Always give yourselves fully to the work of the Lord, because you know that your labor in the Lord is not in vain. (1 Corinthians 15:58)

When you read the phrase "work of the Lord," what comes to mind? If you've inhabited similar Christian circles to myself, there's a good chance your mind immediately jumps to mission work. Paul wants these Corinthian Christians to overflow in their ministries of evangelizing non-Christians and discipling Christians. Many commentators agree with that. Raymond Collins claims:

> In Paul's rhetorical lexis "work" ... and "toil" ... are almost technical terms used to describe the work of evangelization. On the "work" of the Corinthians see 3:10–17. It is a work of building up the community as the temple of God, in which the Spirit dwells.[6]

Similarly, C. K. Barrett writes:

> What is meant is the Christian labour of calling the church into being and building it up. This is especially the task of apostles, but also that of their helpers, such as Timothy, and indeed of every Christian, since all are members of the body.[7]

And they provide good arguments to support that conclusion. Earlier in the chapter, Paul writes of his own "labor" in a context where it's clear he refers to gospel ministry (15:10). A few verses later, Paul refers to Timothy "*carrying on the work of the Lord*, just as I am" (16:10)—and this too most likely refers to his pastoral endeavors. While the verse serves as a final appeal to Paul's argument throughout the whole letter, it also provides the concluding ethical implications of Paul's detailed argument in chapter 15—which began with the content of the gospel and then discussed the reality and nature of the future resurrection.

On that basis, Paul encourages these Corinthian Christians to "overflow" or "abound" or "be excessive" or "be extravagant" in their mission work. That seems inconsistent with the concept of leisured retirement. Even if you still managed to somehow justify ceasing creation work, it would be very difficult, I think impossible, to wiggle out of the superlative language Paul uses here and conclude that it's okay to retire from mission work.

Yet I warned you earlier that I have an aversion to making undue distinctions between the sacred and the secular. While the context favors the above interpretation, I doubt Paul had in mind our distinction between creation work and mission work. I think that's a modern distinction we bring to the text. If we asked Paul whether "the work of the Lord" included creation work, I think he'd answer affirmatively.

Earlier in this letter, Paul wrote, "So whether you eat or drink or whatever you do, do it all for the glory of God" (10:31). Admittedly, he's not talking about work in that context. The issue there is whether I should eat meat offered to idols if by doing so I may offend my fellow Christian. Yet it remains a very broad statement that fails to make the sacred/secular distinction—or, if you prefer, this statement brings everything into the realm of the sacred.

Paul does the same thing in Colossians 3:17: "And whatever you do, whether in word or deed, do it all in the name of the Lord Jesus, giving thanks to God the Father through him." The immediately preceding context refers to ministry within the church. Yet, as Peter O'Brien notes, the breadth of Paul's instruction makes "plain that the injunction ought not to be limited to the context of worship" and that "the point is strongly driven home that the Christian's whole life must be lived in obedience to the Lord Jesus."[8] This becomes clear also from the broader context of Colossians 3, which uses the metaphor of changing clothes to describe the expected transformation that follows Christian conversion. Following this statement, Paul proceeds to discuss relationships in Christian households. In the process he encourages slaves: "Whatever you do, work at it with all your heart, as working for the Lord, not for men, since you know that you will receive an inheritance from the Lord as a reward. It is the Lord Christ you are serving" (3:23–24). And so, returning to 1 Corinthians 15:58, I agree with Gordon Fee that it "may refer more broadly to whatever one does *as a Christian*."[9] That, it seems to me, is consistent with Paul's view of the Christian life.

I don't think Paul compartmentalized his own life. Clearly his priority was to preach the gospel. Yet, in order to be able to do so free of charge, he engaged in what we'd identify as secular work—tentmaking (or leather work). But I don't think Paul saw it in those terms. Let me be clear about what I'm about to do—namely, engage in some speculation to draw out this point. The text of Paul's letters doesn't provide this specific information. This is my reading between the lines.

Did Paul resent those times when he had to support himself by tentmaking? I think not. He tells the church at Philippi that he'd learned to be content in all situations (Philippians 4:11–13). That included times when he had to support his own ministry by making and selling tents.

Did Paul consider the time spent in tentmaking wasted? Again, I think not. Rather than adopt the Hellenistic values of traveling teachers who were paid for their lectures (they thought manual labor below their dignity), he appears to align himself with his Jewish heritage that required rabbis to engage in manual work.[10]

Did Paul consider tentmaking a worthwhile task? I think he considered creation work part of the task God gave humanity. Given the advice Paul gave slaves (Ephesians 6:5–8; Colossians 3:22–25), I assume he put his best efforts into the tents he made and the way he conducted himself with customers.

Did Paul consider tentmaking an interruption to his ministry? I suspect he saw it as an opportunity for a different kind of ministry and perhaps to a different range of people.

Did Paul prefer teaching the gospel to tentmaking? I think so. When he received gifts from churches, he was grateful he could put aside his tentmaking and devote all his time and energies to teaching. He believed that was the prime commission God gave him.

In 1 Corinthians 15:58, Paul writes to a group of Christians in Corinth. They had no specific church buildings. They had few organized church programs. We have no indication that any of them were being financially supported in ministry "positions." Most of their time each week was taken up with whatever creation work they did. Very likely, many of them were slaves. Yes, they engaged in mission work among themselves whenever they met together—that is, they used their gifts and abilities to encourage one another in their Christian growth. But is it likely that Paul here refers only to that small segment of their week? I think not.

I think it's far more likely Paul considered their whole lives to be mission work—including what we now identify as creation work. Because we divide the two, we tend to think of mission work as what happens at church and other activities we identify as "Christian." If we hold a Bible study at work, that's mission work. If we try to evangelize our fellow workers, that's mission work. But we don't think of the job itself as being mission work because we think it's secular. I think that's an unhelpful distinction that promotes aspects of the clergy/laity division that the Reformers tried to overcome. I think Paul identifies the whole lot as part of one package called the Christian life, and that how we conduct ourselves in our creation work is actually part of our mission work. It's part of how we demonstrate God's goodness and the goodness of his creation and the goodness of his presence in our lives. It's part of how we serve others for the common good.

And so I think it's equally a part of "the work of the Lord" that we're fully to give ourselves to as we seek to serve others. Like Ecclesiastes taught us, we don't understand the purpose of all the work God sets before us and how it fits into his eternal purposes—but we can be confident that God has things under control and he uses our work to achieve his purposes, both in our own lives and in the lives of others. And so, why would we want to retire? How will our retirement achieve the work God wants to do through us?

These are important issues: they also relate to the discussions Christians have over the relative places of evangelism and social action in Christian ministry.[11] But whatever conclusion you come to about the definition of "the work of the Lord," I think it opposes pursuing the version of retirement promoted by the Australian (or American) dream.

SUMMARY

As I indicated at the outset, the purpose this chapter was to briefly consider some of the evidence that supports the Bible's presumption that humans will work and thus undermines any encouragement to adopt the practice of retirement. Some of the individual pieces of evidence may be somewhat dubious in themselves, but overall I think they present a strong case that we should continue to work for the common good while we have the ability to do so. This is an expression of our service to God and our love for other people.

16

WHERE TO GO FROM HERE?

As I said in the introduction, my aim in this book is to achieve a paradigm shift—to get you thinking that retirement (at least as we normally think of it) is not God's best for your life. Rather, I believe God's purpose for you is to continue work throughout your life (unless, as I've noted, infirmity or disability prevents this)—that you develop a mind-set that always seeks to serve others for the common good.

We've worked our way through a significant amount of biblical material. In doing so, I've found no concrete support for the concept of retirement. Rather, I've found repeated confirmation of an expectation that humans will involve themselves in work—the task God originally gave humanity at creation.

However, as I indicated in chapter 1, this is only the first part of the project. It seems to me that God gives us considerable freedom in how we structure cultures—including the work aspect of culture. Rather than provide us with a cultural blueprint, God indicates to us what values are important to him and allows us to construct a variety of cultures that demonstrate those values. Thus, while I believe the presumption of work remains, perhaps we are free to structure our culture so that it includes this concept of retirement, provided it also reflects the values that are important to God. Resolving this question is beyond the scope of this book.

THE CHRISTIAN RESPONSE TO CULTURE

But rather than leave the project up in the air at this point, I think it's worth beginning to consider a Christian response to this issue. For even if we conclude that we're free to structure our culture to include retirement, it's quite apparent the present way overlooks values that are important to God. For example, how can I participate in a practice of retirement that focuses on my leisure and personal enjoyment while others in my world lack the basic necessities of life? Surely the communal aspect of the cultural mandate requires that I continue to work for justice for such people.

If we conclude the Bible doesn't support retirement and is perhaps even anti-retirement, what should we do about that? In some jurisdictions, retirement is compulsory at a mandated age. Should we simply disobey the government? Should we start campaigns to overturn all retirement legislation—both voluntary and compulsory? Such campaigns would likely generate persecution against the church—but did not our Master warn us to expect opposition from the world? Should we simply leave it to individuals to find their own way around the problem—to find ways of exercising their vocation beyond the normal retirement age? Should we set up alternative communities where we demonstrate the personal value and communal benefits of living under God's standards? What do we do when church clashes with culture?

The church has a long history of dealing with issues where its values differed from those of the culture in which it found itself. Sometimes the issues were very serious. The early Christians clashed with Rome over all sorts of matters. Rome insisted that people acknowledge the divinity of the emperor. Christians thought that clashed with their allegiance to Jesus as Lord. They refused to conform at the cost of their lives. Roman culture exposed unwanted babies. Christians rescued them and provided them loving homes. Both matters were serious. At one level, the responses are very different. One response was public; the other was done "behind the scenes," as it were. Christians didn't have the option of organizing political rallies. Both responses challenged their culture. Both responses ultimately changed the culture.

Over the centuries, the church has struggled with how to relate to culture. Approaches have varied depending on the cultural issues involved and the political strength of the church at the time. In 1956, H. Richard Niebuhr attempted to systematize the church's approaches. He identified five basic models of relating Christ to culture.

1. Christ against culture (rejection). Christianity and culture are in opposition.

2. Christ of culture (assimilation). Christ and the highest expressions and aspirations of culture are in agreement.

3. Christ above culture (synthesis). There is both continuity and discontinuity between Christ and culture.

4. Christ and culture in paradox (dualism). There is paradoxical tension between Christ and culture.

5. Christ transforming culture (conversion). Culture is sinful, yet it can be turned to Christian purposes.[1]

Niebuhr's preference was the fifth option.

Many have critiqued Niebuhr's work for a variety of reasons. Some "believe Niebuhr caricatures them"; some think his categories need reworking for a post-Christendom context; some counter that he assumes a monolithic culture.[2] For our purposes, the most important issue is that each of the models has its strengths and weaknesses. Each (with the possible exception of the second[3]) can find some biblical support, but none encompasses all the biblical material. And so it's not a matter of choosing one model and sticking with it; rather, it's drawing on the strengths of each and considering which is the better option (or options) in the particular circumstances being considered.[4]

At this point, you may be thinking: "Let's get to where the rubber hits the road and stop beating around the bush with all this theoretical stuff." But the reason I introduce this "relating to culture" material is that I don't think this is a one-solution-fits-all scenario. As I hope I've made clear, I think the modern practice of retirement is a subject where we should be out of step with our culture. Niebuhr's value for us is to demonstrate that there's more than one model for how we may express our "out-of-stepness." Thus I expect many options will be available to us—even more than what I list below. So please don't feel restricted by my imagination. I'd encourage you to use these suggestions as springboards for your own creativity.

Moreover, as Andy Crouch and Tim Keller have pointed out, each of us will likely gravitate toward one of the models. This depends on a number of factors, including our particular gifts and abilities, our theological community, our personal aptitudes, and so on. That means that some of the following suggestions will likely appeal to you more than others. That's okay. God usually expects us to serve him in line with the way he's wired us as individuals. But be aware that this doesn't make the other options wrong—it's just that they're not the best fit for you. And also remember that there's biblical truth in each of the models. Sometimes we need to step out of the model in which we feel comfortable and embrace broader aspects of scriptural truth.

SOME POSSIBLE OPTIONS

So, what could we do if we don't retire? If retirement is not a biblical option, what action should we take? How can we ensure our lives conform more closely to biblical values?

At this point, I paint mainly with large brushstrokes. My aim is to present broad ideas rather than to fill out all the details. Others have presented more detailed ideas. For example, many Christian authors who accept retirement as a legitimate concept and who write to assist people to make the transition into their retirement years also encourage people to use those years both actively and productively—and they often include specific suggestions for how people can do that. Many of those suggestions remain just as relevant if we reject retirement as a biblical option. Thus I refer to some of them below.

Individual Options

Option 1

We could simply refuse to retire. Stay on the job as long as our physical capability to do so remains. This enables ongoing service of others through our jobs themselves. It should also enable increased service of others through giving financially—both from the ongoing wages we receive and through the availability of superannuation funds that would no longer be required for our personal use.

This would require carefully thought-out responses for those who ask why we're doing it, especially our employers and colleagues. We don't want to appear superior or self-promoting—after all, we're thankful for the opportunity to serve others. Nor do we wish to come across as judgmental—we simply rejoice in our relationship with God. Yet we do want to convey that our ongoing work reflects our Christian values based on God's grace toward us.

Option 2 *(a variation of option 1)*

For some, option 1 will be unavailable. Some occupations (such as airline pilots) have mandatory retiring ages; in others (such as surgeons), wisdom dictates ceasing work once one's physical capabilities become reduced; in still other occupations (such as those involving heavy manual labor), the spirit may still be willing but the flesh is now beyond weak. A change of occupation could be considered. In some cases, that change may occur within the same industry—for example, a surgeon might serve in a teaching role. In other cases, a new career path may be an option. Such changes may require some level of retraining.

At this point, you may doubt whether this option is feasible. After all, we may not have many modern-day examples of people who continue to work and even learn a new career after the official retirement age. But such people are out there. In August 2015, *The Guardian* presented an article titled "Not the Retiring Type: Meet the People still Working in their 70s, 80s and 90s."[5] Audrey Gillan provides several examples of ordinary people choosing these first two options (some of their reasons are indicated in the headings she uses).

- "I still have my life force": Ivan Roitt (87) finished as head of immunology at University College London and then set up the cancer research center at Middlesex University.
- "I've been at every night out they've had": Jean Miller (92) finished as a sales representative for a household supplier

and now works three days a week as the cloakroom atten-
dant at a Vidal Sassoon hair salon.

- "The shop keeps my memory going": Tom Swan (79) continues to run Swan's Sweet Shop—an establishment he's worked
in for sixty years.

- "I couldn't live on my pension": In his fifties, Sidney Htut
(now 70) lost his job as a research scientist and then re-
trained as a psychiatrist.

- "My customers know they have to behave": Eudokia Stafford
(90) continues to run the Beehive Inn in South Wales—work
she's been doing for sixty years.

- "To suddenly do nothing would be a disaster": Brian Denney
(82) ran his own insurance brokerage business for fifty-two
years. He sold the business in 2010 but now serves the new
owners as a pensions consultant, as well as doing other voluntary work in his spare time.

- "I feel more tired when I'm not working": Pat Thomson (73)
began her career as a primary school teacher. Over the years,
she continued to study and grow her qualifications and is
now a freelance offshore materials and logistics superinten-
dent, working sixteen-hour days on North Sea oil rigs and
platforms around the world.

Expectations about careers have changed in recent decades. For
many people today, they expect to change careers several times during their working life. Thus option 2 merely continues this practice
beyond our culture's anticipated retirement age.

Option 3

Become involved in voluntary work. The Bible does say the
worker should share in the spoils of their work—whether that be
directly partaking of the produce or being remunerated by other
means. But the Bible doesn't say we can't work if we're not paid. Paul
labored at creation work in order to offer his mission work without
charge. But I see no logical reason why we can't also offer creation
work free of charge.

In my Australian culture, there are many opportunities for voluntary work—both creation work and mission work.[6] These provide great opportunities to serve others for the common good. Christians in the early church gained a reputation for this sort of work. Unlike most other people in their culture, they actively cared for the sick and the poor—even the sick and the poor outside the Christian community. Others were drawn to discover what so motivated Christians to work for the common good. In our current post-Christian culture, that sort of compassion no longer stands out in quite the same way, because non-Christians also participate in humanitarian projects. What does stand out is when Christians abandon this sector and fail to demonstrate care for others.

This, of course, requires the people involved in this work to be funded in other ways. Currently, for retirees in Australia, the latter arrangement happens primarily via government pensions, superannuation schemes, or personal savings. We're in a transition phase while the government tries to reduce the size of its pension budget. I intimated earlier that I think the concept of superannuation savings also requires examination from a Christian perspective—as to whether it's godly to accumulate significant resources for future personal use—but that's beyond the scope of this book. Needless to say, there are further issues to consider in relation to this option.

Option 4 *(a variation of option 3)*

In 1995, when my family first went to Papua New Guinea, we met an older couple who was also a recent addition to the staff. The husband had been retrenched during a company restructure and received a significant golden handshake. That provided the couple the opportunity to use their acquired skills and experience in a new "career" in another culture—and to do so in a voluntary capacity.

This is now part of the changing face of missions. In Australia, the Christian organization Second-Wind Network provides a service to match the skills and experience of "retirees" looking for a new sphere of service with the needs of missions organizations. The aim is to mobilize a valuable (not least because it's self-funding) Christian resource to serve the peoples of our world.[7] Finishers provides a similar forum in the United States.[8] There are also Christian resources for retirees who are looking to become involved in volunteer work, such as Kay Strom's book *The Second-Half Adventure,* which she describes as a "tool for connecting your gifts and interests with organizations that are eager for your expertise."

Option 5

Review (or establish) your life purpose.[9] We are all different—that's the way God made us. We all have different personalities, abilities, aptitudes, and life situations. We all have different functions in how we work for the common good. Also, we are all finite and have finite resources. We can't do all that we're able to do—not even all that we'd like to do. Working out our life purpose helps us prioritize our time and efforts. It helps us focus on those tasks we believe God has equipped us to do—our particular contribution to the common good.

Ideally, we should review our life purpose regularly to check that the various pressures of life don't sidetrack us. But the period leading up to "retirement" (the time when our culture encourages us to focus on self-indulgence) seems a particularly good time to review our purpose and priorities—and to do so "with all the wisdom and experience gained over the years."[10]

Harold Koenig provides a useful discussion of this topic. He doesn't challenge the *concept* of retirement, but rather focuses on how to make the best use of your retirement years for the benefit of God's kingdom. Yet what he writes remains equally applicable under my paradigm. He advises that your life purpose will take advantage of your strength and abilities, be flexible, have the potential for significant impact, and be related to God's will. He also discusses the impact on your purpose of various life changes (such as diminished capacity) associated with advancing years. He is concerned to present "an alternative to retiring to a life of self-absorption, leisure, and inactivity."[11]

Those five options are fairly straightforward. They don't require any real structural change in our society's practice of retirement. They simply rely on the individual choices of individual Christians. There's nothing to stop people exercising those options now. They are real options for people wishing to make the paradigm shift. As you do so, keep in mind Paul Clayton's discovery: "The biggest surprise and lesson about retirement for me was that I had to take the initiative."[12]

Other people also have explored these options—often in greater detail. Especially helpful resources are: Paul Clayton's book *Called for Life*, chapter 5; Harold Koenig's book *Purpose and Power in Retirement*, chapter 5; and Kay Strom's book *The Second-Half Adventure*, which I've mentioned above.

Communal-Type Options

Part of me thinks that's as far as I should go at present—that any communal-type options should await consideration of the broader economic issues. The other part of me feels, perhaps wrongly, that would result in a rather bland concluding chapter. So I've reached an internal compromise: to present some communal-type options that could be pursued at a church level. This is not to say that they couldn't also be pursued at a societal level—just that I'm not considering that possibility at this point.

I haven't thought through all the details of these options. Some may prove unworkable. Some contravene current legislation. They're my poor attempts to think outside the box—especially outside our current cultural box. I hope that they'll elicit even greater attempts by you.

Option 6

Set up alternate work situations for seniors. As noted earlier, not all have the option of continuing in their current job. Thus some seniors may require new positions in a different industry. An entrepreneurial Christian (or church) could establish a company designed specifically to employ seniors.[13] Perhaps some industries are particularly suitable for such an enterprise (though, not being entrepreneurial, I don't know!). A variety of flexible employment packages could be developed to accommodate different senior situations—for example, the company could offer a range of part-time positions to accommodate the reduced capacities of some seniors. The main aim is to provide opportunities for seniors to continue to work for the common good.

Option 7

Encourage an atmosphere in which there's no expectation of retirement. Imagine if Christians entered the workforce anticipating (even hoping) that they'd work (and thereby serve for the common good) for the rest of their lives. How do you react to that? Perhaps it sounds like an added burden rather than a joy. Maybe it evokes feelings of lifelong slavery. Perhaps you think it's just another way Christians will take the fun out of life. And maybe that indicates how far our minds still need to be renewed by God's word. The Bible assures me that work is one of God's good gifts. God says I'll find purpose and joy in life through serving others.

I've no doubt this would be a hard sell. We're hooked by our culture's attractively packaged retirement dream. It's a fight against a well-financed industry. It's one of the few remaining areas where our culture still encourages delayed gratification—put up with the hard work now for the sake of this magnificent reward at the end. It's easy to buy into that package. Work is often hard. We develop resentment toward it. Very often, it doesn't feel like one of God's good gifts. It's easy to trust our culture's assessment rather than God's word. The self-centered natures we've inherited from the fall are more than willing to confirm our culture's assessment.

Imagine the change if we could transform our attitude to work—how that would impact the work itself, those we serve in our work, and those who observe the way we work. It could very well cause those around us to ask why we're so different. And think of the resources that could be freed for the good of others if we didn't have to accumulate so much money to finance our lengthy retirements.

After I completed this book, I came across some more recent work that claims Baby Boomers have a different attitude toward retirement. Amy Hanson writes:

> Research sponsored by Merrill Lynch indicated that 70 to 80 percent of boomers want to keep working in some fashion after they retire. Interestingly, most of them would like to find different jobs

in areas of personal interest where they can make a difference in society. They want work that will allow them the flexibility to travel, spend time with family, participate in leisure activities, and continue learning.[14]

If that's true, this may not be such a hard sell in the near future.

Option 8

In *Baby Boomers and Beyond*, Amy Hanson proposes an altered focus for ministry to older adults within the church. She distinguishes three groups:

- The frail elderly (those requiring the compassionate caring ministry of the church)
- Seniors (the usual target of church seniors programs at present)
- The "new old" (Boomers now entering their retirement years)

She views those in the latter two groups—those with time, energy, experience, and resources—as a relatively untapped resource. She argues that the church should take more initiative to encourage these people to engage in ministry:

> We are talking about a philosophy of ministry in which older adults are engaged in meaningful service and Kingdom impact that have the ability to transcend age.[15]

In chapter 9, she provides four answers to the question of what churches can do to create a serving environment among older adults. She writes that churches can first take advantage of every opportunity to tell the stories of how leading-edge Boomers are making a major impact with their lives; second, raise the value of unpaid work; third, become places that are intentionally outward-focused; and fourth, begin challenging people before they reach retirement. She then provides several practical ways to lead older adults to find their place of ongoing service. This book has plenty of practical suggestions for how a church can move forward in this area. Basically, this is option 3 done on a church level.[16]

I would add one caveat to this approach. On a church level, it's easy to think primarily in terms of mission work. It's also easy to adopt an attractional model—finding ways to get nonchurch people onto our turf in order to minister to them on our terms. In Australia, that's becoming an increasingly difficult task—nonchurch people are increasingly resistant to coming onto our turf. And so thought should also be given to equipping this group for kingdom service through ongoing creation work. I suspect we need to focus more on how to operate effectively as "salt" and "light" on their turf.

Option 9

Encourage a move back toward intergenerational households. My personal situation is that my wife and I live as empty-nesters. We are also a significant distance from our parents and children—our son and his family are the closest to us at 150 kilometers (about 93 miles) away. Why?

When we married, the cultural expectation was that we would form our own nuclear family. At that time, our parents lived in adjoining suburbs in Sydney, but we couldn't afford to purchase a house there. We ended up 30 kilometers (about 19 miles) away. This was also influenced by my wife's employment. Later, our work in pastoral ministry and missionary service took us even farther away. As our children reached maturity, we left them behind when we moved to other churches. Because of their university studies and general connectedness in their current communities, they stayed where they were and we moved away. That's not an unusual scenario.

It's very different from the culture of Bible times. Now, I don't think any of the cultures set forth in the Bible is *the* culture we should all aim to copy. As I noted earlier, the Bible doesn't present one uniform culture throughout. Yet consider some of the possible benefits of intergenerational households:

- Inbuilt childcare facilities—provides work for seniors who are unable to continue regular jobs and releases the younger generation for full-time employment. This also allows the younger generation to benefit more from the accumulated wisdom of grandparents.

- Inbuilt aged-care facilities—the issue of whether seniors can continue to maintain an independent lifestyle has been short-circuited; they are already in an environment where they can receive appropriate care if they become too frail.

- Reduced demand for physical resources since two fully independent households are no longer being maintained.

We think it's too hard—that living in such close proximity may result in old annoyances resurfacing, or the jealousy of other siblings or the danger of interfering grandparents, or a whole host of other possible problems. I won't pretend no difficulties are involved. But earlier generations learned to cope. People in other cultures still cope. It's only our affluence that allows us to choose the alternative of separate households. And maybe learning to cope would facilitate growth in godliness.

Maybe there's scope for developing something similar within the church family. In some cases, there may be legitimate reasons why a family's biological grandparents can't exercise this option. In this case, perhaps families could be linked with "adopted grandparents" who could fulfill some of these roles. Our individualism and strong desire for independence will fight against this—but I think neither of those characteristics features in any of the biblical lists of godly traits.

Option 10

Encourage a culture that values experience. Now, I know that in some industries things change so quickly and so dramatically that experience counts for nothing. Within my working life, I've witnessed whole industries be born and become obsolete. Thus, in some ways, it was inevitable that society's focus shifted to youth. They're trained in the new technologies. They understand the modern environment. Let's use them to replace those out-of-date dinosaurs. And so many are seemingly forced into early retirement.

Yet not all industries are like that. For example, I've just turned sixty and am approaching my government-authorized retirement age—though they continue to move the goalposts and increase the official age. My present grasp of the Bible is greater than it's ever been. I think my sermons have continued to improve throughout the course of my ministry. I have more experience of dealing with people in the church. I'm still in good mental and physical shape. In other words, in many ways I'm still approaching the peak of my game. Yet I'm expected to retire soon. Indeed, I suspect I'm already beyond the age at which many churches would consider employing me. Pastoral ministry is not the only occupation that's like that.

The Bible speaks relatively often about valuing the wisdom of the elderly. While young people occasionally show wisdom beyond their years, the wisdom that comes with experience is unavailable to them. It can come only with age—though it's also true that not all who age grow in wisdom. Where does this wisdom fit on the church's radar? How well does the church show that it values the wisdom and experience of its seniors? Or, like our culture, do we consign them to the scrap heap of outdatedness?

James Houston and Michael Parker argue that a big paradigm shift is required. The church must repent of its ageism. It must recognize the valuable resource present in its mature members. It must develop ways to utilize this resource for the benefit of God's kingdom. They go so far as to claim:

> The aging church is not an accident. It is God himself who has granted longer life for his purposes, and we believe that elders hold the keys to solving many, if not most, of society's problems.[17]

But that won't happen without radically changed attitudes toward the place of seniors in the church. Of course, it also requires those seniors to forsake the vision of retirement promoted by our culture and to resist the pressure to consider themselves beyond their use-by date.

Option 11

One way to develop this greater appreciation for seniors in the church is to focus more on intergenerational relationships and activities. In recent decades, the church has followed our culture's lead by promoting a greater emphasis on age-segregated activities. This may have helped prevent some generational wars within churches, but that's happened at the cost of intergenerational relationships. It's becoming more apparent that it's a high cost to pay. Each generation fails to learn from the experiences and wisdom of the other generations. They know only how to relate with their own age group. They miss out on the richness of God's design for his church—that it's a harmonious community that transcends all barriers erected by human cultures. Today, everyone misses out on the potential growth in godliness and relational skills that come from watching the church work through different generational preferences—of watching how people put aside their own self-interest for the sake of serving others.

Certainly, age-segregated activities have some benefits. We should not completely abandon them. Yet if the church is to display the relational richness intended by God, we must find ways to return to greater interaction between the generations. This will require effort from all age groups—but perhaps seniors can lead the way by demonstrating how to put aside self-interest (especially the self-interest of a self-indulgent retirement) for the sake of serving others. For some practical suggestions about how to achieve this see: Amy Hanson, *Baby Boomers and Beyond*, chapter 9; James Houston and Michael Parker, *A Vision for the Aging Church*, chapter 14; and Ross Parsley, *Messy Church*.[18]

Option 12

Develop an atmosphere that acknowledges self-indulgence as sin. The term "self-indulgence" is used only twice in the NIV. In both cases, it has a strongly negative meaning:

- Matthew 23:25—Jesus pronounces a woe on the Pharisees because inwardly "they are full of greed and self-indulgence."

- James 5:5—James refers to exploitative entrepreneurs who "have lived on earth in luxury and self-indulgence and thus fattened themselves in the day of slaughter."

They're both serious charges, and they should at least arouse in us a wish to avoid being self-indulgent.

But further than that, there are other attitudes often associated with self-indulgence that the Bible warns against. Two are mentioned in those verses: greed and luxury. There are others as well: selfishness, self-centeredness, drunkenness, orgies, debauchery, partying, and so on. I think it's easy to think of it in terms of excessiveness—as being something more indulgent than my current lifestyle, as being the lifestyle of someone like Hugh Heffner. It's easy to find someone I think is far more self-indulgent than I am and then to use that to convince myself that I'm not self-indulgent at all.

Why is it that we don't talk much about self-indulgence in the church? Part of the problem is it's so hard to define. For example, which of the following is self-indulgent?

- Enjoying a luxury cruise
- Taking an extended holiday
- Meeting a friend at a coffee shop
- Going to the movies
- Having a second helping of dessert
- Buying a new pair of shoes
- Eating three meals a day

Would your answers be different if you were a beggar on the streets of Calcutta? Should they be different? Is there an absolute scale for self-indulgence or is it a comparative thing? If I have more resources, does that entitle me to treat myself to more luxuries? Is it only self-indulgent if I can't afford it?

Part of the reason we struggle with self-indulgence is that it's become a way of life. It's like greed. Our economy depends on it. It's part of the air we breathe. We become used to it. We accept it as a normal part of our lifestyle—even though the Bible identifies it as idolatry. Self-indulgence is like that. The advertisers tell us we deserve it simply as a break from our regular routine—it's good for our well-being. It's how we motivate ourselves to get a task done—with the promise of a reward. For some people, the anticipation of an indulgent pleasure is the only way they get through the day. For some, perhaps, the anticipation of a leisured lifestyle upon retirement is the only way they get through their working life. It's difficult to fight the constant bombardment; it's much easier to simply excuse it.

Part of the reason is that we're afraid of the specks in our own eyes when we wish to pull the planks out of the eyes of others. If I point out your blatant and extravagant self-indulgence, what's to stop you pointing the finger at that extra CD I bought last week at the garage sale? It's very easy to generate a sense of guilt in myself when I think about self-indulgence and so I avoid talking about it, don't take steps to discipline it, and become more enmeshed in a self-indulgent lifestyle.

And I mustn't forget one other important truth: God expects me to enjoy his good creation with thanksgiving. This too is God's gift to humanity. It's right that I enjoy the fruits of my labor—that I indulge in the good food God provides and encourage others to do likewise.

How can we identify self-indulgence in ourselves? Ultimately, it's not a question of the brand of our clothing or the size of our yacht (although those things may ring some significant warning bells); it's a question of attitude. Attitudes are not always easy to pin down, and so it's often helpful to have some more concrete "tests." One test is to apply Jesus' words about specks and planks (Matthew 7:2–5) to this situation. I'm often tempted to think someone else is acting in a self-indulgent manner. The question is: Am I willing to apply the same standard to myself? I've discovered that I'm quite skilled in finding reasons to differentiate my own behavior from that of others—and thus to excuse it. Jesus reminds me that such rationales provide a very flimsy covering for hypocrisy and that I'm the only one fooled by them.

A second "test" is to review my attachment to possessions and pleasures. Do I consider myself *entitled* to particular products or experiences because of my status? Am I guided by what I truly need, or by what I can afford? Do I have to update my possessions each time a new model is released? Do I define myself by what I own? Am I living as God's steward (treating my resources as opportunities to serve him), or do I think everything is mine to do with as I please? Are there things I can't live without? Yes, we all have needs and God expects us to use his good gifts to meet those needs—but has my definition of "needs" expanded to include multiple luxuries?

A third "test" explores my ability and desire to help others. How willing am I to use God's resources to supply the needs of others? Do I place any limits on the type of people I'm willing to help? Do I give cheerfully? Have I considered downsizing so that I can give more to gospel ministry? Am I willing to use my time to help others? Am I generous in how I serve others?

There's still plenty of room for me to grow in this area. In the long run, such growth won't come from rules and regulations. Instead, I need God's word continually to remind me that true life is found by being in right relationship with my Creator, and not in the accumulation of material things or the indulgence of my own desires. The latter is an illusion my culture promotes at every opportunity. And having thus renewed my mind by the goodness of God's word, I also need God's grace to enable me to die to worldly passions and to mature in godliness (Titus 2:11–14).

Retirement need not be self-indulgent. Some people are grateful for the opportunities it provides to serve others in new ways— and to do so without charge. John Piper's booklet encourages that attitude.[19] Yet the retirement dream promoted by my Australian culture is completely self-indulgent. And it seems to me that, in this matter, the Australian church is far more influenced by its culture than John Piper's booklet or the arguments of other Christian teachers. We're far too accepting of this sinful attitude—often even encouraging it. That acceptance needs to change. We need to clearly identify the spiritual dangers of self-indulgence and warn people to flee it. At the same time, we should promote the positive values of serving others and the opportunities we already have to do so. As Bruce Waltke rightly notes: "If I were to regard retirement as a time of self-indulgent ease and pleasure I am thinking sensually, not Christianly."[20]

LEARNING TO VALUE WORK

Other options could be added, but that should be sufficient to get the ball rolling. What would prevent us from exercising these options? There's a whole range of factors.

For many, the advancing years bring with them physical and mental incapacities. Sometimes that comes from past work—labor that's taken its physical toll. Sometimes it comes from accidents or other unforeseen circumstances. Sometimes it's the genes we're dealt. Clearly, those things reduce our ability to continue to serve for the common good—sometimes even preventing it altogether. That must be accepted within the context of God's providence. It may be a cause for regret that one can no longer utilize this gift, but it should never be a cause for guilt. My purpose is not to deny the reality that our increasing years bring with them a diminished capacity for work.

Spiritual (and physical) inertia will also keep some people from rethinking their retirement plans. It's just too hard to change things. Perhaps it's too hard to change your thinking. You've grown up looking forward to retirement. You've spent your working life planning and saving for it. It's the reward you deserve. You've promised yourself this for so long. It'd cost too much emotional energy to change course now.[21] Or perhaps it's too hard to buck the system. All your friends would be retired. You'd stand out as different—a real oddball. How would you explain it? I know people for whom this type of criticism is a reality as they continue in overseas mission work in their later years.

For some, it's simply the allure of the dream. It just looks so desirable. Why would I want to resist it? As I wrote in the introduction, that dream resonates with something deep in my being. I can easily daydream about retirement. It seems such a big step to sacrifice it. How do I overcome that? By developing a better dream. That better dream is to appreciate the goodness of God's gift of work and to learn to enjoy it for as long as I can. It's to realize that the essence of the Christian life is to serve other people. It's to acknowledge that my life purpose is to glorify God through the task he's gifted me.

That's why many of the above options focus on the necessary paradigm shift. The battle must first be won in our minds. Our minds must be transformed by God's values and purposes rather than simply adopting the dreams of our culture. Once that happens, finding ways to serve for the benefit of others is not that difficult. Perhaps few organizations are willing to employ people once they've reached retirement age (though I've heard rumors that some employers value older people because they're more reliable), but there are innumerable opportunities available for volunteers. Stanley Hauerwas states the challenge this way:

> As Christians we do not seek to be free but rather to be of use, for it is only by serving that we discover the freedom offered by God. We have learned that freedom cannot be had by becoming "autonomous"— free from all claims except those we voluntarily accept—but rather freedom literally comes by having our self-absorption challenged by the needs of another.[22]

That dream must also be in the context of a world that remains in need, both spiritually and physically. How can I justify a self-indulgent retirement when so many people either remain ignorant of the gospel or lack the basic necessities of life and I still have the ability to do something about it? Can I truly do that in good conscience? As Duane Garrett notes: "Until work becomes a blessing to everyone, God's people are called to struggle for the benefit of all workers."[23]

One final thought goes to the heart of how we view work and whether we consider it God's gift to us. Perhaps one of the reasons we so readily adopt our culture's values surrounding retirement is that we've already adopted their values about work. So often our view of work incorporates self-centered values. It's easy to value ourselves on the basis of our work—or what our work provides. We have a hierarchy of occupations with sanitation engineers (the new title for garbage collectors) at the lower end of the scale and open-heart surgeons at the upper end. We have a hierarchy of lifestyles associated with the various classes of society. We have a hierarchy that's based on our possessions—the size of our houses, the suburb they're in, the number of cars we have and their brand, the size of our entertainment system, the value of our yacht, and so on. These hierarchies stem from our work and the size of our paychecks. This determines our position in society—and thus whether we've succeeded in life.

Those same values transfer into retirement. The desire to demonstrate your success and impress others remains. Many of the

status symbols don't change, but there is one significant new one—
how early you were able to retire. And so not retiring—well, that's
unthinkable; that would demonstrate a big failure in life; that would
put you at the bottom of the pecking order.

But that's not the Bible's view of work. It's God's gift whereby
I may serve others. It's similar to what Paul says about how God
distributes gifts within his church in 1 Corinthians 12. They aren't
given for the benefit of the recipient—to puff up his or her ego or
reputation or place in society's pecking order. They're given for the
common good. God gives them so that others can benefit. And if
we have that view of work—if service of others because of our love
for God is our daily motivation—why would we even consider that
we had reached our limit and want to stop?

NOTES

INTRODUCTION

1. As I hope will become evident in later parts of this book, work includes far more than paid employment. For example, the relationship between paid employment and work is considered in chapter 1.

CHAPTER 1

1. Chad Brand and Tom Pratt suggest that "his purpose . . . was not to empower the people but to make them more subservient and manageable and increase the power of the state." *Awaiting the City: Poverty, Ecology, and Morality in Today's Political Economy* (Grand Rapids, MI: Kregel Digital Editions, 2012), 265.

2. This summary is based on Harold G. Koenig, *Purpose and Power in Retirement: New Opportunities for Meaning and Significance* (West Conshohocken, PA: Templeton Foundation Press, 2007), 11–25; Mary-Lou Weisman, "The History of Retirement, From Early Man to A.A.R.P.," *The New York Times* (21 March 1999), http://www.nytimes.com/1999/03/21/jobs/the-history-of-retirement-from-early-man-to-aarp.html; and Robert McCann and Howard Giles, "Ageism in the Workplace: A Communication Perspective," *Ageism: Stereotyping and Prejudice against Older Persons*, ed. Todd D. Nelson (Cambridge, MA: The MIT Press, 2004), 174–76. Amy Hanson, *Baby Boomers and Beyond: Tapping the Ministry Talents and Passions of Adults over 50*, Leadership Network (San Francisco: Jossey-Bass, 2010), 74–76, also provides a brief history of retirement.

3. Maurice Balme, "Attitudes to Work and Leisure in Ancient Greece," *Greece & Rome* 31, no. 2 (October 1984), 140–52, http://www.jstor.org/stable/642580, provides a full discussion of these issues.

4. A. Delbridge, ed., *The Concise Macquarie Dictionary* (Lane Cove, Australia: Doubleday Australia, 1982), 1086.

5. Centrelink is the government organization that administers the Australian social welfare system.

6. Stephen Sapp, *Full of Years: Aging and the Elderly in the Bible and Today* (Nashville: Abingdon, 1987), 12.

7. John Piper, *Rethinking Retirement: Finishing Life for the Glory of Christ* (Wheaton, IL: Crossway, 2008), http://www.desiringgod.org/books.

8. *Interact* 22, no. 2.

9. Ben Witherington III, *The Rest of Life* (Grand Rapids, MI: Eerdmans, 2012), 32–35.

10. This sort of distinction is made in the prologue of Chris Wright's book, *Living as the People of God* (Leicester: Inter-Varsity, 1983), 12–16.

11. The Hebrew word *shalom* is used in the OT with a variety of meanings (the appropriate meaning being determined by context on each occasion). In this study, I use the term to describe the idea of wholeness and well-being—humans living in harmony with God, each other and their environment; lives characterized by goodness, justice and love; people enjoying God's promised blessings—in short, people experiencing life as God intended it to be. For an example of a description of this sort of life, see God's promised blessings on Israel if they are obedient to his laws in Leviticus 26:3–13.

12. It should be noted that some superannuation funds provide specifically ethical investment options.

CHAPTER 2

1. I lived in Papua New Guinea for five years. Retirement was available within some sectors of the economy, but not for the general populace. I've also ministered in Indonesia (three months) and Tanzania (four months) during short-term mission trips.

2. Todd D. Nelson, ed., *Ageism: Stereotyping and Prejudice against Older Persons* (Cambridge, MA: MIT Press, 2002), provides a good introduction to this whole area.

3. For a more detailed treatment of these last two (and some other similar) points, see Gordon J. Wenham, *Story as Torah: Reading the Old Testament Ethically* (Edinburgh: T. & T. Clark, 2000), 5–15.

4. If you want a more detailed summary of the plot, see Andrew Sloane, *At Home in a Strange Land* (Peabody: Hendrickson, 2008), 25–28. For a still fuller explanation, see Graeme Goldsworthy, *According to Plan* (Sydney: Anzea, 1991).

CHAPTER 3

1. Carol L. Meyers, "The Family in Early Israel," *Families in Ancient Israel* (Louisville: Westminster John Knox, 1997), 18. Jon L. Berquist, *Controlling Corporeality: The Body and the Household in Ancient Israel*

(New Brunswick, NJ: Rutgers University Press, 2002), suggests even lower figures—less than 25–30 years was the life expectancy in ancient Greece.

2. For example, noted by Joseph Blenkinsopp, "The Family in First Temple Israel," *Families in Ancient Israel* (Louisville: Westminster John Knox, 1997), 79–82. This is a controversial issue that's beyond the scope of this book.

3. The above summary is based on material from Leo G. Perdue, ed., *Families in Ancient Israel* (Louisville: Westminster John Knox, 1997); William Dever, *The Lives of Ordinary People in Ancient Israel: Where Archaeology and the Bible Intersect* (Grand Rapids, MI: Eerdmans, 2012); Richards S. Hee and M. Daniel Carroll R., eds., *Family in the Bible* (Grand Rapids, MI: Baker Academic, 2003); Christopher J. H. Wright, "Family," *The Anchor Bible Dictionary*, vol. 2, ed. David Noel Freedman (New York: Doubleday, 1992), 761–69; and Timothy M. Willis, "Family," *The New Interpreter's Dictionary of the Bible*, vol. 2, ed. Katherine Doob Sakenfeld (Nashville: Abingdon, 2007), 427–30.

4. After completing this book, I became conscious that some interpret the expression "common good" as including socialist ideology. That was not my intention in using the expression.

5. In addition to the references in note 3, see Oded Borowski, *Daily Life in Biblical Times* (Atlanta: Society of Biblical Literature, 2003), especially the final chapter, which provides an imaginary description of a day in the life of an ancient Israelite family.

6. This summary is based on Carolyn Osiek and David L. Balch, *Families in the New Testament World: Households and House Churches* (Louisville: Westminster John Knox, 1997); Carolyn Osiek and David L. Balch, *Early Christian Families in Context: An Interdisciplinary Dialogue* (Grand Rapids, MI: Eerdmans, 2003); Ken M. Campbell, ed., *Marriage and Family in the Biblical World* (Downers Grove, IL: InterVarsity, 2003); Hess and Carroll, *Family in the Bible*; Willis, "Family;" Wright, "Family."

CHAPTER 4

1. N. T. Wright, *The New Testament and the People of God* (London: SPCK, 1992), 139–44. This concept is also discussed in N. T. Wright, *Scripture and the Authority of God: How to Read the Bible Today* (London: SPCK, 2005).

2. Robert L. Saucy, "Theology of Human Nature," *Christian Perspectives on Being Human: A Multidisciplinary Approach to Integration*, ed. J. P. Moreland and David M. Ciocchi (Grand Rapids, MI: Baker, 1993).

3. Nahum M. Sarna, *Genesis: the Traditional Hebrew Text with the New JPS Translation*, JPS Torah Commentary (Philadelphia: Jewish Publication

Society of America, 1989), 35–36. Sarna suggests the association of these advances in technology with Cain's line "constitute an unfavorable, or at least a qualified, judgment of man's material progress . . . , a recognition that it frequently outruns moral progress and that human ingenuity, so potentially beneficial, is often directed toward evil ends." I remain unconvinced this is achieved by the association with Cain's line; it seems to me this simply results from the fall, which impacts all humans.

4. As the NIV footnote indicates, the word could also mean *stonemason*. That does not alter the point being made here since the same Greek word is used in Mark 6:3.

5. This is discussed briefly by Andrews J. Köstenberger and Peter T. O'Brien in *Salvation to the Ends of the Earth: A Biblical Theology of Mission* (Downers Grove, IL: Apollos/InterVarsity, 2001), 34–37.

6. The labels are a shorthand way to make this distinction. You may prefer different labels: for the former, ruling work, cultivation work, secular work; for the latter, evangelism work, church work, sacred work. Feel free to substitute your own label if you find that more helpful.

7. Miroslav Wolf, *Work in the Spirit: Toward a Theology of Work* (New York: Oxford University Press, 1991); Darrell Cosden, *The Heavenly Good of Earthly Work* (Peabody, MA: Hendrickson, 2006).

8. Not all Christians would apply all these references to the final state. The discussion of millennial views is beyond our scope here.

9. I acknowledge that this is not the only reasonable interpretation of the biblical material. Paul refers to our transformed resurrection bodies in 1 Corinthians 15:35–57. These bodies may well be suited to a non-earthly existence. Even if this is the case, I don't think it negates the argument that follows.

10. The concept of *rest* is developed more fully in chapters 5–7.

11. Note that some would assign the fulfillment of this passage to a millennial kingdom that is a prelude to the final state.

12. For a fuller discussion of these matters, see N. T. Wright, *Surprised by Hope* (London: SPCK, 2007).

CHAPTER 5

1. David Aaron argues for a third (and original) version of the Decalogue in Exodus 34: David H. Aaron, *Etched in Stone: The Emergence of the Decalogue* (New York: T. & T. Clark, 2006). This version contains nothing similar to the fifth commandment and so will be ignored here.

2. This is an example of typology, where OT events and institutions are considered to prefigure some aspects of Jesus' life and ministry.

3. I noted earlier the principle of using Scripture to interpret Scripture, which I continue to affirm. The issue here is which part of Scripture we should use to help us interpret Genesis 2:1–3—the Sabbath material (covered in the next chapter) or the material covered in the trajectory of rest (covered in the remainder of this chapter). Also, as Willard Swartley notes, it's important not to allow this principle to prevent us from being challenged by the distinctiveness of particular texts: Willard M. Swartley, *Slavery, Sabbath, War & Women* (Scottdale, PA: Herald, 1983), 186.

4. Walter Brueggemann, *Genesis*, Interpretation (Atlanta: John Knox, 1982), 27.

5. George Guthrie, "Rest," *The New Interpreter's Dictionary of the Bible*, vol. 4, ed. Katherine Doob Sakenfeld (Nashville: Abingdon, 2007), 767–69.

6. David L. Allen, *Hebrews*, NAC (Nashville: B & H Publishing Group, 2010), 280–81.

7. William L. Lane, *Hebrews 1–8*, WBC (Dallas: Word Books, 1998), 101.

8. K. A. Mathews, *Genesis 1–11:26*, NAC (Nashville: Broadman & Holman, 1996), 208.

9. Gordon J. Wenham, *Genesis 1–15*, WBC (Dallas: Word, 1998), 128. Interestingly, the narrative highlights this name and its significance in Genesis 5:29. See Mathews, *Genesis 1–11:26*, 316–17, for a discussion of some of the difficulties surrounding the explanation of Noah's name. It would be instructive to explore the significance of Noah's name—whether God uses Noah to bring an element of rest to his creation via the judgment and destruction of his rebellious subjects. I suggest such rest points to the restoration of harmony (*shalom*) rather than inactivity.

10. John H. Sailhamer, "Genesis," *The Expositor's Bible Commentary*, rev. ed., vol. 1, ed. Tremper Longman III and David E. Garland (Grand Rapids, MI: Zondervan, 1990), 79.

11. William L. Holladay, ed., *A Concise Hebrew and Aramaic Lexicon of the Old Testament* (Grand Rapids, MI: Eerdmans, 1980), 231. For further nuances and more detail, see the article by Horst Preuss in *The Theological Dictionary of the Old Testament*, vol. IX, ed. G. Johannes Botterweck, Helmer Ringren, and Heinz-Josef Fabry (Grand Rapids, MI: Eerdmans), 277–86.

12. I suspect this is an unhelpful translation at this point. Due to Greek influence, we tend to think of "soul" as the inner, spiritual component of our beings—separate from our bodies. Jesus' offer is made to whole persons and includes their bodily existence. Perhaps "selves" or "beings" would be a more helpful translation.

13. Donald A. Hagner, *Matthew 1–13*, WBC (Dallas: Word, 1998), 324.

14. For example, those familiar with John Bunyan's imagery are likely to think in terms of the burden of sin under which non-Christians labor.

15. After completing this book, I read Johnny V. Miller and John M. Soden, *In the Beginning . . . We Misunderstood: Interpreting Genesis 1 in its Original Context* (Grand Rapids, MI: Kregel Digital Editions, 2012), esp. 141. Their main thesis is totally unrelated to this book, but their comments about the seventh day seem consistent with my argument.

CHAPTER 6

1. Christopher John Donato, ed., *Perspectives on the Sabbath: Four Views*, Perspectives (Nashville: B & H Publishing, 2011). Willard Swartley's discussion of three views is also helpful in *Slavery, Sabbath, War & Women* (Scottdale, PA: Herald, 1983), 67–96.

2. For example, Donato, *Perspectives on the Sabbath*, 21–22, 301–3.

3. Donato, *Perspectives on the Sabbath*, 303–7, 315.

4. D. A. Carson, ed., *From Sabbath to Lord's Day: A Biblical, Historical and Theological Investigation* (Grand Rapids, MI: Zondervan Academic, 1982).

5. G. K. Beale, *A New Testament Biblical Theology: The Unfolding of the Old Testament in the New* (Grand Rapids, MI: Baker Academic, 2011), 775–801.

6. Beale, 776.

7. Beale, 777.

8. Beale, 778.

9. Beale, 778.

10. Beale, 779.

11. Beale, 780.

12. Finding the text challenged my previously reasoned presupposition. I looked at it afresh. My conclusions from these investigations resulted in new presuppositions that now guide my reading of the text.

13. John I. Durham, *Exodus*, WBC (Dallas: Word, 1998), 289. He further notes that Robinson argues it has "nothing to do with 'rest' as relaxation, but refers instead to 'stopping for settlement' and 'coming to an end' of something."

14. Lawrence O. Richards, *Expository Dictionary of Bible Words* (Grand Rapids, MI: Zondervan, 1985), 519.

15. "It is a different word from *shabath*, which is the word used in 16:30 and in Gen 2:2–3. The word used here refers to resting after becoming tired." Noel D. Osborn and Howard A. Hatton, *A Handbook on Exodus*, UBS Handbook Series (New York: United Bible Societies, 1999), 478.

16. Some of the myths of the origins of the ancient Olympian Games indicate their institution was to honor Zeus.

17. It should be noted that scholars disagree over the exact meaning of this particular Hebrew phrase. Some argue for an interpretation that does not require assembling together—that it's simply a way of indicating that the day is proclaimed sacred; for example, Nobuyoshi Kiuchi, *Leviticus*, Apollos OT (Nottingham, UK: Apollos, 2007), 415, 420.

18. Donato, *Perspectives on the Sabbath*, 295.

19. I think Harold Dressler expresses this well: "This can only indicate that the goal of creation is not mankind, that the crown of creation is not man, but that all creative activities of God flow into a universal rest period. The mystery of this seventh day cannot be explained away in human terms but finds its goal and solution in the revelation related in the New Testament. Thus, the creation account of Genesis 1:1–2:3 proclaims *God's* activity, *his* majesty, and *his* power. Man takes his place within creation at his allotted position. God's last creative act is not the making of man but the creation of a period of rest for mankind. This creative act of God does not take the usual form of decree of fashioning but is simply an act of ceasing, resting, and being refreshed.

"Genesis 2 does not teach a 'creation ordinance' in our opinion; the institution of the Sabbath for the people of Israel, however, was based on the creation account and became a sign of God's redemptive goal for mankind." In "The Sabbath in the Old Testament," 29–30.

20. I would argue that this is another type that Jesus fulfilled.

CHAPTER 7

1. Christopher J. H. Wright, "Jubilee, Year of," *Anchor Bible Dictionary*, vol. 3, ed. David Noel Freedman (New York: Doubleday, 1992), 1025–30; Christopher J. H. Wright, "Sabbatical Year," *Anchor Bible Dictionary*, vol. 5, ed. David Noel Freedman (New York: Doubleday, 1992), 857–61.

2. For a fuller discussion of these issues, see Wright, "Sabbatical Year," 858–59.

3. P. C. Craigie, *The Book of Deuteronomy*, NICOT (Grand Rapids, MI: Eerdmans, 1976), 371.

4. I don't have space here to pursue the related concept of the gospel's call for Christians to be slaves of Christ—and that such is a position of true freedom and *shalom*. The idea of the Israelites being God's servants is also present in the Old Testament.

5. Wright, "Sabbatical Year," 860.

6. For a brief discussion of this issue, see Darrell L. Bock, *Luke 1:1–9:50*, ECNT (Grand Rapids, MI: Baker, 1994), 405–7.

7. Willard Swartley, *Slavery, Sabbath, War & Women* (Scottdale, PA: Herald, 1983), 194.

CHAPTER 8

1. *Qohelet* is an English transliteration of the Hebrew word the writer of Ecclesiastes uses to open this document. Its meaning and significance is the subject of much scholarly discussion. The NIV translates it "Teacher"; the ESV opts for "Preacher." On why these titles are inappropriate, see Daniel C. Fredericks and Daniel J. Estes, *Ecclesiastes and the Song of Songs*, Apollos OTC (Downers Grove, IL: InterVarsity, 2010), 31.

2. Craig G. Bartholomew, *Ecclesiastes*, Baker Commentary on the OT (Grand Rapids, MI: Baker Academic, 2009), 93; Jacques Ellul, *Reason for Being: A Meditation on Ecclesiastes* (Grand Rapids, MI: Eerdmans, 1990), 33–42.

3. Bartholomew, *Ecclesiastes*, 17.

4. Duane A. Garrett, *Proverbs, Ecclesiastes, Song of Songs*, NAC (Nashville: Broadman & Holman, 1993), 271–79.

5. Fredericks and Estes, *Ecclesiastes and the Song of Songs*, 37. Bartholomew, *Ecclesiastes*, 84–92, has a useful discussion of the relationship of Ecclesiastes to other parts of the OT.

6. Stephan de Jong, "A Book on Labour: The Structuring Principles and the Main Theme of the Book of Qohelet," *JSOT* 54 (1992): 107–16. See also Barry G. Webb, "Ecclesiastes: Garment of Vexation," *Five Festal Garments*, NSBT (Leicester: Apollos, 2000), 86–89.

7. Fredericks and Estes, *Ecclesiastes and the Song of Songs*, 38, thinks this claim is too broad; rather, he argues Qohelet confines himself to "the very particular question of difficult toil, . . . 'Why should one work so hard and wisely?'"

8. Roland Murphy, *Ecclesiastes*, WBC (Dallas: Word, 1998), 6–7. The variation "under heaven" found in 1:13; 2:3; and 3:1 is found elsewhere in the OT.

9. Webb, *Five Festal Garments*, 95.

10. Murphy, *Ecclesiastes*, lviii–lix, 3.

11. Bartholomew, *Ecclesiastes*, 105. R. N. Whybray is similar: "Unfortunately it is not entirely clear what Qoheleth meant by it: 'vanity,' 'nothingness,' 'worthlessness,' 'futility,' 'absurdity,' 'mystery,' 'impermanence' are only a few of the ways in which it has been translated." *Ecclesiastes*, Old Testament Guides (Sheffield: Sheffield Academic, 1989), 64.

12. Fredericks and Estes, *Ecclesiastes and the Song of Songs,* 27–28.

13. Webb, *Five Festal Garments*, 90.

14. Compare Proverbs 6:10–11; 24:30–34.

15. Whybray, *Ecclesiastes*, 20. See also (although he doesn't use the word *leisured*) Bartholomew, *Ecclesiastes*, 54.

16. Also noted by Bartholomew, *Ecclesiastes*, 54–58; Whybray, *Ecclesiastes*, 69.

17. Duane Garrett, "Ecclesiastes and Work," 14, www.theologyofwork .org/old-testament/ecclesiastes.

CHAPTER 9

1. John Goldingay, *Numbers and Deuteronomy for Everyone*, Old Testament for Everyone (Louisville: Westminster John Knox, 2010), 23.

2. Gordon J. Wenham, *Numbers*, Tyndale OTC (Leicester, UK: Inter-Varsity, 2004), 97–98, 2n.

3. Timothy R. Ashley, *The Book of Numbers*, NICOT (Grand Rapids, MI: Eerdmans, 1993), 176.

4. B. Maarsingh, *Numbers: A Practical Commentary*, Text and Interpretation (Grand Rapids, MI: Eerdmans, 1987), 32.

5. Anastasia Boniface-Malle, "Numbers," *Africa Bible Commentary*, ed. Tokunboh Adeyemo (Grand Rapids, MI: Zondervan, 2006), 179–80.

6. Iain Duguid, *Numbers: God's Presence in the Wilderness*, Preaching the Word (Wheaton, IL: Crossway, 2006), 118.

7. For a helpful categorisation of the Levites' overall functions, see Baruch A. Levine, "Levites," *Encyclopedia of Religion*, ed. Lindsay Jones (Detroit: Macmillan Reference USA, 2005), 5424–27.

8. For a survey of the issues involved, see D. A. Hubbard, "Priests and Levites," *New Bible Dictionary*, ed. D. R. W. Wood et al. (Downers Grove, IL: InterVarsity, 1996), 956–62; Merlin D. Rehm, "Levites and Priests," *The Anchor Bible Dictionary*, vol. 4, ed. David Noel Freedman (New York: Doubleday, 1992), 297–311; Joseph Blenkinsopp, *Sage, Priest, Prophet: Religious and Intellectual Leadership in Ancient Israel*, Library of Ancient Israel (Louisville: Westminster John Knox, 1995).

9. For a discussion of these issues, see Gordon J. Wenham, *The Book of Leviticus*, NICOT (Grand Rapids, MI: Eerdmans, 1979), 18–29, 161–225.

10. Samuel ben Meir, *Rashbam's Commentary on Leviticus and Numbers: An Annotated Translation*, trans. Martin I. Lockshin (Providence: Brown Judaic Studies, 2001).

11. Dennis T. Olson, *Numbers*, Interpretation (Louisville: John Knox, 1996), 50.

12. R. Dennis Cole, *Numbers*, NAC (Nashville: Broadman & Holman, 2000), 154.

13. Helen Kenik Mainelli, *Numbers*, Collegeville Bible Commentary (Collegeville, MN: Liturgical, 1985), 46.

14. Eryl W. Davies, *Numbers*, NCB (Grand Rapids, MI: Eerdmans, 1995), 79.

15. Walter Riggins, *Numbers*, Daily Study Bible (Edinburgh: Saint Andrews, 1983), 67.

16. Cole, 542; Wenham, *Numbers*, 235.

17. See http://www.thechristianidentityforum.net/downloads/Com plete-Scrolls.pdf.

18. James H. Charlesworth, ed., *The Old Testament Pseudepigrapha*, vol. 2 (Garden City, NY: Doubleday & Company, 1985), 100.

CHAPTER 10

1. Jacob Milgrom, *Leviticus 23–27: A New Translation with Introduction and Commentary*, Anchor Bible (New York: Doubleday, 2001), 2368–69, has a useful discussion of the Hebrew expression used here.

2. J. D. Douglas, "Nazirite," *New Bible Dictionary*, ed. D. R. W. Wood et al. (Downers Grove, IL: InterVarsity, 1996), 809.

3. Tony W. Cartledge, *Vows in the Hebrew Bible and the Ancient Near East*, JSOT Sup (Sheffield, UK: JSOT, 1992), 11–35.

4. For an alternate reading in the LXX and Dead Sea Scrolls that does include the term, see Tony W. Cartledge, "Nazirite," *The New Interpreter's Dictionary of the Bible*, vol. 3, ed. Katherine Doob Sakenfeld (Nashville: Abingdon, 2008), 241.

5. Erhard S. Gerstenberger, *Leviticus: A Commentary*, OTL (Louisville: Westminster John Knox, 1996), 439–40, thinks the substitutionary payment was envisaged from the outset and this simply "represented the traditional manner of speaking of such things." Cartledge, 53, notes: "The promise of a person (who can later be redeemed) seems much more impressive than the promise of money itself."

6. Critical scholars who argue the legal material developed over a lengthy period of time suggest that early in Israel's history, dedication of people to the sanctuary was feasible. What they consider as the later development of Levitical structures made this unnecessary. Philip J. Budd, *Leviticus*, New Century Bible Commentary (Grand Rapids, MI: Eerdmans, 1996), 380.

7. Richard Nelson Boyce, *Leviticus and Numbers*, Westminster Bible Companion (Louisville: Westminster John Knox, 2008), 108; Carol Meyers, "Procreation, Production, and Protection: Male-Female Balance in Early Israel," *JAAR* 51, no. 4 (1983): 585.

8. This was also the amount for redeeming a firstborn male: Numbers 3:47; 18:16.

9. Among others, John W. Kleinig, *Leviticus*, Concordia Commentary (St. Louis, MO: Concordia, 2003), 591. Budd, 381, indicates there may be some suggestion of a "sense of intrinsic worth."

10. Carol Meyers, "Procreation, Production, and Protection," esp. 583–86.

11. Mark F. Rooker, *Leviticus*, NAC (Nashville: Broadman & Holman, 2000), 325.

12. Gordon J. Wenham, *The Book of Leviticus*, NICOT (Grand Rapids, MI: Eerdmans, 1979), 338. Roy Gane, *Leviticus, Numbers*, NIV Application Commentary (Grand Rapids, MI: Zondervan, 2004), 468, and Milgrom, *Leviticus 23–27*, 2370–72, argue against this.

13. Martin Noth, *Leviticus: A Commentary*, OTL (London: SCM, 1965), 204–5, argues the highest value would be set on children if it was a once-for-all payment.

CHAPTER 11

1. Robert J. Karris, *The Pastoral Epistles*, New Testament Message (Wilmington: Michael Glazier, 1979), 89. Ben Witherington III, *Letters and Homilies for Hellenized Christians*, vol. 1 (Downers Grove, IL: IVP Academic, 2006), 265, makes similar comments. Note that Hulitt Gloer, *1 and 2 Timothy-Titus*, Smyth & Helwys Bible Commentary (Macon, GA: Smyth & Helwys, 2010), 182, claims that widows were to be cared for by the state when they had no other support.

2. Bruce W. Winter, "*Providentia* for the Widows of 1 Timothy 5:3–16," *Tyndale Bulletin* 39 (1988), 83–88.

3. Noted by Margaret Davies, *The Pastoral Epistles: I and II Timothy and Titus*, Epworth Commentaries (London: Epworth, 1996), 40. Yet Susan Treggiari writes: "Poor women and even slaves seem to have tried to produce some kind of dowry." In "Marriage and Family in Roman Society," *Marriage and Family in the Biblical World*, ed. Ken Campbell (Downers Grove, IL: InterVarsity, 2003), 150.

4. Luke Timothy Johnson, *1 Timothy, 2 Timothy, Titus*, Knox Preaching Guides (Atlanta: John Knox, 1987), 89.

5. Donald Guthrie, *The Pastoral Epistles: An Introduction and Commentary*, Tyndale (Grand Rapids, MI: Eerdmans, 1990), 113. Also noted by George W. Knight III, *Commentary on the Pastoral Epistles*, NIGTC (Grand Rapids, MI: Eerdmans, 1992), 219; Craig S. Keener, *The IVP Bible Background Commentary: New Testament* (Downers Grove, IL: InterVarsity, 1993).

6. Thomas D. Lea and Hayne P. Griffin, *1, 2 Timothy, Titus*, NAC (Nashville: Broadman & Holman, 1992), 147.

7. Johnson, *1 Timothy, 2 Timothy, Titus*, 94.

8. Luke Timothy Johnson, *Letter to Paul's Delegates: 1 Timothy, 2 Timothy, Titus*, New Testament in Context (Valley Forge, PA: Trinity Press International, 1996), 172, suggests verse 16 may hint at the existence of at least one rich widow in the church at Ephesus. Jouette M. Bassler, *1 Timothy*,

2 Timothy, Titus, Abingdon NT Commentaries (Nashville: Abingdon, 1996), 96, is similar.

9. According to Jay Twomey, the website LadiesAgainstFeminisim. com disagrees. It argues that this passage supports the idea that women should never work outside the home. Jay Twomey, *The Pastoral Epistles through the Centuries*, Blackwell Bible Commentary (Malden, MA: Wiley-Blackwell, 2009), 76–77.

10. For example, E. F. Scott, *The Pastoral Epistles*, Moffatt NT Commentaries (London: Hodder & Stoughton, 1936), 60. Jouette M. Bassler, "The Widows' Tale: A Fresh Look at 1 Tim 5:3–16," *JBL* 103/1 (1984): 34, 39n, thinks this "abandons exegesis in favor of ethos." In essence, this is correct.

11. Davies, *The Pastoral Epistles*, 40–41. See also Guthrie, *The Pastoral Epistles*, 114–15; Thomas C. Oden, *First and Second Timothy and Titus*, Interpretation (Atlanta: John Knox, 1989), 153; John Stott, *The Message of 1 Timothy and Titus*, BST (Leicester, UK: Inter-Varsity, 1996), 129.

12. Gordon D. Fee, *1 and 2 Timothy, Titus*, NIBC (Peabody, MA: Hendrickson, 1988), 119; J. N. D. Kelly, *A Commentary on the Pastoral Epistles*, Black's New Testament Commentaries (London: A & C Black, 1963), 115; Knight, *Pastoral Epistles*, 223.

13. Patrick Fairbairn, *Commentary on the Pastoral Epistles*, Classic Commentary Library (Grand Rapids, MI: Zondervan, 1874), 201.

14. Fee, *1 and 2 Timothy, Titus*, 119; Knight, *Pastoral Epistles*, 223, 225. Note Winter's comments about Roman law requiring widows under fifty to remarry: "*Providentia*," 85, 95.

15. Joseph Reuss, *The First and Second Epistle to Timothy*, NT for Spiritual Reading (London: Burns & Oates, 1969), 64. Twomey, 78, notes this was Tertullian's position.

16. A. T. Hanson, *The Pastoral Epistles: Based on the Revised Standard Version*, New Century Bible Commentary (Grand Rapids, MI: Eerdmans, 1982), 98; Kelly, *The Pastoral Epistles*, 117; Knight, *Pastoral Epistles*, 222, 225–27; Philip Graham Ryken, *1 Timothy*, Reformed Expository Commentary (Phillipsburg, NJ: P & R Publishing, 2007), 214–15.

17. Fee, *1 and 2 Timothy, Titus*, 121; Oden, *First and Second Timothy and Titus*, 157; Philip H. Towner, *1–2 Timothy, Titus*, IVP NT Commentary (Downers Grove, IL: InterVarsity, 1996), 121. Towner also adds the possibility that remarriage may have been "a hasty alternative to genuine repentance for immoral behavior."

18. For example, Fee, *1 and 2 Timothy, Titus*, 115.

19. For example, Bassler, "The Widows' Tale," 31–32.

20. For example, Bassler, *1 Timothy, 2 Timothy, Titus*, 94; Fee, *1 and 2 Timothy, Titus*, 115.

21. For example, Johnson, *Letters to Paul's Delegates*, 177–83.

22. For example, Oden, *First and Second Timothy and Titus*, 153.

23. Hanson, *The Pastoral Epistles*, 96–98; Kelly, *The Pastoral Epistles*, 112, 115–17; Reuss, *The First and Second Epistle to Timothy*, 63.

24. There is evidence of the formal office of widow by the third century, but it is unclear when it first became a formal office: *The Didascalia Apostolorum in English*, trans. Margaret Dunlop Gibson (Cambridge: Cambridge University Press, 1903), 70–78.

25. This was particularly demonstrated by the common purse in the Jerusalem church in Acts 2:41–47 and 4:32–35. We have no evidence that particular level of communal sharing continued indefinitely or that it was practiced in the Gentile churches. Yet, one has the impression they operated with a greater level of communal responsibility than is the experience in modern Western cultures.

26. Ryken, *1 Timothy*, 209–10.

27. Hanson, *The Pastoral Epistles*, 99. Why does Paul mention "going about from house to house" in 5:13? Is it simply a statement of fact—that this is what younger widows would do? Or does it hint at an expectation that enrolled widows visit people in their homes and that younger widows, in their immaturity, would misuse this privilege?

28. Hanson, *The Pastoral Epistles*, 96.

29. Kelly, *The Pastoral Epistles*, 116–18.

30. Karris, *The Pastoral Epistles*, 91.

31. Stott, *1 Timothy and Titus*, 133.

32. Bassler, "A Widows' Tale." Also, Bassler, *1 Timothy, 2 Timothy, Titus*, 92–98. Bassler thinks 2 Timothy was written in the second century. More recently, Deborah Krause, *1 Timothy*, Readings—a New Biblical Commentary (Edinburgh: T & T Clark, 2004), 96–109, has developed this interpretation further, claiming that "[t]he writer has accomplished a coup within his community by attempting to eliminate women with social power, physical health and financial means from eligibility for the office of widow in the church," 100. Power is the main issue.

33. Bassler, "A Widow's Tale." Concerning the shortcomings of this interpretation, I agree with Johnson, *Letters to Paul's Delegates*, 177–79. In addition, I'm not convinced the "solution" proposed in the passage would actually resolve that particular problem.

34. This is not to say that Paul here distinguishes creation work and mission work or gives priority to one over the other; rather, he recognizes that this group is now available for a particular task.

CHAPTER 12

1. Note that this is enumerated as the fourth commandment in Catholic and Lutheran traditions. I have retained the numbering system with which I am familiar.

2. Telford Work, *Deuteronomy*, Brazos Theological Commentary (Grand Rapids, MI: Brazos, 2009), 82.

3. Eugene H. Merrill, *Deuteronomy*, NAC (Nashville: Broadman & Holman, 1994), 153–54.

4. Raymond Brown, *The Message of Deuteronomy*, BST (Leicester, UK: Inter-Varsity, 1993), 58–59.

5. Edward L. Greenstein, "The Rhetoric of the Ten Commandments," *The Decalogue in Jewish and Christian Tradition*, ed. Graf Henning Reventlow and Yair Hoffman (London: T. & T. Clark, 2011), 3. Athalya Brenner disagrees. She claims that "to include [the women] in the address . . . by drawing upon linguistic praxis would be misleading and less than naïve." Athalya Brenner, "The Decalogue—Am I an Addressee?," *A Feminist Companion to Exodus to Deuteronomy*, ed. Athalya Brenner (Sheffield: Sheffield Press, 1994), 256.

6. Greenstein, "Rhetoric," 3.

7. Brenner, "The Decalogue," 257; Judith Plaskow, *Standing Again at Sinai: Judaism from a Feminist Perspective* (San Francisco: Harper Collins, 1991), 6, 82; Greenstein, "Rhetoric," 3–4; David J. A. Clines, "The Ten Commandments, Reading from Left to Right," *Words Remembered, Texts Renewed: Essays in Honour of John F. A. Sawyer*, ed. Jon Davies, Graham Harvey, and Wilfred Watson (Sheffield: Sheffield Academic Press, 1995), 102–5.

8. Plaskow, *Standing Again at Sinai*, 25–26.

9. Brenner, "The Decalogue," 258.

10. Ben Witherington III, *New Testament Rhetoric: An Introductory Guide to the Art of Persuasion in and of the New Testament* (Eugene, OR: Cascade, 2009), 143.

11. Robert Martin-Achard, "Biblical Perspectives on Aging," *Aging*, ed. Lisa Sowle Cahill and Dietmar Mieth (London: SCM, 1991), 35–36. He notes he derives this classification from an article by R. Albertz.

12. Walter Harrelson, *The Ten Commandments and Human Rights*, Overtures to Biblical Theology (Philadelphia, PA: Fortress, 1980), 92–96; Walter Harrelson, "No Contempt for the Family," *The Ten Commandments: The Reciprocity of Faithfulness*, ed. William P. Brown, Library of Theological Ethics (Louisville: Westminster John Knox, 2004), 239–42. To be fair, Thorwald Lorenzen also links these two consecutive words—but his perceived connection has a totally different basis: Thorwald Lorenzen, *Toward a Culture of Freedom: Reflections on the Ten Commandments Today* (Eugene, OR: Cascade, 2008), 85.

13. Assnat Bartor, *Reading Law as Narrative: A Study in the Casuistic Laws of the Pentateuch* (Atlanta: Society of Biblical Literature, 2010), 101.

14. Thomas B. Dozeman, *Commentary on Exodus*, Eerdmans Critical Commentary (Grand Rapids, MI: Eerdmans, 2009), 493–94, and George

V. Pixley, *On Exodus: A Liberation Perspective* (Maryknoll, NY: Orbis, 1987), 136, provide references that indicate caring for aged people was also an issue in the surrounding cultures.

15. The NIV's "man" is imported from verse 15 and is correctly translated generically by the ESV. It fails to indicate the age of the culprit.

16. There are examples of what appear to be flagrant breaches: Abimelech (Judges 9:1–20), Eli's sons (1 Samuel 2:12–36), Samuel's sons (1 Samuel 8:15), and Absalom (2 Samuel 13–18); but no examples of human intervention to execute judgment for those breaches. Perhaps less flagrant breaches include Samson (Judges 14:1–4, 8–9, 16), Michel (1 Samuel 19:11–17), and Jonathan (1 Samuel 20).

17. Here I confine my comments to the rural communities. Those living in urban centers usually enjoyed better work conditions. They were often wealthier and better fed. Their life expectancy was greater. Yet, there is nothing to suggest their approach to the issue of aged parents was any different.

18. Jon L. Berquist, *Controlling Corporeality: The Body and the Household in Ancient Israel* (New Brunswick, NJ: Rutgers University Press, 2012), 114, suggests it could be as low as age twenty.

19. Berquist, *Controlling Corporeality*, 119–23; Daniel I. Block, "Marriage and Family in Ancient Israel," *Marriage and Family in the Biblical World*, ed. Ken Campbell (Downers Grove, IL: InterVarsity, 2003), 98–100.

20. Berquist, *Controlling Corporeality*, 115.

21. Stephen Sapp, *Full of Years: Aging and the Elderly in the Bible Today* (Nashville: Abingdon, 1985), 80–84, provides a brief summary of this position.

22. Gerald Blidstein, *Honor Thy Father and Mother: Filial Responsibility in Jewish Law and Ethics* (New York: Ktav Publishing House, 1975).

23. Blidstein, 1.

24. Jan de Waard and Eugene Albert Nida, *A Translator's Handbook on the Book of Ruth*, UBS Handbook Series (New York: United Bible Societies, 1991), 76.

25. Lorenzen, *Toward a Culture of Freedom*, 82; Johann Jakob Stamm and M. E. Andrew, *The Ten Commandments in Recent Research*, Studies in Biblical Theology (London: SCM, 1967), 95–96. Also mentioned by Brevard S. Childs, *Exodus*, OTL (London: SCM, 1979), 418.

26. Dale W. Manor, "Ruth," *Zondervan Illustrated Bible Backgrounds Commentary*, vol. 2, ed. John H. Walton (Grand Rapids, MI: Zondervan, 2009), 247, suggests Naomi was likely in her mid-forties.

27. Frederic William Bush, *Ruth, Esther*, WBC (Dallas: Word, 1996), 105.

28. Katharine Doob Sakenfeld, *Ruth*, Interpretation (Louisville: John Knox, 1999), 39.

282 RETIRING RETIREMENT

29. Victor H. Matthews, "Marriage and Family in the Ancient Near East," *Marriage and Family in the Biblical World*, ed. Ken Campbell (Downers Grove, IL: InterVarsity, 2003), 18. See also 16, 19–21.

30. S. M. Baugh, "Marriage and Family in Ancient Greek Society," *Marriage and Family in the Biblical World*, ed. Ken Campbell (Downers Grove, IL: InterVarsity, 2003), 121; see also 105–6, 119, 129.

31. Block, "Marriage and Family in Ancient Israel," 94–100.

CHAPTER 13

1. Timothy M. Willis, "Elders in the OT," *The New Interpreter's Dictionary of the Bible*, vol. 2, ed. Katherine Doob Sakenfeld (Nashville: Abingdon, 2007), 233–34, provides a brief summary of these matters. Hanoch Reviv, *The Elders in Ancient Israel* (Jerusalem: The Magnes Press, The Hebrew University, 1989), deals with the issues in more detail.

2. So noted by R. L. Hubbard, *The Book of Ruth*, NICOT (Grand Rapids, MI: Eerdmans, 1988), 235, 18n.

3. Bush, *Ruth, Esther*, 198–99.

4. John R. Wilch, *Ruth*, Concordia Commentary (St. Louis, MO: Concordia, 2006), 325.

5. Daniel I. Block, *Deuteronomy*, NIV Application Commentary (Grand Rapids, MI: Zondervan, 2012), 607.

6. At this point, the issue is: who has the responsibility to redeem the land? Presumably the actual redemption will later be negotiated with the person who has purchased the use of the land.

7. William D. Mounce, *Pastoral Epistles*, WBC (Dallas: Word, 2000), 306–11.

CHAPTER 14

1. Leon Morris, *The Gospel according to John*, NICNT (Grand Rapids, MI: Eerdmans, 1979), 472.

2. George R. Beasley-Murray, *John*, WBC (Dallas: Word, 2002), 139.

3. Irenaeus of Lyons, "Irenæus Against Heresies," *The Ante-Nicene Fathers: The Apostolic Fathers with Justin Martyr and Irenaeus*, vol. 1, ed. Alexander Roberts, James Donaldson, and A. Cleveland Coxe (Buffalo, NY: Christian Literature Company, 1885), 392 (2.22.6).

4. Irenaeus, "Irenæus Against Heresies," 391 (2.22.4).

5. Craig S. Keener, *The Gospel of John: A Commentary*, vol. 1 (Peabody, MA: Hendrickson, 2003), 769.

6. Carol Meyers and Eric M. Meyers, *Haggai, Zechariah 1–8: A New Translation with Introduction and Commentary*, The Anchor Bible (Garden City, NY: Doubleday, 1987), 415–16.

7. T. V. Moore, *The Prophets of the Restoration, or, Haggai, Zechariah, and Malachi: Commentary* (New York: Robert Carter & Brothers, 1856), 192–93.

CHAPTER 15

1. Ben Witherington III, *1 and 2 Thessalonians: A Socio-Rhetorical Commentary* (Grand Rapids, MI: Eerdmans, 2006), 245–49.

2. First Timothy 6:2 would have been a similar opportunity. Paul doesn't instruct believing masters to give their Christian slaves less work. Instead, he encourages the Christian slaves to serve their believing masters even better.

3. See page 195.

4. John Nolland, *Luke 9:21–18:34*, WBC (Dallas: Word, 1998), 685.

5. J. A. Motyer, *The Day of the Lion: The Message of Amos*, BST (Leicester, UK: Inter-Varsity, 1974), 143.

6. Raymond F. Collins, *First Corinthians,* Sacra Pagina (Collegeville, MN: Liturgical, 1999), 583.

7. C. K. Barrett, *The First Epistle to the Corinthians*, Black's New Testament Commentaries (London: A & C Black, 1968), 385.

8. Peter T. O'Brien, *Colossians, Philemon*, WBC (Dallas: Word, 1998), 211.

9. Gordon D. Fee, *The First Epistle to the Corinthians*, NICNT (Grand Rapids, MI: Eerdmans, 1988), 808 (emphasis in the original). Fee goes on to indicate he thinks the primary reference is to "those kind of activities in which believers engage that are specifically Christian, or specifically in the interest of the gospel."

10. William J. Larkin, *Acts*, IVP NT Commentary (Downers Grove, IL: InterVarsity, 1995), 263.

11. For the record, I agree with Michael Bird's statement: "Social action and caring for the poor is not, however, the gospel; it is simply what Christians are expected to do alongside the gospel. Showing compassion and pursuing justice are implications of the gospel, implications of the fact that Christians belong to a kingdom, not simply share a final heavenly destination. As Christians confess the lordship of Jesus Christ, they begin to order their lives according to the story, symbols, and summons of their exalted Master, and that will inevitably impact, often abrasively, the world around them." Michael F. Bird, *Evangelical Theology: A Biblical*

and Systematic Introduction (Grand Rapids, MI: Zondervan, 2013), 58. See also the broader context of this statement.

CHAPTER 16

1. Summary is taken from Doug Hynd, "Public Theology after *Christ and Culture*: Post-Christendom Trajectories." From a paper given at "Christian Mission in the Public Square," a conference of the Australian Association for Mission Studies (AAMS) and the Public and Contextual Theology Research Centre of Charles Sturt University, held at the Australian Centre for Christianity and Culture (ACC&C) in Canberra from 2 to 5 October 2008, 13, http://www.csu.edu.au/__data/assets/pdf_file/0010/94735/Hynd.pdf. Timothy Keller also has a helpful summary in *Center Church* (Grand Rapids, MI: Zondervan, 2012), 194.

2. Keller, *Center Church,* 196.

3. D. A. Carson, *Christ and Culture Revisited* (Grand Rapids, MI: Eerdmans, 2008), 31–36.

4. Carson, *Christ and Culture Revisited,* 31–65; Keller, *Center Church,* 181–247.

5. http://www.theguardian.com/lifeandstyle/2015/aug/01/still-working-aged-in-70s-80s-90s?CMP=ema_632. There are eight similar "reflections" scattered throughout Walter C. Wright, *The Third Third of Life: Preparing for your Future* (Downers Grove, IL: InterVarsity, 2012). Irene Howat, *Stopped Work? Start Living! Encouraging Stories of New Directions in Retirement* (Fearn, UK: Christian Focus, 2005), simply presents the stories of ten individuals/couples who have taken on significant missions work in their "retirement" years.

6. See Harold G. Koenig, *Purpose and Power in Retirement: New Opportunities for Meaning and Significance* (West Conshohocken, PA: Templeton Foundation Press, 2007), ch. 5, for a more detailed discussion of volunteering and its benefits.

7. www.secondwind.net.au.

8. www.finishers.org.

9. There are many good resources available to assist in this process. One good example is Matt Perman's *What's Best Next: How the Gospel Transforms the Way You Get Things Done* (Grand Rapids, MI: Zondervan, 2014), chs. 11–13. This is especially useful because he presents his material in the context of working for the benefit of others (chs. 5–7).

10. Koenig, *Purpose and Power in Retirement,* 58.

11. Koenig, *Purpose and Power in Retirement,* 70.

12. Paul C. Clayton, *Called for Life: Finding Meaning in Retirement* (Herndon, VA: The Alban Institute, 2008), 63.

13. I haven't checked whether this contravenes anti-discrimination legislation. Perhaps it could be argued that this seeks to redress the situation where seniors are generally discriminated against in current employment practices.

14. Amy Hanson, *Baby Boomers and Beyond: Tapping the Ministry Talents and Passions of Adults over 50* (San Francisco: Jossey-Bass, 2010), 10. There are similar comments on page 77.

15. Hanson, *Baby Boomers and Beyond*, xiii.

16. For further practical suggestions, see Emma Lou Benignus, "Challenge to Ministry: Opportunities for Older Persons," *Affirmative Aging: A Creative Approach to Longer Life*, ed. Joan E. Lukens (Harrisburg, PA: Morehouse, 1994), 23–37, and Ian S. Knox, *Older People and the Church* (Edinburgh: T & T Clark, 2002), 186–205.

17. James M. Houston and Michael Parker, *A Vision for the Aging Church: Renewing Ministry for and by Seniors* (Downers Grove, IL: IVP Academic, 2011), 33; Hanson, *Baby Boomers and Beyond*, 8; Kay Marshall, Strom, *The Second-Half Adventure* (Chicago: Moody, 2009), 18, express similar sentiments. I came across this book after I had completed my own. It contains many helpful suggestions.

18. Ross Parsley, *Messy Church: A Multigenerational Mission for God's Family* (Colorado Springs: David C. Cook, 2012).

19. John Piper, *Rethinking Retirement: Finishing Life for the Glory of Christ* (Wheaton, IL: Crossway, 2008).

20. Bruce K. Waltke, "Reflections on Retirement from the Life of Isaac," *The Dance between God and Humanity: Reading the Bible Today as the People of God* (Grand Rapids, MI: Eerdmans, 2013), 414.

21. Perhaps it's worth pointing out that some people slow down because they grow old; others grow old because they slow down.

22. Stanley Hauerwas, *After Christendom?: How the Church Is to Behave If Freedom, Justice and a Christian Nation Are Bad Ideas* (Anzea: Sydney, 1991), 53–54.

23. Duane Garrett, "Ecclesiastes and Work," 14, www.theologyofwork.org/old-testament/ecclesiastes.

About the Hendrickson Publishers/ Theology of Work Line of Books

There is an unprecedented interest today in the role of Christian faith in "ordinary" work, and Christians in every field are exploring what it means to work "as to the Lord" (Col. 3:22). Pastors and church leaders, and the scholars and teachers who support them, are asking what churches can do to equip their members in the workplace. There's a need for deep thinking, fresh perspectives, practical ideas, and mutual engagement between Christian faith and work in every sphere of human endeavor.

This Hendrickson Publishers/Theology of Work line of books seeks to bring significant new resources into this conversation. It began with Hendrickson's publication of the *Theology of Work Bible Commentary* and other Bible study materials written by the TOW Project. Soon we discovered a wealth of resources by other writers with a common heart for the meaning and value of everyday work. The HP/TOW line was formed to make the best of these resources available on the national and international stage.

Works in the HP/TOW line engage the practical issues of daily work through the lens of the Bible and the other resources of the Christian faith. They are biblically grounded, but their subjects are the work, workers, and workplaces of today. They employ contemporary arts and sciences, best practices, empirical research, and wisdom gained from experience, yet always in the service of Christ's redemptive work in the world, especially the world of work.

To a greater or lesser degree, all the books in this line make use of the scholarship of the *Theology of Work Bible Commentary*. The authors, however, are not limited to the TOW Project's perspectives, and they constantly expand the scope and application of the material. Publication of a book in the HP/TOW line does not necessarily imply endorsement by the Theology of Work Project, or that the author endorses the TOW Project. It does mean we recognize the work as an important contribution to the faith-work discussion, and we find a common footing that makes us glad to walk side-by-side in the dialogue.

We are proud to present the HP/TOW line together. We hope it helps readers expand their thinking, explore ideas worthy of deeper thought, and make sense of their own work in light of the Christian faith. We are grateful to the authors and all those whose labor has brought the HP/TOW line to life.

William Messenger, Executive Editor, Theology of Work Project
Sean McDonough, Biblical Editor, Theology of Work Project
Patricia Anders, Editorial Director, Hendrickson Publishers

www.theologyofwork.org
www.hendrickson.com

"This commentary was written exactly for those of us who aim to integrate our faith and work on a daily basis and is an excellent reminder that God hasn't called the world to go to the church, but has called the Church to go to the world."

BONNIE WURZBACHER

FORMER SENIOR VICE PRESIDENT, THE COCA-COLA COMPANY